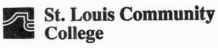

St. Louis Community College

Forest Park
Florissant Valley
Meramec

Instructional Resources
St. Louis, Missouri

GAYLORD

Race in the Hood

Race in the Hood

Conflict and Violence among Urban Youth

Howard Pinderhughes

University of Minnesota Press
Minneapolis
London

Published by the University of Minnesota Press
111 Third Avenue South, Suite 290
Minneapolis, MN 55401-2520

Printed in the United States of America on acid-free paper

Library of Congress Cataloging-in-Publication Data

Pinderhughes, Howard.
    Race in the hood : conflict and violence among urban youth /
Howard Pinderhughes.
        p.   cm.
    Includes bibliographical references (p. 185) and index.
    ISBN 0-8166-2918-8 (hardcover : alk. paper). — ISBN 0-8166-2919-6
(pbk. : alk. paper)
    1. Juvenile delinquency—New York (State)—New York—Case studies.
2. Youth—Crimes against—New York (State)—New York—Case studies.
3. Hate crimes—New York (State)—New York—Case studies. 4. New
York (N.Y.)—Race relations—Case studies. 5. Youth—New York
(State)—New York—Attitudes. I. Title.
HV9106.N6P56   1997
305.8'009747'1—dc21   97-13526

Cover photo: Hmong Teenagers, 1994," by Wing Young Huie, from his book, "Frogtown: Photographs and Conversations in an Urban Neighborhood," Minnesota Historical Society Press.

To my son, Samora, and my daughter, Elena, and my wife, Raquel,
who are the greatest joys in my life and my companions in
our struggle to make the world a better place.

Contents

Acknowledgments

A work of this kind is never a singular effort. It requires the cooperation, support, input, guidance, and mentorship of many people whom I would like to thank.

In the early stages of my research and writing I received outstanding support and helpful critique from several colleagues—Robert Blauner, John Ogbu, David Wellman, and especially Troy Duster. David Wellman read numerous drafts of the manuscript and pushed me to fully develop my theoretical framework. Troy Duster provided extensive and helpful critique in the early stages of the project, kept me focused, and never failed to provide the advice, critique, and encouragement I needed. I also received support from faculty and staff at the Institute for the Study of Social Change, particularly Robert Yamishita, Janice Tanigawa, and David Minkus.

Howard Winant and Becky Thompson reviewed the manuscript for the University of Minnesota Press and provided excellent criticism and comments that helped me to improve the book. I received outstanding support and assistance from the staff at the University of Minnesota Press, including Mary Byers, Robin A. Moir, and Gretchen Asmussen. Lisa Freeman provided important advice, support, and encouragement throughout the process. Kathy Delfosse did an outstanding job of copyediting.

This work was supported by fellowships and grants from the University of California Office of the President, the Community Service Society of New York City, and the Pew Charitable Trusts. Special thanks to Terry Rosenberg and Jaime Casteñeda for their support and encouragement.

Several youth organizations and schools were concerned enough about the issue of racial conflict among youth to allow me access to youth in their programs. I would like to thank the Manhattan Valley Youth Program, especially Chris Boyd; the 61st Precinct YouthDares Program, especially Doug Blancero and Bob Zweig; Central Part East Secondary School, especially Deborah Meier; Christopher Columbus High School, especially Frank Melia and Linda Cetta; and the Panel of Americans, Inc., especially its late director Lawrence Murphy-Stephens, for their cooperation with this study and for their commitment to the youth with whom they work.

I developed a deep respect and admiration for each of these institutions and persons who exemplify the type of leadership and commitment we will need to reduce racial conflict among young people. The members of the Partnership to Advance Intergroup Relations in Schools (PAIRS) were extremely helpful, as were Cyria Lobo and Robert Sherman of the Human Rights Commission of the City of New York, who provided important data and feedback to this project.

I received important intellectual and moral support from many of my friends, including David Eifler, Rachel Morello-Frosch, Michael Gelobter, and Pedro Noguera.

My parents, Charles and Elaine, read the manuscript and supplied valuable critique, but more important they laid the foundation for my interest in race relations and for my lifelong commitment to racial justice.

I would especially like to thank Amanda Berger who was invaluable to the development of this project. It was through our discussions that the idea for this research was formulated. Amanda helped me to gain access to the youth interviewed in this study. She also critiqued the manuscript, provided moral and intellectual support, and taught me a great deal about the issues dealt with in this book.

Most of all, I would like to thank my wife, Raquel, who read and reviewed the manuscript at every stage and provided the most important intellectual input. Raquel constantly pushed me to improve the book, and she afforded me the time and space to write it, often at the expense of her own work. She, along with our two children, kept me sane and nourished my spirit. She is my sustenance and my greatest colleague. I owe her my deepest gratitude for making this work possible. In many ways, this work is as much hers as it is mine.

Lastly, my deepest thanks to all the youth for their enthusiasm, honesty, and openness to struggle with important issues that many adults choose to avoid. Every last one of them provides a hope that even with their differences, prejudices, and various attitudes, young people from different ethnic and racial backgrounds can someday cross racial lines without fear and mistrust.

Introduction

Yusuf Hawkins, a young African American male, is walking through a white neighborhood—some might say he's in the "wrong part of town"—when he's attacked by a group of white kids from the neighborhood. The kids, all male and between the ages of fifteen and twenty-one, are not members of an organized group; they are just a gathering of neighborhood teens who regularly hang out together getting high and partying. The youths are pretty high and drunk when they hear that an African American man is walking through their neighborhood. Somebody in the group vociferously suggests that the group "take care" of the intruder. The weapons of choice are baseball bats and heavy sticks, which have been brought in anticipation of the night's activities. The group finds Yusuf Hawkins easily and attacks him with the bats and sticks, yelling racial epithets and warning him to stay out of their neighborhood.

Since the civil rights movement in the 1960s revealed the brutality of racial violence to the American public, racial attacks have been perceived as particularly heinous crimes. They remind us of the not-too-distant past, when lynchings were an accepted method of social control of African Americans in many parts of the country. Media reports of racial violence pick at the scab on the American psyche, reopening the wounds of racial division to reveal a festering sore that has long been neglected. When news stories about attacks such as the 1989 racial murder of Yusuf Hawkins in the Bensonhurst area of Brooklyn are reported to the American public, the response is shock and disbelief. Most of us cannot imagine how anyone could perpetrate such a despicable act.

This book examines the factors that produce ethnic and racial conflict and violence among youth in New York City. It focuses on the experiences and attitudes of youth between the ages of fourteen and

1

twenty-one in four neighborhoods in New York City between October 1988 and December 1991. During this period, three news stories filled the pages of the city's major newspapers: the Bensonhurst murder trial, the Central Park jogger rape case, and the boycott of two Korean grocery stores in Flatbush. Each of these events symbolized a growing problem in New York City and the nation as a whole: Racial tension, conflict, and confrontation had increased, and hate violence was on the rise. Two of these events—the Bensonhurst murder and the Central Park jogger attack—had profound effects on the youth from the communities examined in this book.

One of the most infamous bias incidents in recent history was the murder of Yusuf Hawkins. In the trial that followed, the incident was presented in the courtroom and through the media as a tragic one-night occurrence that happened almost accidentally, the result of a confluence of factors that included Hawkins and his companions being "in the wrong place at the wrong time"—walking down a street in Bensonhurst where the mob of young whites mistook them for a different group of blacks, who they thought were coming into their neighborhood to cause trouble. Deeper reasons for the tragic incident were never analyzed.

Contrary to the popular view of the Bensonhurst incident as an aberration, data from my interviews with white youth from southern Brooklyn reveal a consistent pattern of racially motivated violence. These youth repeatedly described how they sought out blacks and members of other minority groups as targets for physical assault.

Though the case of the Central Park jogger was not classified as racially motivated, the April 1989 attack swiftly took on sharp racial overtones. In that incident, a white woman who was jogging through Central Park was brutally beaten and raped by a group of African American and Latino young men who had been going through the park attacking people. Despite the fact that there was no evidence that the crime was racially motivated, it was consistently portrayed as such. Analysts in prominent newspapers surmised that the rage these young black males unleashed on the white woman banker was an expression of their frustration and hostility toward the power and privilege of white society, which she represented.

The event shocked New Yorkers and became a powerful symbol for both white and African American residents. For many whites, the event crystallized the image of the violent, unpredictable criminal acts committed by young poor black males, heightening their sense that the violence of poor black ghettoes could not be confined to its residents or its boundaries.

For many African Americans, the case represented yet another instance in which young black males were portrayed as violent and in which attacks committed against whites received more attention from the police, the media, and the mayor than attacks committed against African Americans.

In the past decade, there has been a change in the climate of race relations in the United States as outward signs of racial conflict in the United States have become more visible with the increase in racial violence and racialized politics. The bleak state of the economy has prompted a debate over welfare expenditures and public assistance that has increasingly been marked by racial overtones. Affirmative action has become an extremely contentious political issue. The problem of education reform has been marked by debates over the elimination of measures taken to achieve racial integration and over multicultural curricula. As violent crime has increased, discussions of harsher sentencing, prison terms, and more police protection have been waged using language and symbols that evoke images of dangerous African American males. Developments in the political arena have been accompanied by an increase in reported bias incidents on college campuses throughout the nation, by a resurgence of white supremacist organizations, and by racial clashes among youth in urban neighborhoods—the subject of this book.

In 1990–1991, when I conducted my research, there was a tense atmosphere in New York City. Racially motivated violence had been increasing over the previous five years, and the city had been rocked by a series of high-profile racial incidents. In 1986, 235 bias crimes were verified by the New York City Human Rights Commission. In 1987, the number of bias crimes shot up to 463, and the number reached 550 in 1988. By 1989, the number of bias attacks had reached 566, an increase of more than 120 percent in five years. African Americans were the number one target of bias related crimes: 48 percent of all bias attacks during that period were against African Americans.

Two differences in the character of the bias-motivated crimes that occurred between 1985 and 1990, as compared to those that had occurred during the three previous years, were the racial and ethnic backgrounds of the victims and the types of attacks. In 1982, 50 percent of the confirmed bias-motivated crimes were characterized as anti-Semitic, and the vast majority of these crimes were directed against property. This trend continued until 1985, when blacks became the number one target of bias-related crimes, and the percentage of physical assaults increased significantly. Of the five hundred verified bias attacks in New York City in 1987, 118 victims were white, 220 were black, 82 were Jewish, and 33 were Latino.[1]

The pattern revealed an increase in physical bias-related attacks, with people of color and gays and lesbians as the primary targets of these attacks. Attacks occurred in many different neighborhoods and in all five boroughs of the city. Victims and assailants came from many different backgrounds. One common feature of the assailants was their age. Over 70 percent of those arrested for perpetrating bias crimes in 1987 and 1988 were under the age of twenty. Since schools are not required to keep statistics on racial incidents, the number of racial incidents in the schools cannot be reported. However, interviews with teachers and administrators indicated that there had been an increase in racial tensions, conflict, and violence in the schools as well.

Most people, when they hear of racial violence, think of rednecks in white hoods burning crosses or skinheads in black storm trooper boots with swastikas on their arms. But the reality of contemporary racial violence is that it is ordinary young people under the age of twenty who are perpetrating the overwhelming majority of racially motivated crimes. Most of the violence is random. It is not connected with an articulated racial ideology. There are no organized groups, no clear political objectives.

How can we explain why two teenagers from different racial backgrounds who encounter each other on the street are just as likely to attack each other as they are to talk to each other? How does race come to take on such enormous meaning in the minds of many young people? To say that we live in a racist society is a truism that supplies little information to help us understand the nature of race relations and the process of production of racial attitudes and racial interaction.

This book explores these two questions and examines the factors that encourage ethnic and racial conflict and violence among New York City youth. It focuses on young people, most of whom grew up in similar class backgrounds, facing similar problems and issues, with only one significant difference in their lives: their race or ethnicity. This one significant difference shapes the way these young people see themselves and others. If a young working-class African American and a young working-class Italian American were to meet on the street and talk, they might discover that they are alike in a number of ways. Yet they are just as likely to see each other as enemies because of one significant difference: their race.

This difference is reflected in dress, music, style, language, and, most important, the nature of their life experiences. For African American youth, race is a central element in their daily existence. It is an inescapable reality that profoundly affects their life chances and predetermines most people's initial reactions to their very presence. As a result, their individual identity is imbued with an understanding of racial difference and racial oppression. Many Latino youth must also cope with racial issues on a daily basis. Like African American youth, Latino youth must often deal with stereotypes about them as problematic and dangerous adolescents. For the white youth, race is a more peripheral issue. Most white youth have strong opinions about race, but it is not the primary defining feature in their daily experience. Nevertheless, they too incorporate a sense of ethnic and racial identity into their understanding of who they are as individuals and as group members. Racialized experiences, along with racialized information the youth receive, help shape their perception of themselves and other young people from different ethnic and racial backgrounds.

It is the meaning of race in the lives of young people that provides the foundation for ethnic and racial animosity and conflict among them. It is not the actual racial differences that generate racial conflict; it is the meaning ascribed to those differences and the significance of that meaning in the lives of young people that produce ethnic and racial confrontation.

This book is about race: about how race affects the lives and outlook of youth in New York City, about how young people interpret the state of race relations in our society, about why some of those young people resort to racial violence. This book is about youth: about how young people forge their identities in a racialized society, about how those identities become tied to their attitudes about themselves and others. This book is also about community: about the central role that communities play in the production and reproduction of ethnic and racial attitudes, ideologies, identities, and conflict.

The book examines the causes and consequences of the increase in racial conflict and violence among youth in New York City and analyzes why some youth end up perpetrating racially motivated violence while others develop tolerance and respect for persons of different racial backgrounds. The statements and experiences of the youth in this book help us to understand how horrendous acts like the Yusuf Hawkins murder can occur.

Many young people are growing up with hatred, distrust, and fear of people from different racial and ethnic backgrounds. How does this occur? Why, after decades of obvious progress in the development of racial tolerance among each successive generation, is there an apparent deviation? Scholars who have studied racial attitudes in the last thirty years have reported a strong and steady change in white American attitudes toward the principle of racial equality (Sheatsley, 1966; Taylor, Sheatsley, and Greeley, 1978; Kinder and Sears, 1981; Schuman, Steeh, and Bobo, 1985). Schuman, Steeh, and Bobo (1985) point to an important finding in their study of racial attitudes in America: Positive trends in the attitudes of whites toward blacks have largely been the result of cohort replacement rather than individual attitude change. They predicted that this trend would not continue, a prediction that is consistent with the pattern of increase in racial conflict among youth in New York City. The question is *why* there has been an increase in racial conflict among youth in the last ten years.

Theories about the Causes of Racial Conflict

The search for the causes of ethnic and racial conflict has intensified among scholars in the past decade as a result of the increase in ethnic and racial conflict and violence in this nation and throughout the world. Just as representations of racial conflict and violence in the popular media have been woefully inaccurate, explanations of racial conflict and violence have been inadequate in the academic literature. The predominant theories about ethnic and racial conflict concentrate either on macrolevel social forces and relations or on individual psychological processes. The tendency in social theory has been to search for a primary cause that can explain a social phenomenon. Studies of ethnic and racial relations have produced a variety of explanatory theories on the origin of ethnic and racial conflict. Conflict has been analyzed as a problem of the process of assimilation (Park, 1950; Frazier, 1968; Sowell, 1981); as the product of ignorance, misinformation, and lack of contact (Allport, 1954); as a function of the divide-and-rule strategy of the ruling class (Cox, 1948); as a product of capitalist development (Blauner, 1972; Montejano, 1987); as a product of Western European psychohistorical development (Kovel, 1970); as the result of value and cultural differences (Park, 1950; Frazier, 1968; Myrdal, 1944; Glazer and Moynihan, 1963); as the product of competition for scarce resources (Blalock, 1967; Wellman, 1977; Olzak and Nagel, 1986; Olzak, 1993); or as the result of the structure of class stratification within the economic system (Wilson, 1978).

Arguments between different theories and perspectives about racial conflict have primarily focused on the question: What is the primary factor or precipitant cause for the history of racial conflict, oppression, and inequality in this country and for the present condition of race relations? There is a danger in attempting to isolate the primary or original cause of prejudice, racism, discrimination, and conflict. Each of these paradigms implicitly or explicitly makes the case that either economic, social, cultural, political, or psychological factors are the core or most important determinant of the development of race relations in the United States.

In some rare cases, there is an attempt to discuss the interrelationship among different factors and how they affect one another. Although several sociologists have advocated comprehensive approaches to ethnic and race relations (for example, Myrdal, 1944; Pettigrew, 1985), there are few integrative studies of race relations that bridge the gap between different theoretical paradigms and examine the way in which structural, economic, cultural, and social-psychological factors *combine* to produce tolerance or conflict. An examination of the interaction of structural forces with sociopolitical and social-psychological factors is critical to understanding how individuals and groups act and interact. Human action is the product of many different factors and forces, factors and forces that must be examined together in order to understand why humans behave the way they do. This book provides a model for the examination of how ethnic and racial relations are shaped and determined at the level of behavior. By focusing on ethnic and racial conflict as a *process* that is the result of the combination of structural, social, psychological, and cultural factors, we can better understand the link between structural factors, historical context, political and social influences, and attitudes and behavior. This book examines how these factors converge and combine at the community level to produce racial conflict or tolerance.

The concentration on community processes is not a negation of the importance of more widespread societal factors and forces or of individual factors and forces. These communities exist within a larger social context that provides a historical, economic, social, cultural, and ideological basis for the form and content of racial attitudes, ideas, relations, and behavior. This approach establishes communities as an important location where the processes of race relations and racial conflict unfold. Communities are the locations and institutions where racial ideologies crystallize. Racial beliefs are community constructions, and racial actions are community activities. The community is the nexus where the societal forces combine with the individual factors to influence ethnic and racial attitudes and behavior.[2] The process of racial identification takes place at the community level. It is at the community level that ethnic and racial grouping and bonding take place.

The three predominant theories that have been used to explain the presence of racial conflict are *power/conflict theories*, which analyze racial conflict as a feature of systemic racial and class exploitation (Cox, 1948; Carmichael and Hamilton, 1967; van den Berghe, 1978; Blauner, 1972; Bonacich, 1972, 1973, 1980; Wellman, 1977; Steinberg, 1981; Montejano, 1987); *competition theory*, which sees racial conflict as the result of a struggle over scarce resources resulting from the rising supply of low-wage labor provided by immigrants and African American migrants (Barth, 1969; Blalock, 1967; Lieberson, 1980; Banton, 1983; Olzak and Nagel, 1986; Olzak, 1993); and *psychosocial theories* of prejudice, which find the root of racial conflict in the attitudes of individuals (Myrdal, 1944; Adorno et al., 1950; Allport, 1954; Pettigrew, 1958; Ashmore and De Baca, 1976).

While such approaches may be useful in illuminating different factors that influence race relations, they are incapable of sufficiently explaining the ebbs and flows of racial conflict. Ethnic and racial conflict is the product of a complex mixture of factors that combine to produce either tolerance or prejudice, cooperation or conflict. In order to understand the enduring quality of racial conflict and the present increase in racial conflict and violence, it is necessary to use a multidimensional approach. Violence must be analyzed as a *process* that has its roots in the ongoing interaction among a number of key factors that come together at the community level. Specifically, racial conflict is the product of three primary factors: (1) economic structural conditions that have resulted in heightened competition among groups and the existence of real or perceived inequality, (2) racial ideologies and racial belief systems, and (3) ethnic and racial identity. Structural conditions provide the context and foundation for the development of positive or negative attitudes. Ideology supplies the interpretive lens through which those conditions and the nature of different ethnic and racial groups are understood. Individual and group identities incorporate ideological messages into structured belief systems that connect attitudes toward others with the individual's or the group's sense of self.

The Structural Economic Sphere—Competition and Inequality

Structural economic conditions provide a foundation for racial conflict by shaping the nature of intergroup interaction. When different groups come in contact with each other, the nature of that contact is determined by their position in the stratification order. Groups that occupy the lower rungs of the stratification ladder are thrown into competition with each other.

At first glance, the increase in ethnic and racial conflict in New York City provides a classic example of competition theory (Olzak, 1993; Olzak and Nagel, 1986). Indeed, the decline of the manufacturing sector and the restructuring of the city's economy has laid the foundation for ethnic and racial antagonism through intensified competition for employment and housing. These structural developments have altered the opportunity structure for white youth on the educational and economic margins (Weis, 1990). These conditions have also affected the quality of life in the youths' neighborhoods. Communities that for two or three generations have been stable working-class communities must now cope with rising unemployment, rising poverty rates, and the influx of people from different ethnic and racial backgrounds searching for work and housing. These structural conditions have resulted in increased competition among ethnic and racial groups.

The existence of competition is clearly part of the mixture that results in conflict. Competition theory provides important explanations of how the interethnic and interracial interactions of white youth are structured and determined in a restrictive economic environment. It fails, however, to provide a plausible explanation for the attitudes of African American youth.

The ideas of African American youth have been shaped more by their perceptions of inequality, power, and oppression than by competition with other ethnic and racial groups. Theories of racial oppression provide more useful frameworks for understanding the dynamics of the attitudes and behavior of African American youth. Power/conflict theories analyze racial conflict as the product of a racially stratified economic and social system (Carmichael and Hamilton, 1967; van den Berghe, 1978; Blauner, 1972; Bonacich, 1972, 1973, 1980; Steinberg, 1981). Under this conception, there are two sides to the conflict. Dominant groups seek to maintain their position of power and privilege through coercive policies, laws, and actions that reinforce or establish advantages for the dominant group. Oppressed groups struggle to resist laws, policies, and practices that maintain their inequality and subjugation. The groups are in conflict with each other because of the nature of the economic system, which structures their relations in antagonistic terms.

Both the intensification of economic and political competition and the existence of real or perceived inequality provide a foundation for ethnic and racial conflict and violence. Competition can breed conflict between groups that are at similar levels in the job queue and that are thus competing for resources from an equal or slightly superior position in the stratification order. However, antagonism and conflict can also arise from perceived barriers to equal opportunity and treatment. In this case, the conflict is with those groups that are perceived to hold the advantage.

The difference between the origins and substance of the attitudes of African American and white youth underscores the limitations of structural theories in explaining the production of ethnic and racial conflict. A single theory cannot explain the attitudes and behavior of youth from groups and communities with separate histories, a different social position, unequal resources, unequal power, and relations to different groups. The competition exists because of the existence of inequality and the struggle among those groups on the margins to maintain or gain economic, political, and social advantages.

Structural conditions have both psychological and ideological implications for the youth in this study. On the psychological level, economic hardship and uncertainty foster heightened anxieties and frustrations for youth in economically troubled neighborhoods and circumstances and increase their sense of competition with other groups. Many of the youth in this study who have not done well academically are in this position. Some of these youths have embraced ideas that place the blame for their condition on other groups who are perceived to hold power.

On an ideological level, depressed surroundings seem to contribute to a more negative and oppositional sense of group position. Both white and black youth in this study who live in communities undergoing economic hardship had a sense of being victimized, a sense that was connected to their perceptions of the actions and advantages of an opposing group. Deficient structural conditions increase the likelihood of ethnic and racial conflict but do not guarantee it. With their focus on economic relationships, power/conflict and competition theories illuminate how macrolevel structural forces can create the potential for racial conflict by shaping the interactions of different ethnic and racial groups, but they do not explain why racial conflict actually occurs—why some groups who are in competition with each other become perceived as threats while others do not.

The Political and Cultural Spheres:
Ideology—Defining Who Is the Enemy

By themselves, structural conditions do not produce conflict; they do not explain how conditions are transformed into the ideas and actions of individuals from particular groups. What is missing is an explanation of the link between social structural conditions and the meaning of those conditions for individuals from groups with different amounts of power. The critical link between the structural conditions that shape the nature of intergroup interaction and either intergroup conflict or intergroup tolerance is an ideology that explains the conditions, relations, and interactions and justifies any action taken based on those ideas. Ideology supplies the frame within which the social and economic position of one's own group, the conditions and nature of other groups, and the character of intergroup relations are understood. Young people's interpretation of these conditions is shaped by their exposure to community and societal ideologies that produce negative or positive attitudes toward other groups and that produce racial conflict or tolerance. Ideology plays a critical role in providing a lens through which youth interpret their experiences and conditions. Their attitudes are the product of their exposure to ideologies that define and represent these groups as problematic and threatening. This process of definition and representation takes place at both the societal and community levels.

The definitions and representations of different groups are shaped in part by the history of a community's interaction with those groups, by the social position of those groups, and by their relationship to the community. The historical context of ethnic and racial relations in New York City is an important foundation for current ethnic and racial conflict. This history, of contact and conflict, contributes to the collective ideology of particular communities and provides a foundation for the current conflict.

The relationship between ideology and structural conditions is persuasively analyzed by Robert Miles (1989). Miles contends that individuals form their understanding of other groups through their interaction with other members of their own group. According to Weatherell and Potter: "It is through their activities and interaction with other members of their community that individuals create a social environment which comes to structure their judgements. This material practice and subsequent set of social relations, along with the history of those relations, inexorably direct the attention of social groups to some features and to some behavioral patterns of other groups" (Weatherell and Potter, 1992, p. 41).

Omi and Winant (1986) analyze how groups become racially identified and why racial meanings change over time. These racial meanings supply the interpretive frame through which individuals and groups come to understand the meaning of their economic status and their cross-cultural contacts and experiences. Their analysis of the effects of racial conflict on the pattern of race relations and ethnic and racial group identification provides an important analytical framework for understanding the role of ideology in the construction of race relations and in the production of racial conflict:

> The crucial task is to suggest how the widely disparate circumstances of individual and group racial identities, and of the racial institutions and social practices with which these identities are intertwined, are formed and transformed over time. This takes place through political contestation over racial meanings. (Omi and Winant, 1986, p. 69).

Omi and Winant concentrate on the role of social movements in the production of racial ideologies and racial meanings. Under their theory of racial formation, racial groups organize into social movements, which then agitate for changes in the state's approach to race relations and racial inequality. Omi and Winant provide an important contribution to understanding ethnic and racial conflict by highlighting the importance of the articulation of ethnic and racial identities within social movements that struggle for changes in the dominant societal racial ideology. However, they do not examine the production and role of ideology at the community level—the level at which it is internalized and expressed.

Social movements grow out of community-based attitudes and concerns. The community is a social institution that is critical to the regeneration and reproduction of racial ideology, racial identity, and racialized relations. The community level is where individuals internalize racial attitudes and where ethnic and racial identities are formed. The formation and transformation of "individual and group racial identities, and of racial institutions and social practices with which these identities are intertwined"—which Omi and Winant identify as crucial—take place within the community context.

Just as structural factors alone do not result in ethnic and racial conflict and violence, racialized ideologies provide only a piece of the puzzle. For ethnic and racial conflict to occur, these ideological messages must be incorporated into a belief system that forms the basis of a group identity. Individual and group identities incorporate these ideological messages into structured belief systems that connect attitudes toward others with the individual's or the group's sense of self.

The Social-Psychological Sphere:
Identity—We Have Seen the Enemy and They Are *Not* Us

There has been a growing interest in the construction of ethnic and racial identity since the early 1980s, spurred by the increasing diversification of the U.S. population. Studies of ethnic and racial identity have focused primarily on questions about how and why people think of themselves in one racial or ethnic category or another; they have rarely focused on the role of ethnic and racial identity formation in the production of conflict (Barth, 1969; Glazer and Moynihan, 1963, 1975; Lieberson, 1988; Waters, 1990).

Ethnic and racial identities are not only based on how one conceives of one's own group but also on how one's group is perceived, defined, and treated by other groups. Conversely, ethnic and racial attitudes toward other groups are based not only on beliefs about the nature of another group but also on a conception of one's own group.

Two theoretical approaches to ethnicity and race are useful in understanding the process of identity formation and its role in producing racial conflict: (1) Herbert Blumer's 1958 theory of racism as a sense of group position and (2) cultural studies approaches to the role of difference and representation in the production of identity as exemplified in the work of Stuart Hall and Henry Giroux.

Blumer's theory supplies a framework for understanding the fusion of negative attitudes toward other groups into the ethnic and racial identities of groups and individuals. Blumer's theory was based on the notion that a basic understanding of race prejudice must be sought in the process by which racial groups form images of themselves and of others. Blumer asserted that the genesis for racial prejudice could be found in the relationship between groups rather than in the thoughts and feelings of individuals (Blumer, 1958). Blumer stated that understanding race prejudice requires a focus on "the collective process by which a racial group comes to define and redefine another racial group . . . the process by which racial groups form images of themselves and of others" (p. 3).

The process of ethnic and racial identity formation is a process of understanding and making sense of one's situation and position. This process is a product of historical conditions that shape the conditions of intergroup contact. Blumer's theory of race prejudice as a sense of group position was one of the earliest attempts to explain how ethnic and racial stratification and subsequent contestation and competition over group social and economic position was tied to the content and structure of group identity. Blumer was concerned with the racial attitudes and actions of dominant racial groups. He outlined four basic types of feelings associated with this sense of group position: (1) a feeling of superiority, (2) a feeling that a subordinate race is intrinsically different or alien, (3) a feeling of proprietary claim to certain areas of privilege and advantage, and (4) a fear and suspicion that the subordinate race harbors designs on the prerogatives of the dominant race. The last three of these four feelings were clearly evident in the attitudes and behavior of many of the young people in this book. Surprisingly, I found little evidence of a feeling or sense of superiority among any of the white youth. To the contrary: Many of the young people from different racial backgrounds expressed feelings of victimization at the hands of other groups.

Blumer asserts that the definition of other groups as an opposition and a threat is the key to the development of group prejudice. This process takes place at many levels through complex interaction and communication between members of the same ethnic or racial group.

"Through talk, tales, stories, gossip, anecdotes, messages, pronounce-ments, news accounts, orations, sermons, preachments and the like definitions are presented and feelings are expressed" (Blumer, 1958, p. 5). While Blumer describes the development of this sense of group position, he does not analyze how it gets reproduced. In fact, Blumer's fundamental approach supplies a framework for understanding how both the tolerant and the intolerant racial attitudes of individuals from any ethnic or racial group are formed, transformed, and reproduced.

The view of racial and ethnic identity formation as an ongoing process has been advanced by cultural studies theorists, who see ethnic and racial identities as fluid and changing over time and according to context (Hall, 1991). According to Hall, an individual's identity is al-ways emerging, constantly being reshaped or reinforced to adapt to ex-isting or new social conditions, intergroup and interpersonal relations, and cultural articulations about ethnic and racial groups. He analyzes the importance of understanding identity as a process of identification:

> We've assumed that there is something which we can call our identity which, in a rapidly shifting world, has the advantage of staying still. . . . It's a kind of fixed point of thought and being, a ground of action, a still point in a turning world. . . . In fact, identity is something that happens over time, that is never absolutely stable, that is subject to the play of history and the play of difference. (Hall, 1991, p. 10)

For Hall, identity is formulated through discourse and interaction both within one's group and with those outside who get defined as the Other. The process of identification is also a process of affiliation and differentiation. The basis and meaning of inclusion and exclusion, the definition of who is different, and the meaning of that difference are defined within one's chosen group. Individuals do not decide on their own who they are and who they are not. They do so through their interaction in a community of peers.

According to Hall, the construction of one's identity is a quest to give authenticity to one's experience (Hall, 1991). This quest is under-taken together with other individuals with whom one identifies and from whom one desires acceptance. The result is the adoption of the group's norms as individual values and of the group's construction of identity as individual identity. One's attitudes toward other groups be-come one of the bases for affiliation within one's own ethnic or racial group. Hall states that "one critical thing about identity is that it is partly a relationship between you and the Other. Only when there is an Other can you know who you are" (Hall, 1991, p. 16). You have to know who you are not to know who you are.

The formation of an identity is not a process of identification that is isolated from relations and forces outside of the community context. Rather, it is a process that takes place in and is affected by larger societal relations, processes, and ideologies. Those relations include a racially stratified economic order that has placed certain groups in competition with each other, societal ideologies that de-emphasize the importance of class membership and inflate and distort the importance of ethnicity and race, and cultural messages about the meaning of ethnic and racial group differences.

The class backgrounds of the young people examined in this book have a bearing on how they think and act, not specifically because of their economic status but because of a whole set of factors that go along with that economic status: economic and employment anxiety, perception of threat, competition with other groups, proximity to other groups, and differences in economic, political, and social power among different groups. Consequently, it is some of the poor and working-class youths who displayed the most intolerant attitudes toward other groups. At the same time, the most tolerant attitudes of any of the youths were displayed by working-class and poor youths who were exposed to different messages about the meaning of their class position, ethnic and racial group membership, and the problems their communities faced. Their stories help to illuminate the importance of ideology, language, and meaning in the production of ethnic and racial conflict. They learn either racial tolerance, intolerance, or hatred, which is linked to their understanding of their group position, their ethnic and racial identities, and their perceptions of other ethnic and racial groups.

For many of the working-class youths in this study, part of the process of ethnic and racial identity formation was making sense of their marginal economic and social position. They did not identify themselves as working-class or poor persons who were victims of an economic system that afforded them limited opportunities. They adopted a racialized basis of identification, which was the dominant source of affiliation and identification in their communities. In the United States, race is a far more salient ideology than class. Community-based ideologies have been shaped by the centrality of race in U.S. culture and consciousness. The result has been the formation of identities that embrace oppositional attitudes toward other ethnic and racial groups who become defined as the perpetrators of oppression or the holders of economic, social, and political advantages.

The process of identification is also illuminated by the ideas and attitudes expressed by the more tolerant youths in this book. Their understanding of who they are was developed through their social interaction with other young people in a peer group that functioned as a multicultural community. Though these youths were exposed to similar images of other ethnic and racial groups within their community and at their school, the meaning they ascribed to ethnic and racial difference was different. This demonstrates why projections of stereotypes in the media and within different social interactions do not a priori result in the adoption of those images as individual attitudes about another group. These images are filtered and interpreted through the lens of a community-based ideology that provides a guide as to the meaning of that image.

Racial animosity is one of the most enduring of all social phenomena. This is precisely because racial attitudes toward other groups are grafted onto the cultural norms and values of ethnic and racial groups in competition and in conflict with each other. Over time, these attitudes become a part of the group's values and part of the defining characteristics that help to demonstrate membership and loyalty to an ethnic or racial group.

In the present period, the deterioration of economic prospects for youth has raised anxieties, fears, and competition among many young people. Community sentiment and peer group participation channel these anxieties and fears against other ethnic and racial groups by encouraging an oppositional sense of group position and linking membership in the community and peer group to particular attitudes toward other groups. Popular and community-based ideologies supply information to youth about how to interpret their experiences, their identities, and their relationships with other groups. Peer groups provide the arena in which young people internalize their attitudes toward other groups and in which they express these attitudes in the form of intergroup interaction, avoidance of interaction, or ethnic and racial conflict.[3]

Concentric Spheres of Reproduction

The conditions, attitudes, and actions of the youths in this book demonstrate the complexity of the process of ethnic and racial conflict. The ethnic and racial relations among these young people are the result of numerous factors. These factors converge and combine at the community level to result in racial conflict or tolerance. I have labeled this process "concentric spheres of reproduction."

Understanding current race relations in the United States requires that we explain the continual regeneration and reproduction of factors within several different spheres: cultural, political, social, psychological, and economic. There are concurrent processes of reproduction that take place within each sphere and that account for the continuity of ethnic and racial relationships and conflict. Structural relationships among groups are reproduced within the economic sphere. These structural conditions and relations in the economic sphere shape the nature of intergroup interaction, which results in competition among groups or the perception of oppression of one group by another. Attitudes are reproduced and concretized as ideologies in the sociopolitical sphere. Racialized ideologies and racial belief systems, which are generated in the sociopolitical sphere, provide the explanations of that interaction, explanations that place the blame for a group's position on the actions and power of another ethnic or racial group. These ideologies are communicated through various forms of expression: community social interaction, political ideology, school curricula, music, media imagery. Group interaction and institutional socialization promote perspectives and ideas that reproduce racialized group identities in the psychosocial sphere. Ethnic and racial identities that are formed in the psychosocial sphere incorporate negative or positive attitudes toward other groups as a part of the group's norms and values.

It is at the intersection of these spheres that these different reproductive processes combine and interact to produce opposition or acceptance; conflict or tolerance; violence, avoidance, or interaction. Ethnic and racial conflict is the result of concentric spheres of reproduction in which structural, ideological, and cultural relations and orientations are reproduced and combined.

This theory builds on theories of society as social formations (Althusser, 1971, 1977; Coward and Ellis, 1977; Hall, 1980); these theories advance a notion of a society as an articulation of three levels (the economic, the political, and the ideological), and society is viewed as a structural unity in which each level has relative autonomy but is linked and connected to the other two (Weatherell and Potter, 1992). Although the sociopolitical, social-psychological, and structural-economic spheres are interrelated and affect and determine one another, each sphere has its own regenerative and reproductive processes. The unifying factor across spheres is the existence of, maintenance of, and struggle against power and domination. Racial conflict occurs when there is convergence of unequal conditions, racialized ideologies, and oppositional ethnic and racial identities. In this situation, the racialized action is taken either in defense of power, privilege, and position or in resistance to power, oppression, and domination.

Structural position and the economic and social relationships of groups are reproduced within a capitalist system that promotes the reproduction of class, status, and privilege. These relationships in the structural economic sphere are regenerated and reproduced through the natural workings of the economic system. Changes in these relationships come about only through changes in the economic system's distributive policies and mechanisms, which equalize initial conditions and opportunities. As a result, in the absence of systemic change, racial and ethnic inequality can persist despite social and political ideals of egalitarianism and equality. However, the mere existence of inequality does not produce conflict. Ethnic and racial groups must coalesce and define themselves in relation to their position in the stratification order. There must also be an ideology that defines the inequality as a problem to be remedied or as an advantage to be maintained; this definition provides the basis for group action to defend against the agents of change or to attack the perceived source of domination and privilege.

Although structural economic conditions and relations can affect the cultural values and ideological expressions of particular groups, these cultural norms and values can be reproduced and regenerated even in the face of economic and political changes. Negative attitudes toward other groups can exist without those groups posing an actual or perceived threat. However, these attitudes only become important and provide the basis of action when a threat is perceived.

Changes in the dominant societal ideologies may not result in changes in group norms or attitudes at the community level. This formulation helps explain the maintenance of negative and oppositional ethnic and racial attitudes in communities like Bensonhurst and Gravesend despite the ideological shift in the dominant racial ideology in the 1960s and 1970s. The reproduction of ethnic and racial identities that incorporate negative attitudes toward other ethnic and racial groups is a continual process at the community level. The economic decline of the late 1970s and 1980s increased the salience of these racial attitudes, which provided an outlet for economically based anxieties, frustrations, and anger.

Where do the antagonistic ethnic and racial attitudes come from in times of economic and political uncertainty? The answer to this question lies in the structure and content of ethnic and racial identities that are perpetuated and determined at the community level. The reproduction of oppositional attitudes toward other groups over time in the face of state-sponsored attempts to alter that orientation is powerful evidence of the importance of community-level ethnic and racial ideologies.

These community-level ideologies and sentiments can then be articulated as larger societal ideologies that are concretized and espoused through the development of broader social movements. These social ideologies, which began as community-based attitudes, can exert influence on the political and economic arrangements of power, as has been the case with the development of neoconservative ideology and the rise of the new Right.

The factors and forces present in Bensonhurst, Gravesend, East Harlem, and Pelham Parkway exist in numerous other communities in New York City and throughout the country. The politics of ethnic and racial exclusion and reaction became a powerful community movement in the 1970s and 1980s in New York City, and it has become a powerful societal movement in the United States in the 1990s.

The Production of Racial Violence

For many young people, race has become a wall between themselves and other people of different backgrounds, a wall that they not only will not cross but are prepared to defend. In this context, racial attacks are the probable result of encounters between youths from different ethnic and racial backgrounds. Racial violence is a particular form of racial conflict, perpetrated by those for whom violence is a legitimate form of conflict resolution. The form of conflict is determined by the arena of interaction and the context of the perceived threat. All types of racial conflict have increased. On the political level, struggles over redistricting, economic resources, and political representation have intensified as the number of people of color increases in many regions of the country; political campaigns have included explicit and implicit ideological racial messages. In the judicial arena, there has been a continuing battle over affirmative action, discrimination, and civil rights legislation. In the economic arena, competition for employment has spawned conflict over racially based hiring policies and immigration. In the educational arena, there are debates over school vouchers, public educational policy, multicultural curricula, and Afrocentric education in primary and secondary schools and about admissions, hiring, curricula, and codes of conduct at colleges and universities. Highly charged slogans and ideas, such as "reverse discrimination" and "Our time has come," clearly delineate the racial lines of battle in the public policy and political arenas.

The racial violence among young people appears in *two* forms: (1) neighborhood-based attacks by groups of youths hanging out on the street and (2) conflicts between two or more groups at schools, conflicts that were often part of an ongoing battle between those groups. The neighborhood-based racial attacks were described by white youth in southern Brooklyn. The vast majority of these attacks are perpetrated by young males. The street is, for the most part, a male domain. I heard just two stories of young women engaging in neighborhood-based racial attacks. The racial conflict in the schools was mentioned by the majority of the youths interviewed regardless of gender or racial background. Numerous young women described involvement in racial conflict and violence at school.

It is important to distinguish between racial violence and the violence that is commonplace among many youths in New York City. Both types of behavior can be motivated by a desire to defend turf, by a desire to feel power, and by a desire to validate identity. But acts of racial violence have additional causes, motivations, and meanings for these youths. Racial attacks take on a broader significance in communities where there are widespread sentiments against particular groups. Whereas normal neighborhood-based clashes between groups of youths may be construed as an attempt to control physical turf, racial attacks are linked to a defense of turf, culture, and way of life. The ideas of the youth who perpetrate these attacks are often extensions of widely accepted community sentiments. As we shall see, this link lends a powerful moral aspect to the perpetrators of a racially motivated attack, for they view their actions as consistent with the values, norms, and wishes of the rest of their community. Fights between groups of youths of the same ethnic or racial background do not hold the same moral significance for them.

Altercations, attacks, or fights involving two youths from different racial backgrounds are not always racial violence. They are often conflicts that have little to do with the race of the antagonists. However, I heard numerous stories of personal conflicts escalating into racial confrontations at schools where friends join the conflict on either side and rumors quickly characterize the conflict in racial terms. The people involved differentiated between the pervasive violence among youth and racially motivated violence.

The major difference is the significance that those involved attached to the racial clashes. The racial attacks are far more intimidating for the victims, whereas they are often more affirming for the perpetrators since they serve to bolster the perpetrators' sense of importance and their identity and image among their peers. Racial clashes are more significant for the youths because they involve issues that are larger than they are. The acts take on a larger meaning because of the school, community, and societal context.

The current increase in ethnic and racial conflict among youth in New York City is understandable when placed in the context of overall ethnic and racial relations in the city and the nation. Youth in New York City are coming of age in a time of simultaneous racial progress and regression, of economic growth and decay, of neighborhood cooperation and retrenchment, of prosperity and poverty, of optimism and despair, of tolerance and prejudice.

The differences in the attitudes and behaviors of the young people in this study reflect differences in how they have experienced these times. Alone, these experiences do not determine their ethnic and racial attitudes and behavior. It is how they process and understand these experiences that determines how they think and act toward other groups. There is a direct connection between the attitudes and actions of young people in these neighborhoods and the climate of race relations across the country. There is a grassroots component to the ideologies and policies that have been advanced in the national political arena. Indeed, the racial appeals that have become standard in political campaigns are meant to appeal to this grassroots sentiment.

On the neighborhood level, black nationalism and white backlash provide a backdrop for the development of the ethnic and racial identity of many of these young people. They are reacting to the societal context of racial conflict and expressing their identification with one side or the other in the realms in which they interact: in schools and on the streets, and over issues of turf, neighborhood, dating, and relationships.

The increasing racial polarization in society is mirrored by a polarization of the most racially isolated youth in the study. This polarization begins early. The attitudes that adults exhibit, and that become the basis for adult actions, are already well developed in adolescence. White youth of southern Brooklyn and black youth of East Harlem are already on opposite sides of the fence attitudinally, politically, and ideologically. These differences already form a basis for their distrust and hatred of other groups and provide a motivation and rationalization for their behavior toward those groups.

The youths who perpetrate racial violence receive sanction and support for their activities from their peer groups, families, and neighborhoods. The tendency is for us to demonize these youths, their families, and whole communities—such as Bensonhurst—with the label "racist," as though they are aberrations. This allows us to maintain a more comfortable distance between ourselves and those who perpetrate the violence. It allows us to maintain the illusion that racial violence is not a logical outgrowth of our economic and social system. In fact, these attacks can only be analyzed as a product of the societal racial climate and the structure of economic, social, and political relations among different ethnic and racial groups.

There has been significant outrage expressed by the residents of Bensonhurst, who resent their community being labeled as racist. The difficulty in discussing community collusion with the violent activities is that the neighborhood becomes an exception: It appears to be more racist than other neighborhoods. Labeling Bensonhurst a "racist community" diverts the analysis from a study of racially motivated violence to an analysis of the people of Bensonhurst—from a more systemic and generalizable examination of the problem and factors that produce the present reality of racially motivated violence to a more microscopic, individual analysis. What sets Bensonhurst apart from other communities with similar demographics is simply that Yusuf Hawkins died there. The statements of youths from other white neighborhoods whom I interviewed clearly indicate that racially motivated attacks occur regularly in other white ethnic communities.

The attitudes and behavior of the youths in this book help us to understand the functions of racial hatred. Certainly there is a psychological component. Racial hatred and fear fulfills a function for many human beings. This is not a biologically based, predetermined predisposition but, rather, a learned set of attitudes and beliefs that help individuals define who they are and are not; manage anxieties, fears, and frustrations; and feel power and worth in their lives. That it fulfills a psychological function is only a small part of the picture. Racial hatred also fulfills a societal function. Within a capitalist society, the maintenance of racial stratification allows for a permanent surplus labor force (presently labeled "the underclass"). Through the psychological processes outlined above, racial hatred and fear serve as a safety valve for disenchantment and anger over position in the class stratification order. It fulfills the political and economic functions of some groups through the maintenance of racial privilege. It also fulfills a social control function: The demonization and dehumanization of people of color, particularly African American males, has made possible repressive activity by officers of the state and private individuals, which contributes to the preservation of the existing racial stratification order. Finally, racial hatred also fulfills a social function. The process of grouping and bonding into a group is enhanced if there is an enemy. Patriotism is always highest in times of war and conflict. Likewise, ethnic and racial identification at the community level is heightened during times of perceived socioeconomic threat and intergroup conflict.

Why is race so important to so many young people? Race achieves its importance in the minds of young people through a process of articulation that results in antagonistic racialized identities. This process takes place at many levels: the production of racial meanings; the formation of racial images; the dissemination of information, ideas, and ideology; the internalization of ideas as attitudes and values; the construction of ethnic and racial identities; the psychological processes that take place at the individual and group levels and that facilitate or necessitate the development of racial antagonisms and racist behavior.

The book is organized to provide a coherent picture of how the ethnic and racial attitudes and behavior of youth are shaped and determined. Chapter 1 provides an account of the composition and history of New York City and the three neighborhoods that are the primary focus of this analysis: Bensonhurst in south Brooklyn, East Harlem in Manhattan, and Pelham Parkway in the Bronx.[4] Structural conditions in New York City and in the neighborhoods are examined to illuminate the relationship among socioeconomic factors that have historically been viewed as the necessary conditions for ethnic and racial conflict in New York City.

Statistics are presented about the structural conditions of each neighborhood; these include employment rates, crime rates, dropout rates, average income, socioeconomic status, the settlement patterns of ethnic and racial groups in the areas of study, and demographic changes over the past twenty years in the racial and ethnic makeup of the residents.

Historical information about the development of the ethnic and racial makeup of the neighborhoods studied is supplied as a context for an analysis of the attitudes and actions of the youths who live in those communities. Additionally, a short history of relations between different ethnic and racial groups in New York City is presented in order to provide a context for an analysis of the contemporary situation.

Chapter 2 introduces us to the youth. The book concentrates on three groups of young people drawn from a larger sample: the Avenue T Boys in Bensonhurst, who are white and predominantly Italian American; Schomberg Plaza youth, who are black, predominantly African American; and Albanian youth from Christopher Columbus High School in Pelham Parkway, who are white and ethnically Albanian. These three groups provide case studies of youths from three different ethnic backgrounds and neighborhoods. Their attitudes and experiences are compared to those of youths of diverse backgrounds who attend high schools in these neighborhoods and live in these communities.

Chapter 3 examines the ethnic and racial attitudes of these youths. The role of the structural conditions which they face, the ideological messages they receive about those conditions, and their developing ethnic and racial identities are analyzed. All of these factors emerge from the content and substance of the attitudes expressed by the youths, and the complex picture of the process of ethnic and racial conflict among them comes into sharper focus.

Chapter 4 presents the youths' descriptions of the types of action they take, if any, based on their beliefs. A number of youths describe frequent racial attacks, which they have perpetrated or witnessed. These actions are clearly related to the youths' own sense of ethnic and racial identity and the meaning they ascribe to ethnic and racial difference. The role of community and societal support is analyzed in the production of racialized activity. The analysis of the behavior and actions of the youths is drawn from descriptions they provided of activities they engaged in. To analyze the factors that facilitate the expression of negative attitudes in the form of racial violence, the racial attacks and conflicts engaged in by some of the youths are contrasted with the behavior of others who do not engage in similar action. Additionally, activities undertaken by youths to promote ethnic and racial understanding and harmony are analyzed and compared with the activities of youths who engaged in racial conflict. This comparison underscores, once again, the critical role of peer groups and communities in the production of racial conflict.

The final chapter (Chapter 5) describes the significance of this research for practical efforts to reduce ethnic and racial conflict. Attempts to reduce ethnic and racial conflict and violence must redress each of the factors that combine to produce the conflict. These attempts should include the amelioration of structural economic conditions, the presentation of alternative, ethnically and racially inclusive ideologies, and the promotion of ethnic and racial identities that reject an oppositional and differentiative orientation. Central to the discussion of what can be done are theories about the importance of cultural messages in the development of conceptions of identity and difference. These theories provide important insights into the role that changes in the structure and content of education can play in the promotion of ethnic and racial tolerance.

Traditionally, social science examinations of race relations and racial attitudes have focused either on adults or on young children. Little has been written about the attitudes of adolescents, although adolescence is obviously a crucial period for identity development and attitude formation. The focus on young people is significant. The increase in racially motivated violence has been primarily fueled by the actions of young people.

We are unaccustomed to listening to young people. Yet young people are a mirror of the hearts and minds of our society. They will speak plainly about issues that adults will avoid, distort, or lie about. This is especially true about the issue of race, which is one of the most difficult issues to discuss in U.S. society. Whereas adults may speak in code words, hedging their answers and tailoring their responses, young people are more likely to speak their minds. The attitudes and actions of young people reveal the essence of the contemporary problem of race relations in the United States.

The youths presented in this book are not exceptional. They are average young people who are struggling to make sense of a difficult and tumultuous world. The communities they live in are not abnormal. They resemble communities in other parts of New York City and in other communities throughout the United States. The ethnic and racial attitudes of these youths and the actions they take based on those attitudes are reflections of attitudes prevalent in communities across the United States. In our efforts to understand and solve the dilemma of ethnic and racial conflict and violence, we would do well to listen to our youth. They have much to teach us about ourselves.

one

The Neighborhoods

I entered a house which was for sale in Bensonhurst followed by the watchful eyes of a number of neighbors, some of whom pointed fingers in the direction of the house to alert other neighbors to my presence. I emerged from the house to ask the neighbors about the merits of buying a house in that neighborhood. A middle-aged man in the first group of neighbors responded "People do all right here in this neighborhood as long as they fit in, people around here like to live around people who look and act like them, if you know what I mean." The second group of neighbors turned around and ignored me, speaking to each other in Italian as if I wasn't there and the third group went inside their house and closed the door as I approached to ask them a question. A day later I received an unsolicited phone call from the real estate agent who offered to show me another house in a different neighborhood.

—Author's field notes from 6/12/90

New York City's neighborhoods are an amazing collection of cultural enclaves established by waves of immigrants who settled in different parts of the city. Going from one neighborhood to another can feel like a journey from one country to another. Each neighborhood has its own unique atmosphere, forged from the combination of cultures brought from distant lands and diverse aspects of U.S. culture. From the goods and foods sold in the stores and restaurants to the languages spoken by their residents, New York City neighborhoods reflect both the rich history of their inhabitants and their fate and fortune as groups in U.S. society.

Founded in the 1660s, New York City has never been a homogeneous city. A primary entrance point for new immigrants, it developed as a mushrooming combination of ethnic enclaves. As waves of immigrants arrived, people sought areas where they could live among relatives, friends, and people with similar languages, customs, and cultures (Glazer and Moynihan, 1963). These groups had to compete for jobs and other scarce resources while being the targets of prejudice and disdain from already established immigrants and native-born Americans. Each group was not only the object of prejudice but also the recipient of negative stereotypes and information about other groups—groups with whom they were competing for jobs, housing, education, and political power (Steinberg, 1981). While this in itself may not have created racial conflict, it did create the necessary conditions for its development.

The composition of New York City's population varied and changed with shifting migration patterns. As the primary entrance point for European immigrants in the Northeast, over the last century and a half New York City's population has been shaped by repeated waves of immigration. In the 1840s, Irish and German immigrants fleeing dismal economic situations in their homelands settled in the city in large numbers. By 1890, the Irish-born and German-born and their offspring made up 52 percent of the city's population (Rosenwaike, 1972). Many of the Irish who immigrated were peasants: landless farmers and laborers who left Ireland in the wake of the passage of the Irish Poor Laws in 1838 and the disastrous potato famine that began in 1845. Lacking both resources and skills, Irish peasant immigrants were forced to take jobs at the lowest end of the labor market; they were disproportionately represented among unskilled laborers, construction workers, and household servants (Rosenwaike, 1972). This pattern was repeated by successive waves of immigrants. The German community grew even faster than had the Irish community, with Germans settling in ethnic enclaves. As the Germans moved into a neighborhood, the Irish began to move to other neighborhoods, prompting the resettlement of established native-born Americans. This process and pattern of neighborhood transition was repeated by later waves of immigrant groups. The most recently arrived and poorest immigrants settled in areas with cheap housing—those with the oldest housing stock—which were generally located in the center of the city. By the 1880s, large numbers of Jews and Italians began to arrive in the city, surpassing Germans and Irish as the largest groups to settle in New York City at the end of the nineteenth century. By 1925, Jewish and Italian immigrant residents of New York City outnumbered those of German and Irish descent.

By 1890, a geographic snapshot of the distribution of different ethnic communities in New York City would have shown Italian and Jewish immigrants highly concentrated in a few areas in the center of the city: Italians were scattered in Manhattan enclaves distinguished by their province of origin; Eastern European Jews were concentrated in the Lower East Side of Manhattan. As the "Jewish quarter" expanded northward, Germans moved farther uptown, to Brooklyn and to suburban districts, joining the "old stock Americans" (whites of native parentage) who had already established themselves in better neighborhoods. Similarly, as Italian neighborhoods in lower Manhattan began to expand northward, Irish residents moved further north on the West Side of Manhattan. Jews and Italians who wished to escape the tenements of lower Manhattan established enclaves several miles to the north of the borough in Central and East Harlem (Rosenwaike, 1972). By the turn of the century, the Irish were the least concentrated of the large immigrant groups, and Germans were becoming increasingly less ghettoized.

Though there was a sizable African American population in New York City at the turn of the century (60,666 persons; Bloch, 1969), between 1900 and 1930 the number of African American residents more than quadrupled. This expansion resulted from a large immigration of Caribbean blacks from the West Indies and from the influx of African Americans from the South who migrated north in large numbers after World War I. African Americans migrating to New York City settled in areas where they could obtain housing. Before the large migration of African Americans to New York City, African American residents of New York City were less segregated, living in substantial but highly scattered clusters (Bloch, 1969; Handlin, 1959). However, as large numbers of African Americans moved north, what Bloch characterized as a "circle of discrimination" began to materialize, limiting African American access to most areas of the city and segregating them residentially. Due to housing discrimination, large numbers of African Americans migrating to New York City entered a housing market that severely restricted African American settlement and geographic mobility. As a result, the vast majority of African Americans living in Manhattan settled in Harlem, and those living in Brooklyn settled in Bedford-Stuyvesant. By 1930, 72 percent of African Americans living in Manhattan resided in Harlem, accounting for half of all African Americans in the city (Ford, 1936). Previously, Central Harlem had been inhabited largely by Jews and East Harlem by Italians; but as

African Americans moved into Harlem, Jews and Italians moved north to Washington Heights and the Bronx and east to Queens and central Brooklyn, into neighborhoods such as Crown Heights, East New York, and Brownsville.

After World War II, New York City's ethnic and racial population changed even further as a result of three factors: (1) the movement of middle-income whites to the suburbs, (2) the growth of African American migration to the city, and (3) the rapid increase in the number of immigrants from Puerto Rico. During the period from 1940 to 1970, the net outflow of whites from New York City was over 2.2 million, while the city's Puerto Rican population grew to almost 700,000 and the African American population increased to more than 1,300,000 (Rosenwaike, 1972). Between 1940 and 1960, Brooklyn's African American population grew from 107,000 to 371,000 (Rosenwaike, 1972).

The pattern of Puerto Rican settlement was analogous to that of previous immigrant groups: first concentrated in lower Manhattan, then moving to formerly Jewish and Italian neighborhoods in East Harlem, then to the Bronx and central Brooklyn. At about the same time, African Americans began to settle in new areas, expanding north from Harlem into Washington Heights and the Bronx and moving into what were previously Jewish and Italian neighborhoods in Brooklyn, such as East New York, Brownsville, Williamsburg, Red Hook, Crown Heights, and Bushwick.

In the 1950s and 1960s, New York City experienced another wave of new immigrants, this time from nations in the Caribbean and Asia. The Cuban Revolution in 1959 resulted in a mass exodus of white Cubans from the island, many of whom settled in New York City and neighboring New Jersey. The U.S. invasion of the Dominican Republic in 1965 contributed to a large migration of Dominicans to the United States, most of whom settled in New York City. By 1975, Dominican immigrants constituted the single largest group of newcomers to New York City (Bailey and Waldinger, 1991). Dominican immigrants settled in Puerto Rican neighborhoods in East Harlem, the Bronx, and Washington Heights. The Immigration Act of 1965 served as a catalyst for a surge of immigrants from Jamaica, Trinidad and Tobago, Barbados, and China. And in the 1970s, large numbers of Southeast Asian and Korean immigrants settled in the city. These recent waves of immigrants followed the well-worn path of previous immigrant groups, settling in ethnic enclaves throughout the city and establishing communities in Queens, the Bronx, and Brooklyn and in the city's suburbs (Harris, 1991). Political scientist John Mollenkopf supplies a focused snapshot of New York's ethnic and residential composition by the late 1980s:

> The growing but relatively poor black and Latino populations are concentrated in and around ghetto centers like Central and East Harlem, the Lower East Side, the South Bronx, and Bedford Stuyvesant in Brooklyn. Whites, who tend to be much better off, have held onto their East and West Side enclaves in Manhattan. During the 1980's, they invaded some minority areas, such as the Lower East Side, and transformed loft factory districts like SoHo and Tribeca. Middle class Italians and Jews have also formed enclaves on the city's periphery, from Riverdale in the Bronx to Bayside in Queens around to Canarsie, Bensonhurst and Bay Ridge in Brooklyn. Areas of immigrant influx punctuate this pattern, most notably the Chinese settlements in Chinatown, Flushing and Elmhurst in Queens; Dominicans in Washington Heights; and the Latin American zone of Jackson Heights, Queens. (Mollenkopf, 1991, p. 339)

Since the early 1800s, when New York became a mecca for immigrants, competition for housing has been an issue of major contention between immigrant groups. Each incoming group had to find an area in which to settle, and the paucity of land led to either the ethnic integration of neighborhoods or the displacement of settled communities.

Of course, this phenomenon is not unique to New York City. Many of the nation's industrial urban centers experienced similar patterns of ethnic neighborhood transition with the arrival of new immigrant groups. This process of neighborhood transition has been analyzed as a process of invasion and succession (Burgess, 1928; Duncan and Duncan, 1957; Grodzins, 1958). The ethnic or racial composition of neighborhoods, composed of primarily or exclusively one group, changes with the influx of another group and the movement of the previous group to another location. The first part of the process is characterized as an invasion phase in which a few members of a new group settle in a neighborhood dominated by another ethnic or racial group. The outward movement of the original group is triggered by two factors: (1) the natural outmigration of members of the original group who have achieved an improvement in their economic position, prompting them to move to neighborhoods with better living conditions; (2) prejudice against the newcomers on the part of members of the original group, prompting a plethora of fears and a motivation to move to new areas. This fear is often based on perceptions of the incoming group as bringing crime and violence to the area. The fear of the immigrant as criminal has been well documented in accounts of xenophobia in New York City going back to the 1840s (Sowell, 1981). It has shaped perceptions of various generations of immigrants, from the Irish (hooligans and terrorists), to the Italians (criminals and mafioso), to the Eastern European immigrants of the early 1900s (vagrants, criminals, and anarchists), and most recently to African Americans and Latinos (violent criminals, drug dealers, and rapists).[1]

The history of residential settlement patterns in New York City is filled with examples of the process of residential succession. Neighborhoods in the Lower East Side and the lower parts of Manhattan were the primary residential destinations of numerous groups, starting with the Irish and German immigrants who settled there in the 1800s. These groups were followed by large numbers of Italians and Jews and by smaller numbers of Chinese in the latter part of the nineteenth century. These groups were then succeeded by Puerto Ricans, African Americans, and Dominicans. Although these last groups came in large numbers, the transformation of lower Manhattan was not total; small Jewish and Italian enclaves still remain. Chinatown continues to thrive and expand with the influx of large numbers of Chinese since the repeal of the Chinese Exclusion Act in 1965.

The settlement pattern in Brooklyn has been similar to that of Manhattan. Central Brooklyn, the part of the borough that lies closest to the East River and Manhattan, was settled first, with communities relocating toward the borough's periphery with the arrival of new groups. Central Brooklyn is now a combination of different enclaves with a wide band of mostly white ethnic communities on the periphery.

Race relations in New York City's neighborhoods have been profoundly shaped by this historical process. The racial sentiments and ideologies embraced by communities in New York City have been affected by the history of relations between specific groups and have been molded by the pattern of group settlement in different parts of the city. Relationships between Italian or Jewish communities on the one hand and African American communities on the other are a by-product of the contact and competition that resulted from the repeated migration of African Americans into Italian and Jewish communities. As we shall see from the attitudes of the youth from these neighborhoods, each community has a different set of impressions about the reasons for and the effects of neighborhood ethnic and racial transition. Italians and Jews in southern Brooklyn experienced the transition as an encroachment. Working-class Jews and Italians sometimes equate the influx of African American residents as the precursor to increased levels of crime and violence, to neighborhood deterioration, and to lower property values, despite the fact that the few African Americans who move into the heart of their communities are solidly middle class (Rieder, 1985).

On the other hand, many African Americans who reside in neighborhoods that have changed from Italian and Jewish to African American believe that their community has remained in the control of Italians and Jews who moved their residences but maintained ownership of the buildings and businesses. Many African Americans view these white ethnic groups as direct agents of racial exploitation, oppression, control, and disrespect.

The result of these settlement patterns can be seen in the demographic, economic, and social composition of neighborhoods in southern Brooklyn, East Harlem, and Pelham Parkway. The structural conditions that have shaped the nature of intergroup contact provided a firm foundation for the development of ethnic and racial conflict in these neighborhoods. In fact, each of these neighborhoods has been involved in highly publicized incidents that have contributed to the worsening of racial tension in New York City.

Southern Brooklyn

Bensonhurst, Gravesend, Sheepshead Bay, and Canarsie are adjacent communities; they are part of a strip of white ethnic neighborhoods, primarily working class, predominantly Italian American and Jewish, that stretches across the southern section of Brooklyn.

For the most part, these four neighborhoods are stable working-class communities; they have some of the lowest in-migration (influx of new residents) rates of any of the predominantly white communities in New York City (Stegman, 1988). All four neighborhoods are composed of residents who used to live in central Brooklyn. In a classic case of neighborhood racial succession, many of these families moved out of their previous neighborhoods thirty to forty years ago when African Americans, Puerto Ricans, Asians, and West Indians began to move in. This historical experience profoundly affected the attitudes and sentiments of the white residents toward these groups. All minority groups, but particularly African Americans, were perceived as a direct threat to the quality of neighborhood life, as intruders who had the potential to ruin the stable, close-knit, safe, ethnic niche the white community had taken years to establish.

These attitudes and sentiments have been well documented by Jonathan Rieder in his book *Canarsie: The Jews and Italians of Brooklyn against Liberalism* (1985); Rieder's book focuses on the Canarsie community, which has a history and demographic composition similar to those of Gravesend, Sheepshead Bay, and Bensonhurst. Rieder found that Italian and Jewish residents in Canarsie viewed maintenance of the ethnic and racial composition of their neighborhood as the most important factor for community harmony. Canarsie residents viewed African Americans and Puerto Ricans with mistrust, fear, and loathing as the harbingers of neighborhood deterioration, crime, decay, and chaos.[2]

Both Bensonhurst and Canarsie include a housing project, on the fringe of the neighborhoods, whose residents are primarily African American. In both communities, these housing projects have become focal points of racial animosity and conflict. White residents view the projects as the first foothold gained by poor African Americans encroaching on their communities. For their part, African American residents in the projects describe their situation as reminiscent of the European Jewish ghettoes where residents could not venture outside after dark for fear of being attacked. The Marlboro housing project, located on the border between Gravesend and Bensonhurst, is the center of much of the racial conflict in these two predominantly white communities.

Rieder documents a deep distrust and antagonism toward racial minorities on the part of the residents of Canarsie. These sentiments are clearly evident in the attitudes of the young people interviewed for this study. As we shall see, the history of the neighborhood and the collective community ideology has had a profound effect on the ideas and behavior of the youth of the community.[3]

At a high school in Bensonhurst and at one in Canarsie, there were separate, major racial confrontations, involving interracial violence, in 1976 and 1979. Racial incidents have been regular features of life in Bensonhurst, Sheepshead Bay, Gravesend, and Canarsie. Each community has had its turn in the media spotlight over high-profile racial incidents. Willie Turks, an African American transit worker, was beaten to death by a group of white youths in Gravesend in 1982. Yusuf Hawkins was murdered on the streets of Bensonhurst in 1989. Most recently, Canarsie experienced a series of racially motivated attacks in the summer of 1990.

A walk through Bensonhurst reveals a lively ethnic enclave. There is a vibrant, active retail corridor on 86th Street at the community's southern boundary. Eighty-Sixth Street is a typical New York City commercial area with stores, pizzerias, and street vendors selling everything from discount clothes to fruits and vegetables. The street is teeming with shoppers, and a subway train roars overhead. The crowd on 86th Street is overwhelmingly white, with a few Asians and a handful of African Americans. At the corner of 86th Street and Bay 4th Street, Dyker Beach Park, which is frequented by residents from the surrounding communities of Bensonhurst, Bath Beach, Fort Hamilton, and Dyker Heights, provides a glimpse of the community's culture. With the exception of the young people playing basketball at the far end of the park, nearly everyone in the park speaks Italian. One corner of the park has the feel of a town in southern Italy, with middle-aged and elderly Italian American men playing cards and boccie ball. The games are lively and boisterous, as old men in sleeveless undershirts argue over strategy in the boccie ball pit. The neighborhood is made up mostly of neat, well-kept, modest two-family brick and wood row houses, which line the streets on both sides with tiny patches of lawn or cement patios in front. The streets are clean, with primarily economy and midsize American cars on the street. On the corner of 23rd Avenue and 84th Street, a yeshiva (a school for Jewish religious instruction) across the street from statues of the Virgin Mary and Saint Christopher serves as a reminder of the white ethnic mix of the neighborhood.

In 1990, Bensonhurst was 80.3 percent white; of all the neighborhoods in Brooklyn, it was third (behind neighboring Bay Ridge and Sheepshead Bay) in its percentage of whites (New York City Department of City Planning, 1993). It was one of only three areas in the entire city of New York where there was no appreciable African American population. There were a few Asians living in Bensonhurst, some Latinos, and almost no African Americans. Economically, Bensonhurst was solidly working class with some whites living below the poverty line. In 1990, the median household income in Bensonhurst was $27,125 (New York City Department of City Planning, 1993). Bensonhurst has always had a reputation as a quintessential working-class community. Ralph Kramden and Ed Norton hailed from Bensonhurst on the television show *The Honeymooners*, which depicted the life of the blue-collar working man in an industrial city.

The heart of Bensonhurst is 18th Avenue, which runs right through the middle of the community. Eighteenth Avenue is quite different from 86th Street. It is almost exclusively white, seemingly all Italian. I rarely heard more than a few words of English on 18th Avenue. It is also a lively retail street, with a number of Italian cafés and bars where men gather. (In my many visits to the area, I saw very few women present in any of the establishments.)

At the corner of 18th Avenue and 62nd Street stands Public School (PS) 48, now a landmark, where the group of neighborhood youths gathered with baseball bats and clubs the night Yusuf Hawkins was killed. Though I got an eerie feeling each time I was in Bensonhurst gazing at the school with the knowledge that it served as the staging area for the murder of Yusuf Hawkins, I have detected only a couple of instances of apparent hostility toward me as an African American as I walked through the streets of Bensonhurst. Otherwise, I observed two distinct reactions to my presence: Most people studiously avoided looking at me until I had walked past them; at that point, a number of people would stare at me as I continued down the street. The most blatant instance of this reaction was in a pizzeria I had entered to buy a slice of pizza. There were five men in their twenties and thirties sitting conversing in Italian. As I entered, they shifted in their seats, turning their backs toward me. Others did not wait until I passed to stare but monitored my progress on the street quite openly. The only outward hostility I encountered in my time in Bensonhurst was when I went into the house that was for sale.

By day, much of the atmosphere is dominated by middle-aged and elderly Italian Americans. At night, 18th Avenue has a different character. Groups of neighborhood youths gather at several different corners outside bars or liquor stores along 18th Avenue. On summer nights, young people cruise 18th Avenue and 86th Street with music blaring from car stereos. By night, Bensonhurst appears exclusively white, with little evidence of the small minority population.

The Sheepshead Bay and Gravesend areas appear physically like Bensonhurst. But, though in these neighborhoods too the majority of residents are Italian American and Jewish, the neighborhoods have a character different from Bensonhurst's. Along Coney Island Avenue, Jewish shops abound, evidence of a thriving Jewish enclave that stretches across Ocean Parkway to the eastern section of Bensonhurst. Hasidic men with long, curled sideburns can be seen walking the streets around Ocean Parkway, and religious items like sukkahs (houses for the harvest festival Sukkoth) or menorahs (religious candelabras) are readily visible during different Jewish holidays. The commercial section of Gravesend appears more mixed than 18th Avenue in Bensonhurst, with Asian- and Indian-owned shops along with Jewish and Italian businesses. There is a small African American section in Gravesend and a slightly larger area in Sheepshead Bay. In 1986, the Sheepshead Bay and Gravesend areas were 84 percent white with an African American population of 2.3 percent (Stegman, 1988). In 1986, the median household income in Sheepshead Bay and Gravesend was $20,000.

Canarsie is set in the marshlands of Jamaica Bay, with a history and demographic composition much like the rest of the white ethnic neighborhoods in southern Brooklyn. Once again, the neighborhood's cultural mixture reflects its Italian and Jewish residents. Jewish delis, frequented by Orthodox Jews in skullcaps, can be seen close by stores bearing the red, green, and white of the flag of Italy. Like Bensonhurst, the character of the neighborhood shifts with nightfall. Older members of the community dominate the landscape during the day, creating an ambiance of their European roots. At night, the youth of the community are out in full force, transforming the main commercial strip from an old-world marketplace to a teen hangout.

Canarsie, with a 76.8 percent white population, had the largest African American population of the four southern Brooklyn neighborhoods at 14.3 percent (Stegman, 1988). This percentage is misleading since the overwhelming majority of African Americans lived in two housing projects on the edge of the neighborhood. The African American population in Canarsie was concentrated in three census tracts in the northern section, which included the Breuklin housing project; the remaining twenty-eight tracts were almost entirely white (Rieder, 1985).

East Harlem

The contrast between the old-world–new-world hybrid form of Italian American and Jewish cultures found in southern Brooklyn and the Puerto Rican and African American cultures and the predominance of the Spanish language in El Barrio provides a vivid example of the extraordinary conglomerate of, and contrast between, entrenched ethnic communities that make up New York City. These two neighborhoods exist in the same city, but they seem a world apart.

East Harlem is a predominantly Puerto Rican and Latino neighborhood in the north central section of Manhattan. Few whites can be seen.[4] In 1990, the population of East Harlem was 38.9 percent African American, 51.9 percent Latino (40.9 percent Puerto Rican), and 7.1 percent white (non-Latino) (New York City Department of City Planning, 1993). Most of the whites are concentrated in the southern sections of the neighborhood, where gentrification has been moving northward from the Upper East Side, and the eastern portions, where there is a shrinking Italian enclave. Outside these areas, the only whites I encountered were either construction workers, shop owners, or police officers. There is a vibrant commercial corridor along 116th Street that also expands along 3rd Avenue. Shops catering to the Puerto Rican and African American communities have signs in English and Spanish for Caribbean as well as American goods. The atmosphere in the neighborhood is friendly, with lots of children on the streets. Spanish is spoken by the majority of people on the street.

Old brownstones and tenements are mixed with multibuilding high-rise projects throughout East Harlem. Abandoned buildings and vacant lots dot the landscape. There is debris in many of the vacant lots and abundant trash in the streets. The community appears to be in decline, with only a few isolated signs of renovation.

As one walks down Lexington Avenue toward 96th Street, one sees the Lexington Houses at 99th Street, a large housing project. On the corner of Lexington and 110th Street, there is a lively street life, with thirty to forty young men and women hanging out, listening to music and drinking. What is striking is that this scene occurs on a Tuesday afternoon at 2 P.M. The large number of nonworking young adults is conspicuous.

A walk southward from 125th Street across 96th Street is a trip from the harsh reality of life on the margins to the picture of wealth and the American dream. Crossing 96th Street is like crossing the great American race-and-class divide. On one side, urban decay and poverty; on the other, prosperity and wealth. One crosses from an area where dilapidated housing, mom-and-pop bodegas, and run-down corner stores predominate to a world of doormen in exclusive apartment buildings, condos, cafés, and upscale gourmet shops; from old Chevies and Fords to new luxury sedans and sports cars. Park Avenue changes from a barren landscape cut in half by the train tracks that rise out of the ground north of 96th to the most exclusive street in New York City.

The link between the mostly poor African American and Puerto Rican residents of East Harlem and the working- and middle-class Italian American and Jewish residents of southern Brooklyn can be found in the history of their neighborhoods. At the beginning of the twentieth century, residents of East Harlem were predominantly Italian and Jewish, and there was also a sizable Irish and German population living in Central and East Harlem. It was an important, long-standing Italian neighborhood that produced many prominent Italian American politicians, including Fiorello La Guardia, until the population of the area changed as a result of the influx of African Americans and Latinos into the area after World War II. Many of the new migrants moved into East Harlem as the Italians and Jews moved to parts of Brooklyn, Queens, and the Bronx and to more suburban areas outside of the city.

Directly adjacent to East Harlem, Central Harlem had already become a mecca for African Americans migrating to New York City from the South during the 1920s and 1930s. As the numbers of African American migrants to New York City increased, the black population of Harlem began to expand eastward. At the same time, migration from Puerto Rico increased dramatically in the wake of World War II, from 11,000 in 1944 to 40,000 in 1946. East Harlem was the destination of many Puerto Rican migrants, and the neighborhood eventually earned the name "El Barrio" (Glazer and Moynihan, 1963).

The large influx of African Americans and Puerto Ricans since the late 1940s was fueled, in part, by urban redevelopment projects that resulted in the construction of high-rise housing projects for poor and working-class residents. The most obvious result of this development was a concentration of eight housing projects in East Harlem stretching from 5th Avenue to the East River. This area is presently characterized by high levels of poverty and unemployment and by overcrowded housing. In 1990, the median household income in East Harlem was $14,882—ranking fifty-fourth out of fifty-nine neighborhoods in New York City and well below the citywide average of $29,823 (New York City Department of City Planning, 1993).

Though Jews and Italians moved to other parts of the city as early as the 1940s, many of the shops, stores, and buildings continued to be owned by Jews until the mid 1970s. By the 1980s, many of the shops and stores were bought or rented by Koreans and Arabs.

Since the beginning of the 1980s, there has been some gentrification in the southern sections of El Barrio where the Upper East Side has expanded northward, through condo conversions, housing renovations, and the expansion of businesses north from midtown Manhattan. Though the process slowed somewhat in the later part of the 1980s, the result was a neighborhood "culture clash" between affluent whites from the Upper West Side and poor African Americans and Latinos from East Harlem. In contrast to the persistent, concentrated poverty that characterizes East Harlem, the Upper East Side's median household income—$53,000—was by far the highest of any New York City neighborhood.

The Schomberg Plaza housing project sits at the corner of 110th Street and 5th Avenue, overlooking a vacant lot and abandoned buildings. It is set in a sparse, stark urban landscape that contrasts with the lush green abundance of Central Park stretching southward from the opposite corner. There are very few stores in the immediate vicinity of Schomberg Plaza, and it is much quieter than the projects I observed earlier.

Schomberg Plaza houses mostly poor families, with a small percentage of middle-income families. The vast majority of the project's residents are African Americans who have lived in the housing project for at least five years. Schomberg Plaza became the center of media attention in the wake of the Central Park jogger case. Three of the six youths put on trial for the rape lived at Schomberg. Several stories appeared describing Schomberg as a middle-class apartment complex with a "doorman." In fact, the "doorman" is a security guard not unlike those found in other, predominantly low-income projects throughout New York City.

Pelham Parkway

While East Harlem, Bensonhurst, Gravesend, and Canarsie are virtually racially segregated communities, Pelham Parkway in the Bronx appears to be the picture of the melting pot that New York is supposed to be. Pelham Parkway is an ethnically mixed area, located in the northwest Bronx. It is home to a range of ethnic communities: Italian, African American, Puerto Rican, Dominican, Jamaican, and the largest population of Albanians in New York City. The vast majority of Albanians immigrated to the United States after 1960, fleeing ethnic persecution in Yugoslavia and a Stalinist government in Albania. Historically, the north central Bronx was populated by groups moving north from Manhattan as new groups of immigrants settled in their old neighborhoods and the process of neighborhood succession took place. The area became home to Jews and Italians who moved north as African Americans and Latinos succeeded them in East Harlem, Washington Heights, and the South Bronx. There was an influx of African American and Latino residents during the 1960s and 1970s, but the area did not undergo the full transition of ethnic succession characteristic of so many New York City neighborhoods. The white community shrank by 23 percent, from 77.1 percent of the neighborhood's population in 1980 to 59.8 percent in 1990. The Latino population increased from 13.1 percent of the neighborhood's population in 1980 to 24.1 percent in 1990. The African American population increased from 7.8 percent in 1980 to 12 percent in 1990 (New York City Department of City Planning, 1993). Consequently, Pelham Parkway has remained a mostly white community with significant African American and Latino populations. After spending time in East Harlem and southern Brooklyn, one is struck by the ethnic and racial diversity of Pelham Parkway. Along the main streets, Allerton Avenue and White Plains Road, the people on the street reflect the diversity of the community. Whites, African Americans, and Latinos can be seen shopping side by side in stores that are owned predominantly by Italian and Albanian merchants.

But the racial and ethnic diversity in the commercial areas is not evident in the residential areas. Many of the African Americans, West Indians, and Puerto Ricans live in projects on the neighborhood's west side. In contrast, the east side of White Plains Road is mostly Italian and Albanian and has a more suburban flavor, with cleaner streets, single-family houses, and row houses.

Christopher Columbus High School is the only public high school in Pelham Parkway. Its ethnic composition is quite different from that of the surrounding communities, which are mostly white. In 1988, 34.7 percent of the students were Latino, 19.2 percent were African American, 9.2 percent were Asian, and only 36.8 percent were white, down from 47.3 percent just four years earlier. The ethnic and racial mix at Christopher Columbus High School and the changing demographics of the school provided the context for the development of either ethnic and racial tolerance and awareness by the students of the school or ethnic and racial conflict and violence between different groups in the school.

There have been numerous incidents of racial violence at the high school. In January 1990, Pelham Parkway became a landmark on New York City's map of high-profile racial incidents when a group of white youths who call themselves the "Albanian Boys" attacked an African American youth and a Latino youth in separate incidents.

The attitudes and behavior of the youth in these neighborhoods are an outgrowth of their community's culture and their physical surroundings. Economic conditions in their communities provide the bedrock for the perceptions that community residents have about other ethnic and racial groups. Each neighborhood has a community history and a set of collective experiences, ideas, and values that help shape the common outlook of its members. Part of that outlook is a community ideology about different racial and ethnic groups. This dimension of community sentiment is often neglected in analyses and discussions of race relations and racial conflict. Yet the communities themselves play a vital role in the production of racial behavior. Communities, particularly strong ethnic enclaves, provide the context for the development of ethnic and racial identities among young people. To understand who these young people are, it is imperative to examine the economic conditions, the historical development, and the current dominant racial ideologies of the communities that have helped shape their identities, attitudes, and actions.

Economic Conditions in New York City

Revolving settlement patterns at the neighborhood level and the struggle between ethnic and racial groups for "turf" have contributed to a history of ethnic and racial conflict in New York City. German and Irish immigrants were embroiled in violent clashes with native-born Protestants who resisted the influx of these new groups into their neighborhoods (Katznelson, 1981). Ethnic gangs frequently battled one another defending neighborhood territory. During the period when Jews and Italians were immigrating into the city, street fights erupted between Irish and Jews and between Irish and Italians in the formerly Irish neighborhoods where Jews and Italians settled (Bayor, 1988). Before World War II, whites determined to maintain and enforce patterns of racial segregation participated in race riots (Steinberg, 1981). In the mid 1960s, Italian youths in East New York organized the "Society for the Prevention of Niggers Getting Everything" and violently resisted the settlement of African Americans in their community (Rieder, 1985).

These conflicts have had an undeniable element of class conflict. Competition for jobs has been a major precipitant of ethnic and racial conflict. Most immigrants and migrants arrived impoverished, with few skills, no education, and meager resources, which placed them at the bottom of the occupational ladder and ethnic hiring queue and the hierarchy of ethnic and racial stratification in the city. Lieberson (1980) describes occupational queues as early as 1900 in the different occupations that existed in northern cities. Whites whose parents were native-born occupied the highest positions on the ladder, with a disproportionate percentage in professional occupations; Germans and Irish came next, holding a significant share of trade and transportation occupations and of manufacturing and mechanical occupations; south and central European groups came next, with a high representation in manufacturing and mechanical occupations; and African Americans were last, with high representation in domestic and personal service occupations. It is well documented that African Americans were the victims of widespread economic discrimination by unions, employers, and the government, severely limiting their access to many occupations (Abrams, 1966).

Each new group of immigrants to New York City has had to compete for jobs with groups who hold positions on the lowest rungs of the stratification ladder. The new immigrants' presence only represented a direct threat to those ethnic groups who occupied the same socioeconomic level or the stratum just above them. Stephen Steinberg wrote that the conflict was "fundamentally one between the haves and the have-nots—or more accurately, between the have-nots and those who have little" (Steinberg, 1981, p. 218). Race riots occurred in New York as early as 1863, when large numbers of Irish attacked and killed African Americans in the streets (Abrams, 1966).

Foreign immigrants and African American migrants were often used by employers as a surplus labor force to maintain low wages and as strikebreakers to undermine union attempts to gain better working conditions (Steinberg, 1981). Historian Allan Spear wrote, "Nearly every overt racial clash in the North in the early twentieth century involved conflict between African Americans and working-class whites" (Spear, 1971, p. 163).

Though racial conflict has received the most attention, as this review of settlement patterns shows, there has also been persistent conflict between different ethnic groups of the same race. Early Irish immigrants encountered bitter resentment because of their role as strike-breakers and were hated and kept out of the unions as a result. After the Irish were accepted as members of the unions, Italians, along with African Americans, were the newcomers who encountered hostility as strikebreakers and blockbusters. Irish complaints that Jews controlled all the good jobs and businesses contributed to anti-Semitic violence in the 1930s and 1940s (Bayor, 1988).

Conflict between ethnic and racial groups in New York City has also taken place in the political arena. Glazer and Moynihan (1963) state that the single most important fact about ethnic groups in New York City is that they are also interest groups. Each group has organized in an attempt to influence or control the political policies and institutions from which their group could benefit. The struggle for political control in New York City mirrors the city's history of population expansion and residential succession. In the 1850s, Irish and German immigrants began to challenge the native-born Protestant elite of English and Dutch descent who had controlled the city since its founding, and they eventually gained political power in the 1870s. By the turn of the century, the rapidly growing Italian and Jewish communities began to vie for political power and influence with the more established Irish who dominated the political machine. They succeeded in gaining hegemony in the 1950s (Mollenkopf, 1991). Since the early 1960s, Italian and Jewish groups have been increasingly challenged by the growing African American and Puerto Rican community, as evidenced by struggles over redistricting. Struggles for political power have been marked by violence between the groups in competition (Mollenkopf, 1991).

One essential ingredient for the development of ethnic and racial conflict in New York City seems to be the *perception of a threat posed by another group:* the threat of competition for employment and housing, of displacement from a neighborhood, of a decline in property values and subsequent monetary loss, of an increase in crime, or of a loss of political power.

Although much ethnic and racial antagonism has endured between groups over time, levels of conflict have fluctuated with the fiscal health of the city. When unemployment is high and jobs are scarce, competition between groups is more intense. Shortages of housing may intensify competition for dwellings (Abrams, 1966). Periods of economic hardship tend to jeopardize a group's position in the stratification hierarchy, producing insecurity and anxiety and a perception that the group's future may be threatened (Silver, 1973; Bayor, 1988). As a result of the Great Depression, for example, competition for scarce resources became sharper. The result was an increase in the 1930s in ethnic tensions and conflict that had been relatively submerged during the 1920s (Bayor, 1988). During the 1950s and early 1960s, a period of relative prosperity for the city, the level of overt conflict waned. The passions and attention of the nation were focused on the southern states, where racial conflict had exploded into a war of attrition between the civil rights movement and supporters of racial segregation. New York City's uneasy relative calm was broken in the mid 1960s, when the economy experienced a sharp downturn, and African Americans began pressing for changes in the pattern of racial segregation in housing and the schools of the North.

Current Structural Conditions

New York City's economy underwent a profound restructuring beginning in the late 1960s, a restructuring that has been analyzed as a simultaneous process of decay and growth (Drennan, 1991). Whereas the manufacturing sector has been in serious decline during the last two decades, during the same period the finance and service industries have experienced rapid expansion. Between 1969 and 1977, New York City lost over 600,000 jobs, most of these in the manufacturing sector (Drennan, 1991), with the largest decline in manufacturing jobs in Brooklyn and the Bronx (Harris, 1991). As a result, after a decade of expansion in the 1960s, employment decreased steadily from 1969 to 1977. Although the numbers of workers increased from 1978 to 1984, this increase was almost exclusively in the service sector. The highest percentage of these jobs were in business and related professional services. Jobs in business, professional social and religious services, education, media, and health care accounted for 76 percent of the increase. While some of these were certainly clerical, janitorial, and support jobs, the prospects for working-class and poor youth remained severely restricted. Many of these jobs were likely to be occupied by persons who had moved back into New York City or by white women, who were entering the labor force in large numbers.

Although some sectors of New York City's population benefited from this decade of economic expansion, poverty increased from 15 percent in 1975, about 20 percent above the national average, to 23 percent in 1987, almost twice the national average (Mollenkopf and

Castells, 1991). Unemployment rates have consistently been higher in New York City than in the rest of the state and the nation. Among young people under twenty, unemployment rates are as high as 22.2 percent for whites and 47.5 percent for African Americans. In 1990, 49.1 percent of whites, 47 percent of African Americans, and 42 percent of Latinos were working. Among those below the age of twenty, fewer than 20 percent of the young people were working, compared to the national average of almost 44 percent.

While competition for employment intensified, the dropout rate among the city's youth increased from 13.5 percent in 1983 to 25 percent in 1987. The situation was worst for African American and Puerto Rican youth, with official dropout rates of 24.3 and 31.3 percent respectively (New York City Board of Education, 1989). The percentage of white students in the New York City schools decreased steadily, from 62.7 percent in 1960 to 23.7 percent in 1980. Whereas whites were the majority in 1960 and the single largest group in 1970, they were a distinct minority in New York City schools by the 1980s (New York City Board of Education, 1984).

These trends have been accompanied by significant demographic changes in the composition of the city's population. From 1970 to 1980, the population per square mile declined in four of the five boroughs by between 5 and 20 percent, with an overall reduction of 800,000, or 10.4 percent, as a result of a massive out-migration of New Yorkers to the suburbs and other parts of the state and nation. Much of this movement was due to "white flight"—middle- and upper-income families moving out of the city to escape the rapidly increasing numbers of African Americans and Latinos who were settling in the city. During the same period, the population of people of color grew by 1 million. From 1965 to 1980, the foreign-born population also increased by almost a million. Most of these immigrants arrived from Third World nations; of the 772,040 immigrants who are classified by their country of origin, close to 80 percent, 598,500, were from Third World countries (New York City Department of City Planning, 1985). The demographic changes since the 1960s have made the non-Latino whites a minority of the city's population (Mollenkopf and Castells, 1991).

Meanwhile, working- and lower-class families in New York City have found it increasingly difficult to find or maintain decent housing. Since the late 1970s, in all five boroughs, neighborhoods have been steadily converted from lower- and working-class tracts to middle- and upper-income tracts. Wealthier people—whose resources allowed them to leave an area when threatened with the encroachment of "undesirable" groups and the problems of crime, violence, and overcrowded neighborhoods—have returned to the urban areas from which they fled in the 1950s and 1960s (Harris, 1991). By 1987, vacancy rates for inexpensive apartments throughout the city were extremely low (Stegman, 1988). The result has been an intensification of the housing shortage for lower- and working-class people and a dramatic increase in the number of homeless people.

Economic and demographic changes in New York City were accompanied by significant political change. In the 1989 Democratic mayoral primary, David Dinkins defeated the three-term incumbent Ed Koch, who for twelve years had led the dominant electoral coalition based on the support of ethnic whites in the city.[5] Koch was hurt by a number of scandals involving members of his administration and county party leaders. This, combined with the heightened racial tensions as a result of the Central Park rape case and the racial murder of Yusuf Hawkins in Bensonhurst, allowed Dinkins to appeal to the most liberal whites in Koch's coalition. After Dinkins won the primary, 51 percent to 43 percent, he faced Republican Rudolph Giuliani in the 1989 general election, wherein record numbers of white Democrats voted for the Republican rather than Dinkins, almost resulting in a Giuliani victory (Mollenkopf, 1991). Nevertheless, Dinkins was able to pull enough white liberal votes, combined with his massive support in the African American and Latino communities, to eke out a victory by 43,000 votes out of 1,780,000 ballots cast.

The election of David Dinkins as mayor marked a significant deviation from the existing political control of city hall by the established order dominated by a conservative, predominantly white electoral coalition (Mollenkopf, 1991).[6] Dinkins was elected New York City's first African American mayor in a campaign marked by racially polarized voting. His victory was forged through a coalition made up of African Americans, Latinos, Asians, and liberal Protestants and Jews (Mollenkopf, 1991).

These changes in the economy of New York City have helped to create conditions for increased racial tensions in the six neighborhoods being examined. For the impoverished neighborhood of East Harlem, these changes have meant increased unemployment, diminished job prospects for young people, and more severe overcrowding in substandard housing.[7]

In southern Brooklyn, the decline in the manufacturing sector has had a negative effect on the working population and the structure of opportunity for the youth of these neighborhoods. This is particularly true for young people who have dropped out of school or who do not attend college. The traditional progression into low- and semiskilled industrial jobs is no longer an option in these neighborhoods. Each of the neighborhoods in southern Brooklyn experienced an increase in the number of residents living in poverty between 1980 and 1990 (New York City Department of City Planning, 1993).

Residents of Pelham Parkway experienced similar effects from the economy. A majority of the residents experienced a loss in income between 1980 and 1987 (Stegman, 1988), and the number of residents living in poverty increased from 1980 to 1990 (New York City Department of City Planning, 1993).

Based on this combination of economic problems and demographic and political changes, the necessary structural conditions for ethnic and racial conflict were all present in these neighborhoods in the mid 1980s: economic inequality; the threat of intense competition for jobs and the displacement and scarcity of housing; the ever present specter of crime; and competition for political influence and control.

Within communities organized around ethnicity, there are accepted ideas and attitudes that compose a community ideology or sentiment. This community ideology becomes a part of the values and norms that community members ascribe to their ethnic culture. The experiences of young African Americans in East Harlem, the Italian and Jewish young people in southern Brooklyn, and young Albanians of Pelham Parkway profiled in this book exemplify the conflicts between their ethnic groups. There can be little doubt that each of the neighborhoods examined in this book has an ethos, an ideology, a mind-set that pervades the experiences of these young people and shapes their interpretation of their sense of self and others. Communities determine the attitudes and behavior of their youth. In all circumstances, young people's sense of self, both individually and as members of peer groups, is based on their attitudes and disposition toward others—a disposition shaped by the structural economic conditions of their communities, the ideologies that are dominant in their communities, and a sense of ethnic and racial identity that is tied to a larger community identity.

two
The Youth

Adolescence is an unsettling time for most young people. It is the time when they begin to forge an identity, when they try to understand how they fit into the world around them. It is a time when young people try to figure out who they are and who they are not, and when peer groups become as important as families for many. The adolescent world is a world of acceptance and rejection. Identities are formed in relationship to membership in peer groups: jocks, burnouts, eggheads, nerds, greasers, homeboys, Crips, Bloods. All young people face these issues in their lives. The result is an intense level of anxiety. The institutions and factors that affect their sense of self and their orientation toward others are the same for all youth. It is the differences in the content, substance, and effects of those institutions and factors that account for differences in attitudes and behavior among young people within and across ethnic and racial groups.

Growing up in New York City in the 1990s can be a daunting task.[1] Schools are failing youth at an increasing rate, and the dropout rate is steadily increasing, especially among Puerto Rican, African American, and Italian American youth in New York City. At the same time, employment opportunities for young people have severely constricted, leaving many without opportunities after they leave school.

The sense of anxiety and uncertainty that is a part of adolescence is heightened by structural factors that affect the lives and outlooks of those growing up on the economic margins. Those who grow up in impoverished families in poor neighborhoods have to contend with bleak employment prospects and physically dangerous surroundings. As a result of economic changes in inner cities, young people from stable working-class families now also face uncertain futures. Some have been labeled "at-risk" simply because of the neighborhood or the conditions in which they live (Sullivan, 1989). They are at-risk of dropping out of school, of drug abuse, of juvenile delinquency, of engaging in criminal activity, of unemployment, of violence, of death.

The three main groups of young people interviewed in this book, the Avenue T Boys in Bensonhurst and Gravesend, those from Schomberg in East Harlem, and the Albanians in Pelham Parkway, could all be counted in the at-risk category. This sets them apart from most of the other young people examined in this book, from Central Park East Secondary School in East Harlem, Sheepshead Bay High School and John Dewey High School in southern Brooklyn, and Christopher Columbus High School in Pelham Parkway.

Their lives are marked by poverty, academic failure, violence, and criminal detention. If these young people met and compared their lives, they would probably find that they shared some similar experiences at home and on the street. What is more likely is that, if they met, they would see each other as the embodiment of their individual and group problems—and they would fight.

Boys and Girls in the Hood
The Youth of Southern Brooklyn

The young people interviewed in southern Brooklyn can be separated into two distinct categories: those who have dropped out of school or who are attending alternative school programs and those still attending comprehensive public high schools. Most of the out-of-school youths from southern Brooklyn were from Italian or Jewish working-class backgrounds. Their fathers were salesmen, bus drivers, carpenters, electricians, sanitation workers, maintenance workers, plumbers, truck drivers, butchers, cab drivers, factory workers, and mechanics. A small number, 19 percent, had fathers who were professionals, managers, or administrators, but about 20 percent of these did not live with their fathers. Sixty-five percent of the young people interviewed in southern Brooklyn reported that their mothers worked. Of those, 19.3 percent had mothers who were professionals, managers, or administrators, and 52.1 percent had mothers who were salespersons, secretaries, factory workers, waitresses, or service workers. Only 45 percent lived with both their parents; 45 percent lived with one parent, and 10 percent lived with neither parent. Three-quarters of the young people interviewed were male.

Most of the at-risk youths reported spending significant time on the streets with neighborhood-based peer groups. There are a number of groups who identify themselves according to the neighborhoods they live in and the streets where they spend most of their time. There are groups in almost every working-class or poor section of New York City regardless of race. In southern Brooklyn, the turf is divided along neighborhood lines into numerous groups like the Kings Highway Boys, the Bath Beach Boys, Avenue U Boys, the Avenue X Boys, the Dyker Park Boys. These groups often clashed over turf disputes or in conflicts that erupted at school. The young people interviewed in southern Brooklyn included those who hung out with street groups in Bensonhurst, Gravesend, Canarsie, Sheepshead Bay, along Kings Highway, along Bath Avenue, and in Coney Island.

Most of these neighborhood-based groups are loosely organized. A group of neighborhood youths, mostly male, congregate at a regular hangout spot. The composition of the group is very fluid. The groups do not have official names like many of the "posses," "crews," and gangs that exist throughout New York City. They are not organized gangs in the traditional sense. There is no official membership, no specific initiation rites, no street names, and no official leaders. These youths get together because they live in the same neighborhood. The participants on any particular night vary. The Avenue T Boys were one of these groups.[2]

The Avenue T Boys take their name from the turf that they frequent and defend. There is nothing extraordinary about the young people who hang out on Avenue T. They look and act like teenagers from any part of New York City. When I first met them, they were standing at one of their regular "hangs," outside a pizzeria in the heart of Bensonhurst. Most of the guys dressed in baggy blue jeans or khaki pants and high-top basketball shoes. The young men all had short to medium-length hair. Ronnie was wearing a New York Giants T-shirt underneath a denim jacket that had been hand-painted with an elaborate design of dragons, snakes, and a devil and that had his name brightly emblazoned across the back. Vinnie was wearing a Knicks baseball cap and a St. John's sweatshirt. Vinnie's girlfriend, Rose, wore a jean jacket over a bright green tank top and a pair of black spandex stretch pants with sandals. Frank wore an unzipped grey hooded sweatshirt over a white V-necked T-shirt, and Rocco had on a worn leather motorcycle jacket over a tank top muscle shirt. Mario, whom the rest of the group called Pee Wee (because his impersonation of Pee Wee Herman was legendary), was dressed in a jean jacket with hand-painted designs as well. Sal was the best dressed of the bunch, in slacks and shoes, with a brightly striped, collared shirt and a stylish leather bomber jacket. Maria, Sal's girlfriend, was dressed in tight blue jeans, a lacy halter top, and a purple jacket.

My initial encounter with the group gave me a firsthand glimpse of the attitudes they held toward African Americans. I was invited to meet some of the group by Ronnie, whom I had met and interviewed at the youth project office. After spotting Ronnie with seven other youths, I parked my car across the street and approached the group. Ronnie's back was turned, and Rocco was the first to see me. He pointed in my direction and said to the rest of the group, "Check it out. There's a black guy over there who's eyeing us. Let's take care of him." Ronnie turned, saw it was me, and grabbed Rocco, "That's the guy I told you was coming to talk to us. He's cool."

The Avenue T Boys are not a clearly defined group or organization. Although their reputation in New York City is widespread and many people think of them as a street gang, in fact they are an informal collection of neighborhood youths who hang out together along Avenue T near the border of Bensonhurst and Gravesend. Group identity and participation are determined by geography and race. All of them live in the surrounding neighborhood. The group is all white and is made up primarily of Italian youths with a couple of Jewish and Puerto Rican youths, and one Irish youth. There is no fixed number in the group; it varies according to who comes and hangs out on any given night. There are about eight regulars who are out on the street every night, and there are others who hang out periodically, mostly on weekend nights. The numbers swell in the summer when some school-going young people join the group on a regular basis. Most of those who hang out with the group are between sixteen and twenty-one years of age. There are a couple of older "veterans" of the group who come around from time to time and lend a kind of continuity with the groups who hung around Avenue T in years past. The group is made up mostly of young men. There are also young women who hang out with the T Boys, but their attachment to the group is a result of personal relationships with regular group members.

There is no defined leadership in the group, but there are youths who are held in particularly high esteem who exert significant influence on the actions of the group. Most of the Avenue T Boys are drop-outs. Though several of the weekenders are in school, none of them are successful academically. The group's main activity is to hang out, smoking cigarettes and drinking beer. Sometimes they go to a local park and play basketball or go to a movie, but mostly they just hang out. The action gets most intense on weekend nights and hot summer nights. At these times, there are more young people hanging out until late at night. Almost all of them have been arrested at least once, for offenses ranging from car theft and burglary to assault and battery.

The Avenue T Boys are a community institution, having existed for years, with its membership being continually regenerated by the newer, younger members from the community. The community has an ambivalent relationship to these young people. They are from the neighborhood and are consequently well known by most people. The group is made up mostly of youths who are not in school. Some of the T Boys work during the day, though most of these are in menial jobs with little future. A few of the T Boys at the time of my interviews still attended school, but only one of the youths maintained a C average. Most of them planned to go to college and were planning to take the GED exam to qualify.

Ronnie was a Bensonhurst youth who ran with the Avenue T Boys. Ronnie's life story is typical of the youths who hang out on Avenue T. Ronnie was an eighteen-year-old third-generation Italian American living with his older brother. He was born in east Flatbush but grew up almost entirely in Bensonhurst. He moved out of his parent's home when he was sixteen after repeated disputes over his failures in school and his activities on the street, which landed him in the juvenile justice system. He had spent time in jail, with a short stint in a youth correctional facility. Ronnie had been expelled from several schools for fighting and disruptive behavior. His father, a construction worker, had dropped out of school and begun work when he was sixteen as a carpenter's apprentice—a job he secured through family connections. Though his parents had encouraged him to stay in school and go to college, Ronnie dropped out of school when he was sixteen and tried to find work. He had held a succession of short-term jobs and was now trying to get his GED, with the intention of going to a computer-repair academy.

Ronnie's troubles finding long-term secure employment were typical of the experiences of most of the T Boys. These young men and women face uncertain futures. Since the late 1960s, industrial jobs, which were traditionally available for white youth from these communities, have been disappearing from the city's economy at an alarming rate. Between 1969 and 1981, New York City lost 650,000 jobs, most of them in the manufacturing sector (Steinberg, 1981), and the prospects for employment for working-class youths, particularly males, were definitely constricted.

Competition for employment in the city has been accompanied by an increase in the dropout rate in New York City from 13.5 percent in 1983 to 25 percent in 1987. Although the situation is considerably worse for African American and Puerto Rican youths, with official dropout rates of 24.3 and 31.3 percent respectively, the dropout rate has also increased for Italian American students (New York City Board of Education, 1989). Italian Americans are now the third most likely group to drop out of high school.

Ronnie was unable to follow the path his father had taken after leaving school. The family and community network that had landed his older brothers jobs in construction and a factory were no longer available to him. In fact, one of Ronnie's brothers was laid off from his job and remained unemployed for eleven months until he decided to take a job in a gas station.

Ronnie was an outgoing young man, who introduced me to the rest of the T Boys. He was one of the most liked and respected of the group, and he was the closest to an established leader in the group.

Vinnie had spent his entire life in Bensonhurst. He was a nineteen-year-old third-generation Italian American who lived with his mother and two younger sisters. His father had died when he was six years old. Vinnie was a tall, thin young man with a pencil moustache. He had worked since he was thirteen, sweeping and cleaning up at a couple of local businesses to supplement his mother's income from waitressing. When he was sixteen, he got a job stocking shelves at a local store. He was one of the few T Boys without some kind of criminal record. Though he had been arrested once, he was never charged:

> VINNIE: I guess I've been part smart, part lucky. It's not that I haven't done my share of stuff, but I won't go stealing something or getting into a fight if I think I might get caught. And since I figured out that I want to be a cop, I don't do any of that stupid stuff anymore.

Despite his independence, Vinnie remained a central member of the group by virtue of his fighting prowess. He was acknowledged as the toughest kid in the group. His reputation was firmly established in an ongoing battle with the Kings Highway Boys, a group of street youth from an adjacent neighborhood. Vinnie had been a regular with the Avenue T Boys since he was fourteen, but he had recently been hanging around with them less frequently. He attributed this to his ambitions to finish high school and to get a good job:

> VINNIE: I've had some great times with these guys on the street. But if you spend too much time down here, you ain't going to get nowhere. A lot of the guys are getting older and what are they going to be able to do? There ain't no jobs for kids who haven't finished high school and if you don't have no job, the only thing you can do is steal. I realized that if I was going to get anywhere, I better spend less time out here hanging out. Now, I've got a job and I am finishing school. I've got to do good in school because I fucked up early on and that's going to count against me.

Rocco, nineteen years old, was the opposite of Vinnie. He was a large, dark, handsome young man with the build of a football player. Rocco had been out of school since he was sixteen, when he was expelled for hitting his teacher. Nobody messed with Rocco, who had a reputation as the craziest of the T Boys, a reputation that he earned through a series of criminal activities ranging from car theft to assault to grand larceny, which had landed him in jail several times.

Rocco lived alone in a small apartment in Bensonhurst about seven blocks away from where he grew up. He made his money by fencing stolen property, as a small-time drug dealer, and by fixing cars on the street outside his apartment. He had been raised by his aunt after his mother died and his father landed in prison. Rocco was the least friendly of the group to outsiders, though other youth described him as a funny, loud practical joker.

Maria was a seventeen-year-old whose parents were Italian American and Jewish; she lived with her mother, who worked as a secretary. Maria had left school recently and was attending hairdressing school. She had been hanging around with the Avenue T Boys since beginning a relationship with Sal two years earlier. Maria only hung out with the group when they partied in their neighborhood. Neither she nor any of the other young women regularly participated in any of the illegal activities that many of the boys were involved with. (The street was by and large a male domain. Although I did find evidence of young women who accompanied the young men during these activities, this was not the norm.) She did, however, get in trouble numerous times at school, where she had been suspended at least three times for fighting and stealing.

Maria's boyfriend, Sal, was a tall, muscular, twenty-year-old Italian American youth who lived on Avenue T and drove a bright red Chevy Camaro. Sal had grown up on Avenue T and had moved into a house his father owned three doors from where he grew up. Sal's father was a contractor, and his mother had stayed home to raise Sal and his six brothers and sisters. Sal was the only one of the T Boys with long-term employment. He had been working for two years in his father's business doing construction. Sal was, nevertheless, a regular with the group and had been hanging out on Avenue T since he was eleven years old.

Mario was a relative newcomer to the group. All the other regulars had grown up in the neighborhood and had known each other since they were little kids. Mario had moved to Bensonhurst from Flatbush when he was sixteen. An eighteen-year-old second-generation Italian American, he had been hanging out with the T Boys for about a year. He had met Ronnie and Gino (another Bensonhurst youth who hung out with the Avenue T Boys) in the GED program they were all attending. His friendship with Ronnie had helped him gain entrance into the inner circle of regulars.

Mario had left school when he was sixteen and had worked at a series of short-term jobs. Periodically he had worked construction for Sal's father and had worked at a few of the local businesses, but he had no steady employment.

Frank was an aberration among the regulars. He was the only one who was not at least part Italian. Frank was a seventeen-year-old Irish American youth who had lived in Bensonhurst his entire life. He was, according to the rest of the group, "as Italian as any of us." Frank was proud of his adopted ethnicity; he had learned conversational Italian and even claimed to cook the best Italian food of any of the group.

Frank lived at home with his mother and younger brother. However, he spent many nights sleeping at friends' houses because he and his mother fought constantly. Frank attended a nearby high school, where he was barely passing his classes.

Most of the youth blamed the school system for their academic failures. Most of them told stories about having had problems in school and having been labeled "troublemakers" by teachers throughout their school careers. Rocco was expelled from several schools before finally dropping out:

> ROCCO: I never liked school. The teachers all hated my guts because I didn't just accept what they had to say. I was kind of a wiseass, and that got me in trouble. But that's not why they kept kicking me out of school. Either I didn't come to school or I got in fights when I did come. It got so I got a reputation that people heard about and there was always some kid challengin' me.

Mario echoed Rocco's perspective:

> MARIO: I didn't give a shit about school. I never got along with the teachers. It didn't matter what I did, they didn't like me. So I just said, fuck it. And I stopped going to class and hung out outside the school. After a while, I didn't go to school at all.

A number of the youths were skeptical about the value of school even though they were still attending school. They viewed it as a waste of time that would not result in any increased job opportunities, an attitude not uncommon for working-class white city youth (MacLeod, 1987; Willis, 1977). Maria's attitude was typical of the alienation from school that many of the youth expressed:

> MARIA: I was a pretty decent student until seventh or eighth grade. School was boring and I couldn't see what I was going to get out of it. My mother finished high school and even went to community college and all she could get was a job as a secretary.

> RONNIE: I thought it was a big waste of time. I knew older guys who had dropped out of the tenth grade and within a couple of years were makin' cash money as a mechanic or a carpenter. My brothers did the same thing. I didn't think I was learnin' no skill that I could get a job with in school. I wasn't very good in school. It was pretty damn boring. So I left.

One exception was Vinnie, who regretted not having taken school more seriously and felt that his attitude toward school had cost him dearly. Vinnie wanted to become a police officer or enlist in the Marines, which required a high school diploma:

> VINNIE: When I was thirteen or fourteen years old, I didn't know what I wanted to do. I thought it was cool to talk shit to the teacher and to act tough. I got in my share of fights—I won almost all of them. And I got sent around from school to school and finally ended up in an alternative high school. Now I wish I had done better in

school because it's fuckin hard to get a job. I want to go to the police academy but I have to graduate high school first.

All of the youths reported that when they left school they had felt excited at their newfound freedom and the chance to find a job and make some substantial money. This feeling was replaced by disappointment and reassessment when they realized that long-term, secure jobs were virtually unreachable for young, unskilled, high school dropouts. Most of them decided to take courses to prepare for the high school equivalency test and intended to apply for admission to college or technical school. Ronnie had expected to follow in his father's and brothers' footsteps when he left school. It was a rude awakening when he found that avenue closed to him:

> RONNIE: My older brothers left school and got good jobs right away. They had to learn on the job and pay their dues by doing some of the shit work, but they did pretty fuckin' good. My oldest brother Pat has been working construction for seven years now. My other brother Joey got a factory job right away, but he lost that job last year. It probably was a dumb move to leave school, but my grades were pretty fucked up, so it probably wouldn't have made a difference if I stayed.

The group helped to reinforce and define each individual's ethnic identity. Their ties to the community and the neighborhood were linked to their activities and membership in the Avenue T Boys. The T Boys were proud of their ethnic heritage. For these youths, the meaning of being Italian and Jewish was linked to their experiences on the street and in their community. They drew their sense of the meaning of their ethnic identity from their interactions within the T Boys and their interpretation of how they fit into their neighborhood:

> VINNIE: What does it mean to be Italian? It means that you take care of your family and your neighborhood. You learn from older guys who tell you how they used to have to defend the neighborhood against the blacks and kids from other turf, and now you know its your turn. If you walk around Bensonhurst, you'll see everybody knows each other, they look out for each other. We Italians are crazy, you don't mess with us. So being Italian means taking care of your own, not taking any shit, having a good time, eating good food, and, you know, doing what you have to do to keep the neighborhood safe.

> MARIO: It's not just about bein' Italian. We're Italians from Bensonhurst. That means you put your friends first, your neighborhood

first. You don't let nobody get down on your people and you don't let nobody in the neighborhood who's gonna fuck it up.

The boys didn't view other neighborhood youths with a difference in ethnic background as a problem. This may have been because the people they knew who were from different ethnic backgrounds generally adopted the dominant ethnic identity as their own. Frank was the most extreme example of this process. Frank admired Italians more than any other group. He denigrated the Irish, his parents' ethnicity, and adopted as many Italian cultural traits as he could. He spoke Italian reasonably well—better than most of the other youths—and he had even cultivated an Italian accent. In response to a survey question that asked respondents to rate twenty-four different ethnic groups from 1 to 10 (with 10 as the highest and 1 as the lowest), Frank ranked Italians as 10 and all other groups, including the Irish, as 1. Frank's attitudes and identity provide an example of the central importance of community norms and ideas in the construction of ethnic and racial identities and attitudes. Ethnic and racial identity formation is a community process—defined and established in the context of a group. Young people develop their sense of identity based on the cultural norms and values associated with membership in the group.

The T Boys provide an interesting contrast to the Italian and Jewish youths in Canarsie described by Rieder (1985). The Italian and Jewish youths described by Rieder did not mix. In this case, although youths from Irish, Jewish, and Puerto Rican backgrounds hung out as part of the group, Italian American was clearly the dominant cultural group and defined the cultural norms and identity of the group.

The vast majority of the white students (76 percent) interviewed at Sheepshead Bay High School and at John Dewey High School came from working-class backgrounds similar to the backgrounds of the youths interviewed in Bensonhurst and Gravesend. The young people from Sheepshead Bay and John Dewey High Schools came from a variety of different races and ethnicities. Fifty-seven percent reported that their fathers were sales workers, clerks, craftsmen, transport operatives, or service workers, or self-employed workers. The remaining 38 percent were either professionals, managers, or administrators. Twenty percent of the in-school white youths reported that their mothers were professionals, managers, or administrators. Sixty percent reported that their mothers were sales workers, clerks, service workers, or self-employed workers. Three were housewives. Sixty-seven percent of the white youth at Sheepshead Bay High School live with both their parents.

However, the young people from Bensonhurst, Gravesend, Sheepshead Bay, and Canarsie who were still in school had a distinctly different daily life. Though a few of them were involved in street groups, most of them had primary peer groups that were school based. For many of those in school, ethnic or racial identity was not as central an aspect in their identities as it was for the T Boys. Their affiliations and peer groups were organized around interests and lifestyle as well as around cultural background. The street and the neighborhood were not fundamental elements in the organization of their peer groups. Consequently, few of these youths were involved in the ongoing battles among groups from different neighborhoods trying to defend turf. Some had been the unfortunate victims of attacks by neighborhood-based groups like the Avenue T Boys, and they all knew of the T Boys.

A second major difference between in-school youths and youths in groups like the T Boys is their daily exposure to young people of many different races and ethnicities. The Avenue T Boys had little daily contact with young people outside of their community, except for Sal, whose construction job sometimes took him to other neighborhoods. Both Sheepshead Bay High School and John Dewey High School are very diverse: at the time of these interviews, Sheepshead Bay High School was 40 percent black, 37 percent white, 10.5 percent Asian, 9 percent Latino, and 3.5 percent other.

The Youth of East Harlem

A world away in East Harlem, African American and Puerto Rican youths struggle with some of the same adolescent problems and issues in markedly different surroundings and conditions. The two groups interviewed in East Harlem came from dissimilar backgrounds and were on separate life trajectories: youths from the Schomberg Plaza housing project and youths attending Central Park East Secondary School.[3]

The young people interviewed at Schomberg Plaza were a close-knit group who hung out together around the housing project and participated in activities organized by the Schomberg Plaza Youth Program.[4] All but two lived in the Schomberg Plaza housing project. Most identified their ethnic backgrounds as black or African American, with one who was of Jamaican descent and one from St. Thomas. Only one youth identified himself as racially mixed.

Almost all of the youths came from poor, single-parent families. The most startling aspect of this group was the family composition of their households: Only 16 percent of them lived with both parents; 58 percent lived with one parent, 16 percent lived with neither parent, and 10 percent lived alone and were over eighteen. Only 21 percent of these youths reported their fathers' occupations, which included a professional, a bus driver, a cab driver, and a subway employee. Their mothers were secretaries, day care workers, private household workers, self-employed workers, and unemployed. Most of these youths still attended school, and though most of them reported earning passing grades in school (68.5 percent reported earning a C average or better), the coordinators for the youth project reported that, with few exceptions, they did poorly in school and had dim prospects for attending college or of future employment.

The Schomberg youths, like the Avenue T Boys, valued fighting ability and thought it was imperative to gain a reputation for toughness in their neighborhood. Most of them, including the young women, had been involved in fights on numerous occasions. This was a matter of necessity and survival rather than preference. Virtually all had been detained by the police, though only a few had actually served time in juvenile facilities. They viewed the streets of East Harlem as both friendly and dangerous. Violent conflicts with other young people were a frequent reality. They all knew young people who had been killed and others who were doing "serious time for serious crime."

The youth program at Schomberg Plaza was established in 1989 in the wake of the Central Park jogger attack. Activities at the youth program included job fair and employment information, discussion groups and workshops on different issues, counseling, and trips to basketball or baseball games, swimming, and other forms of recreation. Mostly, the youth program supplied a safe environment for the youths to gather and hang out.

Before the youth program was available, these young people spent almost all their free time on the streets around Schomberg Plaza hanging out with their friends. A number of them speculated that the availability of the youth program had prevented them from getting involved in criminal activities. These young people were not members of any youth gang. They all knew others who had been involved in the Central Park jogger attack, and a couple of them had participated regularly with groups who went on harassment, assault, and crime sprees through the neighborhood, which became known in the media as "wilding." However, most of these young people were not involved in such activities. The program served both young men and women. However, there were few young women who hung out at the program office on a regular basis. For the most part, the young men and women hung out separately.

The Schomberg youths dressed in the typical New York City teen hip-hop style: The young men wore hooded sweatshirts, baggy pants, baseball caps or Malcolm X caps, unlaced high-top basketball shoes or Timberland hiking boots, Africa medallions; the young women wore baggy pants and extra-large T-shirts or stretch bicycle shorts and stretch tank tops. The booming bass and the syncopated poetry of rap music was ever present. "Conscious rap" was the music of preference, and the lyrics of groups like KRS-One, Public Enemy, Big Daddy Cane, and Queen Latifah were standard knowledge among the youth.

There was no discernable leader in this group. Most were longtime friends who had grown up together in the housing project. A few had spent a lot of time on the street with groups of youths from some of the other housing projects in El Barrio. But most hung around with others from Schomberg. There was little rivalry or animosity evident toward youths from other housing projects in East Harlem. In earlier years, there had been a lot of conflict with groups from different projects, especially with Puerto Ricans from the Tres Unidos housing project. But that had cooled out in the late 1980s, and some of the young people now had good friends at some of the other projects.

A normal day for most of these young people began with attendance at school. They went to a few different schools, and two were attending community college. Two had graduated from high school and were searching for work, as were a couple of youths who had dropped out of school that year. They would converge on the youth program office in the afternoon and hang out there through the evening hours. When the program closed at 9 P.M., a few would go back home while others would hang out on the street outside the housing complex. On weekends, the program often offered activities that they would take part in. When they were not hanging out at the youth program, most either hung out on the street with friends or went to the movies or to some event in the city. They spent most of their time in local African

American communities in East Harlem and Harlem, venturing into midtown and lower Manhattan infrequently and almost never going to Brooklyn, the Bronx, or Queens.

Most hung out at the youth program office to escape the streets. They were all trying to stay out of trouble and to figure out their futures despite difficult surroundings, limited opportunities, and low aspirations. There was also, by their own acknowledgment, a very thin line separating them from some of their friends who were regularly involved in violence and criminal activity:

> TERRELL: When you grow up around here, that's what you do. You try and get over. Everybody's schemin', tryin' to run a game, or learn a game or somethin'. Most of us used to hang out with a lot of the guys who are robbin', and stealin', and bangin'. Take a good look at some of those guys, that could've been any of us. I was on that road, hangin' out, schemin'. I don't know exactly why I stopped and they didn't.

Terrell was a nineteen-year-old resident of the Schomberg housing project. He was a medium height, dark-skinned youth with a stocky build and square face. He had a hint of a beard and moustache and a bright, piercing gaze. He lived with his mother, who was a secretary in a city agency. Terrell was still in school, and though it had been a struggle, he was going to graduate, after which he planned to attend Borough of Manhattan Community College.

Terrell had lived in Schomberg since he was eight years old. He had never known his father, who did not stay with his mother after she became pregnant with him at age seventeen. He was extremely outgoing, with a sense of humor that kept the rest of the youth laughing.

Terrell had mixed feelings about where he lived. He liked the people but he hated the conditions:

> TERRELL: You know, a lot of people have dogged the youth here at Schomberg and in East Harlem. Young black males from this neighborhood have been targets of media lies, police harassment. By what you see on TV and in the paper you'd think everybody here was a drug dealer, a gang-banger, or a crack addict. Now, you know that ain't true. Most of the people who live around here are just trying to survive, just trying to live. And they are doing the best that they can. There are a lot of hard workin' folks that live here.

Terrell, like his friends, saw little chance that he would be able to change his economic condition. He was not sure what he wanted to try to do as a career. Every time I talked to him, he had a different idea of a career possibility based on a conversation he had with somebody or on a commercial, advertisement, or brochure he had seen somewhere. The types of jobs he considered gives an indication of the low aspirations he had for his future: security work, park maintenance, asbestos removal. He was not very optimistic about his future:

> TERRELL: I don't know what I am going to end up doing. I figure I'll major in communications but that's like everyone else. Everybody wants to work in show business. It's not terribly realistic, but I don't know what else to do.

One of the reasons for his and some of the other youths' low aspirations was their perception of the difficulties of working for white people. A number of them recounted experiences they had had when applying for work, experiences that made them uncomfortable with the idea of working in a white environment:

> TERRELL: When you work for white people, they are always watching you waiting for you to mess up or steal something. They expect that you are going to fail or that you're going to steal somethin'.

> JEFFREY: It's hard to get a job downtown. You go in there, and all those white people stare at you like they want to know what the fuck are you doing there. And when you get a job, you get some white guy looking over your shoulder doggin' you about what you should be doing. I had a job downtown last summer and I quit it because I couldn't take all those white people.

Jeffrey, known as "J," was one of the most vociferous young men at Schomberg Plaza. He was outspoken in his ideas and in his dress. Jeffrey usually sported brightly patterned colored shirts, with baggy black pants and Timberland hiking boots. A medallion with a red, black, gold, and green image of the African continent was ever present around his neck. Jeffrey was a tall, thin, dark-skinned eighteen-year-old whose mother worked two jobs to support herself and three children. Jeffrey hardly knew his father, who had never lived with the family and had not visited Jeffrey in seven years.

Jeffrey had lived at Schomberg Plaza since he was five years old. He was a senior in high school who was preparing to graduate on time, a rarity among his peers. After graduation, Jeffrey planned to go to City College and get a degree in business:

JEFFREY: I'm going to start my own business. That is where it's at. We need more African American business owners who care about the people they serve and the community which supports them.

Jeffrey had never been involved with any "serious criminal activity," though he had been picked up or stopped by the police numerous times. This experience with the police was common among Schomberg youth:

JEFFREY: I did a lot of stupid little stuff you do when you're young and trying to hang, like shoplifting. But when some of my friends started getting into serious crimes like selling drugs and robbing people, I said forget about it. . . . I've been stopped by the cops a bunch of times. Pretty much everyone I know will tell you the same thing. Anytime something big happens around here that involves a black kid, they just stop every one of us they see until they find the guy who did it or at least someone who is scared enough to confess to it whether they did it or not. They lean on the brothers hard around here.

Shaneequa was a sixteen-year-old who had lived at Schomberg for ten years. Shaneequa was a short, thin, dark-skinned young woman with sharp features and a bright smile. Her hair was straightened and styled close to her head, and her face was framed by greased bangs that hugged her forehead and the sides of her face. She lived with her mother, who was on public assistance, and her younger brother and sister. Shaneequa did not hang out with the guys, but she was one of two young women who were regular participants in activities at the youth program. Shaneequa was an average student in the ninth grade who worked after school at a fast-food restaurant. She spent much of her free time helping her mother with her brother and sister.

Tania was Terrell's half sister and Shaneequa's best friend. The two young women hung out together regularly and frequently came by the youth program office when there were activities. Tania was a gregarious seventeen-year-old with light brown skin and long wavy brown hair who wore large gold earrings and a small diamond stud in her nose. She was in the ninth grade, in the same class as Shaneequa.

Tania had had several problems in her early teens. She was constantly in trouble in school because of fighting and "behavior problems," and at home she hung around with older street youths from some other projects. She started indulging in petty crimes: purse snatching, shoplifting. She was arrested three times and spent a short stint in a juvenile corrections facility for her involvement in a burglary. She had stayed out of trouble for a year and a half after she stopped hanging out with her old friends.

Carl was a heavyset twenty-year-old who had lived at Schomberg for fourteen years until he had moved out at age nineteen. Carl always wore a heavy jacket, even on warm days, work boots with open laces, and a bandanna covering his head. He had dropped out of school when he was seventeen but found it difficult to find long-term work. After returning to school and obtaining his high school diploma, he finally got a job through the youth program with a researcher at City College. He enjoyed the work and had become interested in going to college and possibly getting a graduate degree.

Oscar was chronologically the youngest of the group at fourteen years old. He was, however, among the most mature of the group. He was an excellent student and had also developed critical thinking skills seemingly beyond his years. Oscar's father was a well-known activist in the African American community, and his mother ran her own graphic arts business. Oscar was a chubby, clean-cut young man with a traditional short Afro haircut. He stood out among the rest of the youth, who dressed more fashionably and had more stylish fade haircuts, shaved on the sides and back with very short hair on top.

Yet Oscar had the respect of the other young people. They respected his knowledge and said they learned a lot from him. Oscar had an Afrocentric perspective, which he articulated fervently. He was an intense young man with a high-pitched voice that cut through the constant drone of the music and the loud banter of the rest of the youths. When the discussions turned serious, Oscar always became a primary participant.

Habib was a sixteen-year-old who lived with his mother and brother at Schomberg. Habib appeared to be a child in a man's body. He had a tender face that made him look two years younger, set on a 6-foot, 170-pound frame. Habib was still in school, although he was not doing well academically. He still planned to stay and graduate and go on to college. Habib was probably the toughest of the Schomberg youths. The rest admired his fighting ability and street smarts. He was the only one who had been seriously injured in the streets: He had been shot in his left side during a dispute with a youth from another project when he was fourteen years old. He used to hang out with other youth in East Harlem who went "rushin'":[5]

HABIB: I've been with a bunch of kids when we go out and just bum-rush people. That's when you go up to somebody and you knock them around, take whatever they got, and get outta there. I never saw nobody get hurt bad, they might get punched a few times and knocked down, but that's about it. I stopped doin' it because I realized it was wrong. I got bum-rushed over at 1099 [another housing project], and first it made me mad and I wanted to go out and fuck up somebody. But then I started to think about it and I could see how people felt who were getting attacked. Also, I stopped hangin' out with those guys on 4th Avenue, and some of the fellahs here who I was friends with threw down some knowledge around what I was doin'.

Although Habib had changed his behavior in the streets, he continued to struggle academically. He had been in a special education classroom since the fifth grade. He said that he had been placed in that class because he was labeled a "troublemaker" by one teacher whom he did not get along with and that he carried that reputation through school and was treated accordingly:

HABIB: I was never very good in school but I did okay until the fifth grade. That's when I had this teacher who hated my guts. She transferred me into the special ed class and that's where I've been ever since. In that class, they treat you different than in a normal class. They expect you to fuck up and they treat you like real little children and it pissed me off so much that I would go off. And they would just act like, "I knew you were like that."

Virtually all the youths complained about school. They criticized the teachers and the school system for being unresponsive to the needs of African Americans. They felt they were the victims of racism, as each one described being stereotyped and typecast as a failure because he or she was African American:

TERRELL: I hated school. And the school hated me. I didn't learn anything that's relevant to myself and my peoples. I wasn't dumb or anything. I just couldn't get behind learning all that European history. You know, the teachers didn't respect any of the brothers. As a matter of fact, they were all scared of black men. So they did their best to tear us down, to not let us feel powerful.

Even Oscar, who excelled in school, had similar criticisms:

OSCAR: I get excellent grades, but most of my teachers don't like me because I'm always asking questions. I am always critical of the European perspective that the classes have. I'll learn what they are teaching us and then I'll raise questions about it. They hate that.

Oscar's attitude about the Eurocentrism of his school's curriculum reflects a strong African American identity, which was evident with all the youths. Although Oscar was certainly the most fervent and articulate member of the group when expressing his pride in his African American heritage and culture, the rest were also proud of their racial backgrounds:

SHANEEQUA: I'm proud to be black—African American. We are strong people. We have survived everything—slavery, murder, miseducation, racism. There aren't many people in the world who could survive what we been through. There are some problems in the African American community. But the biggest problem is that white people keep trying to keep black people down.

OSCAR: Being African American means understanding your culture, your history. White people have tried to take that away from us, but a lot of African people are waking up. We are the descendants of kings and queens. We come from the continent which is the cradle of civilization where mathematics and science and language were developed. We get no credit for these achievements, we are not taught this in school, but African people are starting to teach themselves and each other the true nature of our people.

CARL: Most people think that black people are criminals and welfare mothers. That's how they treat us. But being black means you struggle against racism and hatred to survive and thrive. Being black means making something out of nothing. You care about your community and you try to fight for social justice. Black people are the conscience of this country.

TERRELL: Where would this country be without black—African Americans? We built this country. This country was built from the blood and sweat of African Americans. We have not been rewarded for our labor but it's true, this country was built by African Americans.

HABIB: Black culture is the richest in America. Everybody listens to black music. There's a lot of white people who steal our music. Black dancing is the best. Black writers are the best. Everybody be listenin' to our music and reading our books, but they still want to dog us as a people.

Young people in Schomberg Plaza live in a world controlled and dominated by the issue of race, and their identity, ideas, and attitudes reflect this reality. What sets these African American youths apart from their counterparts in white communities is that race dominates their daily life. Unlike the Avenue T Boys and the Albanians, who spoke with each other about race often but not as a primary issue dominating their lives, race was a primary topic of discussion for the Schomberg youth. It was ever present, as a specific topic of conversation, as a side comment, or as a central theme in the rap music:

> HABIB: Every day, every minute, there is something that happens or something you see which reminds you that you are black and it's a white world. Every time you see a police car, you wonder if they are going to stop and hassle you. Every time you go in a store the owners are hawkin' you because they think you're gonna steal something. When you walk down the street in midtown or downtown, the women clutch their purses and cross the street. It seems like everybody's eyeing you all the time.

> JEFFREY: Being black means having to deal with bullshit all your life. Whether it's the police, teachers, politicians, or just white people on the street. And if you are a black male, you can expect to be the object of intense suspicion like the police who are always hasslin' us, you know what I'm saying. When you're a young black male from Harlem then you are guilty 'til you prove you're innocent.

The life conditions, aspirations, and visible opportunities of the black youth at Central Park East Secondary School was in glaring contrast to those of the young people at Schomberg Plaza. The black young people at Central Park East Secondary School were from several different neighborhoods. The majority of those at Central Park East Secondary School lived in East Harlem, Harlem, or the Upper East Side. Those who did not lived in the South Bronx, Flatbush in Brooklyn, and Tremont and the Grand Concourse in the Bronx. They also came from a number of different ethnic backgrounds: African American, Trinidadian, Jamaican, and mixed ethnicity. Many of them came from very different socioeconomic backgrounds than did those interviewed at Schomberg Plaza. Forty-six percent of the black students at Central Park East live with both parents; significantly more than the 16 percent of the Schomberg youths. Sixty-one percent of the black students from Central Park East reported their fathers' occupations, which included professionals, managers, an insurance salesman, a data entry clerk, a welder, and a machine operator. The differences in the occupations of the youths' mothers was even more striking. Among the black youths at Central Park East, 54 percent had mothers who were professionals. There were also one manager, one secretary, and one housewife. Finally, 31 percent were racially mixed. All of the African American youths are doing well in school, with 92 percent maintaining a B average or better. They excelled academically, and almost all were college bound.

Violence was not as significant a part of their lives. They were certainly affected by violence in their community and throughout the city. As at Schomberg, there were those at Central Park East Secondary School who had to cope with crime and with the death of young people they knew. A number of the Central Park East Secondary School students grew up in East Harlem or in communities that had severe economic and social problems and where violence was a severe problem. But their sense of self and their daily activities were not as affected by violence as were those of the Schomberg youths. They spent less time on the street, had more opportunities for escape, and most important, formed their sense of self, their identity, and their circle of friends primarily at school.

The young people from Central Park East Secondary School also displayed a strong racial identity that was marked by pride in the African American tradition of strength, social justice, and struggle and pride in the richness of African American culture.

The Albanian Youth from Pelham Parkway

The Albanian students at Christopher Columbus High School were all residents of Pelham Parkway and Williamsbridge. Most were first- or second-generation Americans; a few had moved to the United States as children. The vast majority (76 percent) lived with both parents. Most were from working-class or middle-class socioeconomic backgrounds, and a large majority of their fathers owned small amounts of real estate or ran their own small businesses; a few of their fathers were skilled craftsmen, salesmen, and unskilled laborers. Most of their families were traditionally structured, with their mothers staying at home working in the house. Only one youth had two parents who worked. Academically, most of the Albanian youths were barely making passing grades. Teachers who worked closely with them reported that although some of the girls were doing fairly well, many of the boys missed class frequently and would have to struggle to graduate. Though many were having academic difficulties, they remained in school.[6]

The Albanian youths from Pelham Parkway are a tight group. As first- and second-generation Americans, they still subscribe to many of the traditions and values that their parents and grandparents brought with them from Albania. The Albanian community is extremely insular, frowning on mixing with other racial and ethnic groups.

These youths dressed more conservatively than the rest of the young people I encountered in New York City. Most of the young men wore slacks or neat blue jeans, T-shirts or button-down dress shirts, and shoes rather than sneakers. Many of the T-shirts were emblazoned with a black falcon, the emblem from the Albanian flag. Most of the young women wore skirts and dresses. Those who did not wore loose-fitting button-down shirts neatly tucked into loose but not baggy pants.

They spent their free time hanging out in their neighborhood, gathering at one of the local pizzerias or parks to talk, drink, and hang out. In this particular group, drugs were frowned upon. While many of the young men used alcohol excessively, they disdained the use of drugs.[7]

Most of these young people were not involved in criminal activity and did not get in trouble with the police. (The exception were two young men who hung out with another group of Albanians when they were not in school. These two had been involved in car thefts, burglaries, and assaults. As a result, each had spent a small amount of time in jail.) Many were, however, involved in violent incidents at school. The majority of them had been suspended from school at least once.

On weekend nights they went to clubs frequented predominantly by Albanians. At the clubs, they listened both to rock music and traditional Albanian music, to which they would do a circle dance. The circle dance was reserved for Albanians only. Should a non-Albanian break into the circle during one of these dances, they were told once to leave. After the first warning they were physically removed:

> FEYZI: The circle dance is special, it's only for Albanians. Sometimes when we start the circle at a club, somebody will try to join who is not from the community. We let them know that this is only for us. If they don't leave then we put them out of the circle. There have been fights started by people who did not respect our circle.

Feyzi, a Muslim, was the unofficial leader of this group of Albanian young people. At nineteen, he was the oldest of this group, who all attended Christopher Columbus High School. He commanded the respect of the entire group of twenty-four. When Feyzi spoke, everyone was quiet. In the middle of a raucous discussion in which everyone seemed to be talking at once, he would hold up one hand to indicate he had something to say, and the group would defer to him immediately. Many of the younger Albanians took their lead from Feyzi. He would be the first to answer questions, and his word was almost never challenged. Feyzi's authority came not just from his being one of the oldest students at the school but also from his father's position as an influential and important man in the Albanian community.

Feyzi was a senior at Christopher Columbus High School, but he was in academic trouble and was in danger of not graduating. He was a thin, medium height youth with dark hair and a radiant smile. He talked slowly and softly, which contrasted with the fast-paced, loud speech of most of his friends. He lived with both his parents and his younger brother and sister in a house in Pelham Parkway. His family had left Albania in 1965 and had lived in Italy until 1976, when they immigrated to the United States. Feyzi was born in Italy and was four years old when his family settled in the Bronx. He had an older brother who had gone into the family business, managing the apartment buildings that his father owned.

Feyzi's younger sister, Yasmine, was fifteen years old. She was a loquacious, opinionated young woman with a quick wit. She was one of the most popular of the young women because of her outgoing personality, her physical beauty—with long wavy hair, dark eyes, and fair skin—and her family. She was a straight-A student with no academic future. Yasmine's future was as the wife of one of the Albanian men in their community. She understood that this was her role, and she did not question it:

> YASMINE: It is likely that I will not finish high school and I will definitely not be going to college. I will be married sometime in the next three years. One guy has already asked my father to marry me, but my father decided he was not suitable for me and that I was not ready. People ask me all the time if it bothers me. I don't even think about it. That's the way it is, and that's the way I want it.

Drita, a sixteen-year-old sophomore, was in a situation similar to Yasmine's. She was a very good student who was destined to be a housewife. Drita, however, was not as unquestioning of her fate as Yasmine:

> DRITA: I know that I will have to marry and I will accept that when it comes. I would like to become an actress but that is certainly not pos-

sible. So I hope to go to college and to become a teacher. I don't like the fact that I can't choose my own husband, but I know that is the way it is. If I don't go along with my father's decision, I will lose my family.

Drita lived with her father, who owned a small retail business, her mother, who was a housewife, and her three younger brothers. She spent most of her time at home working with her mother in the house and doing schoolwork. Drita was one of the few Albanian students in the group who had friends from other ethnic and racial groups. She did not see these friends outside of school because of the restrictions on intergroup mixing that were a part of the community norms:

> DRITA: I have a few friends in my classes at school who are not Albanian. There are a couple of Italian girls and a black girl who I like very much. But we can't see each other in my neighborhood because people would start talking if I brought them to my house. It's a shame but that's the way it is.

Mediha, an eighteen-year-old first-generation Albanian American senior, was the polar opposite of Drita. She hung around exclusively with the Albanian young people and had encountered problems at school. Mediha was a poor student, with a C- average, but she was on schedule to graduate with her class. She had been in several fights with youths from other ethnic and racial backgrounds as part of ongoing conflicts between these groups. When any of the Albanian young women at the school got into altercations, she was the first to join in.

Mediha lived in a rented apartment with her mother and younger sister; they had immigrated to the United States in 1981 from Yugoslavia by way of Italy to join relatives. Her father had died in an accident before they left Yugoslavia for Italy in 1978.

Ramazan was a seventeen-year-old sophomore at the high school who was not doing well in school. Like many of the other Albanian youths, he aspired to work in the family business. Ramazan's father owned a pizzeria, where Ramazan worked after school and on weekends. Ramazan was a Muslim Albanian who had immigrated to the United States when he was thirteen with both parents and his two brothers and two sisters. He was a large, muscular young man, which set him apart from the majority of his peers, who had much smaller frames. Ramazan was one of the "Albanian enforcers" at the school. Anybody who had a conflict with one of the other Albanian students eventually had to deal with Ramazan. As a result, Ramazan had been suspended from school several times, placing his academic advancement in jeopardy.

Lehmi was an eighteen-year-old first-generation Albanian American. He lived with his mother and three sisters. His father had left the family for a younger woman and had moved away after being ostracized by the community. His mother worked as a secretary for a small Albanian-owned real estate company. Lehmi was a handsome young man with a dark full beard and a lightening-quick sense of humor. He was a sophomore at the high school, and though he was short and slight, he also played the role of enforcer for the Albanian school community. He was placed in a special education class in ninth grade after being kept back for the second time in three years.

Lehmi was one of two young men in the group who also hung out with the Albanian dropouts and recent graduates of the high school. This group would hang out across the street from the school and was described by the other Albanian students as "the really bad kids." A number of these young men, including Lehmi, were members of a street group who called themselves the "Albanian Boys." Lehmi was on the verge of dropping out of school and looking for work:

> LEHMI: I'm going to get outta here. I ain't learning anything and the teachers all think that I'm not smart. You don't learn anything useful here anyway. Look around here. I'm tired of wasting my time here when I could be making money on a job somewhere.

Phillip was a seventeen-year-old Catholic youth who lived with his father, mother, and younger sister. His father worked as a truck driver, and his mother was a housewife. His parents had moved to the United States as children and had met in the Albanian community in Williamsbridge. They lived in a large apartment in the predominantly Albanian northeast section of Pelham Parkway. The rest of the youth called him "Guido" because of his Italian appearance. With his green eyes, thin build, and black hair slicked back over his head, he looked as if he would fit right in with the Avenue T Boys.

Phillip, unlike most of the young men, was doing reasonably well academically. He had planned to graduate and attend college to study law. Phillip was unusual among his friends in that he articulated a desire to go to college. Most of the young people expressed aspirations to go into their family business or to learn a trade. College was not seen as necessary to pursue the life courses they envisioned. Most of their parents never went to college, nor did their older brothers and sisters. Phillip's ambition to become a lawyer was still linked to the Albanian community:

> PHILLIP: I hear my father and other people in the community say all the time that there are not enough Albanian lawyers. We have to go outside the community to find lawyers. When my cousin was arrested and we needed a lawyer, we had to hire this Jewish guy. So I want to be a lawyer and work in our community.

At fourteen, Sabri was the youngest in the group. He was a second-generation Muslim Albanian American in the ninth grade. He was a short, stocky youth with short, thick black hair and heavy eyebrows. Sabri was the best student among the boys in the group, maintaining an A average. His grades had slipped slightly since entering Christopher Columbus High School, partially as a result of hanging out with this group and neglecting his studies. His aspirations for the future were loftier than those of any of the other youths. Once again, they centered around the Albanian community:

> SABRI: I want to be the first Albanian politician in New York City. All the other groups have politicians but we don't have any representatives. I want to be the first.

The Albanians lived in a very tight-knit community, which the young people described as extremely traditional—a community governed by the norms, rules, and customs of the "old country." Community members are very religious; approximately 70 percent are Muslim; the other 30 percent are Catholic:

> FEYZI: We have a very closed community. The traditions and rules from the old country still apply for us. A lot of people don't understand that and they think we are strange. We grow up learning that the only people we can really trust are our own people. So we stick to our own.

Many of the norms and rules that govern the lives of these young people are remnants of indigenous Albanian culture. Male–female relations, for example, are structured and circumscribed. Women are viewed as subordinate to men and are responsible for serving their fathers and brothers and eventually their husbands. Marriages are arranged by the girl's father. This is true for Catholic and Muslim families:[8]

YASMINE: One thing people here seem to find strange is that we still have arranged marriages. The way it works is if a boy from the community wants to marry a girl, he goes and asks her father. He tells the guy to come back in two weeks when he will give his decision. That's just how it is. A girl has to be a good girl at home to show that she will be a good wife. I wait on my brothers and my father because I love them, but also because I want to have the reputation as a good woman to marry.

Drita had an enormous amount of work around the house because she was the only daughter with three brothers. Despite feeling that the arrangement was not fair, she diligently fulfilled her womanly duties:

DRITA: I don't think it's fair. None of the girls I know at school have to do it. They get to date and go out with their girlfriends. But, it's what I have to do if I want to get married.

This meant that most of the Albanian young women never hung out with the guys, never drank alcohol, and never went on dates. Only the young women from less traditional families had boyfriends. The young women who did go to the club only went with their boyfriends, but they would not touch alcohol and danced only with their boyfriends. Most of the young women stayed home. Those who did drink and hang out were labeled loose and undesirable for marriage:

YASMINE: There are some Albanian girls who go to the clubs and hang out with guys and drink. Everybody knows who they are. These girls are for the guys to have fun with before they get married. They [the girls] will never get married to an Albanian. They are considered trash and they will not make a good wife. These girls usually end up leaving the community and marrying somebody who is not Albanian because no guy will even look at them when they think about who to marry. And once they marry some guy who is not Albanian, that's it. They are no longer Albanian.

For these young Albanians, traditional norms and values circumscribe and limit the amount of contact and interaction they have with people outside the Albanian community. Both boys and girls are expected to marry within the Albanian community. An Albanian who marries outside of his or her community is frequently banished from the family and the community. Even marriage to Italians, who are otherwise held in high regard, is frowned upon.

Perhaps the tradition most relevant and important to an understanding of racial attitudes and conflict among Albanian youth in Pelham Parkway is the five-hundred-year-old Canon of Albanian Law, which determines how disputes and conflicts in the Albanian community are resolved.[9] This canon was developed in the fourteenth and fifteenth centuries as a strategy for maintaining order in Albanian society. According to the canon, an individual or family who has been the victim of violence has the right and the obligation to retaliate, by taking the life of a male member over the age of seven from the offender's family.

According to the youths, the law still dictates how conflicts are resolved in their community. They spoke of a Council of Elders, composed of older Albanian men who are well respected in the community, that has the authority to decide on appropriate punishments. If a family does not abide by the decision of the Council of Elders and continues the violence, the council can dictate that all male members of that family over the age of seven be killed. Although none of the youths interviewed recalled a time when this ultimate form of punishment had been enforced in the United States, a few recalled its recent usage in Albania:

RAMAZAN: I have an uncle who still lives in Albania. He was stabbed by another member of their village. So they went and killed the sixteen-year-old son of the man who did it. Well, this guy came back and shot my cousin. The Council of Elders decided that this man had gone too far. Members of the council, my uncle's family, and other men from the village went to this man's house, allowed all the women and children under six to leave, and then burnt the house to the ground with all the men inside.

The youth reported that in the United States, a more common form of punishment for a family or individual who has transgressed is physical and social banishment from the Albanian community:

FEYZI: We have a Council of Elders made up mostly of men who moved here from the old country. They still stick to the old laws and old rules. Some things have changed over time. If it is not a physical act of violence, then the person will be banned—no one will deal with them. But sometimes they do it the old-fashioned way. So if someone messes with someone else, they should expect that revenge will come and they better accept it.

During the interviews, many Albanian youths spoke about the problems they faced as they attempted to abide by these laws in a new multicultural society and multiethnic school. Although they did not expect outsiders to uphold the precepts of Albanian law, the canon was still enforced to regulate disputes in the Albanian community. The interactions these young people had with outsiders were clearly influenced by traditional Albanian laws and values. Both the girls and boys talked proudly about how they never backed down from a conflict. Their perceptions about conflict were tied to knowledge about the existence of blood feuds in Albania and were based on a principle of retaliation. Many spoke about how verbal insults had to be paid for "in blood":

RAMAZAN: I was suspended for fighting with this black kid and when I went home my father asked me what happened. When he heard that I had been in a fight with this guy, he says, "You know what you have to do now." I explained to my father that I couldn't kill every kid I had an argument or a fight with. But I can't back down either.

LEHMI: In our community, everybody knows what the deal is. If you break the rules and you hurt somebody, you have to pay. But people outside our community don't know our laws, so of course we can't expect them to abide by them. There are also laws in this country which are not the same as ours which we must take into account. But the bottom line is don't challenge us or you'll have to pay the consequences.

MEDIHA: People know we are the toughest folks in the school because we never back down. We can't back down. When someone insults you or attacks you, they are insulting and attacking your whole family, your whole community. That's why if an Albanian loses a fight, and that don't happen too often, that's never the end of it. There are fights and feuds that have gone on for hundreds of years in Albania.

The Muslim and Catholic Albanian youths mixed freely while at school but said that there was less mixing among these groups in their neighborhoods. There was little intermarriage across religious lines in the Albanian community. The tradition of separation between the religions was not as prevalent among the young people who identified together as Albanians. Their ethnic identity was strong, forged by the immigrant experience. Theirs was a community that intentionally strove to maintain their customs. As immigrants and first-generation Americans, they kept the customs, traditions, and practices intact. The Albanian community in Pelham Parkway reinforced their cultural reproduction through their cultural practice of exclusivity. By restricting contact with other groups and imposing sanctions on those who ventured outside the group, the community maintained control on the amount of change and assimilation its members could undergo.

The youths' sense of ethnic identity was inculcated through all the institutions that they came in contact with: their families, their friends and peers, their church, and their neighborhood. The peer group played a very important role. It extended into the school to maintain elements of control on contact, and it encouraged behavior deemed appropriate in the context of their community's culture. So the school, which is often the primary agent of cultural assimilation for youth, was "controlled" by the Albanian young people. Very few Albanian students came through the school and did not associate with the rest of the Albanian students:

> FEYZI: There are one or two Albanians here who do not hang around with us. They think they are better than us. They want to be different, they don't want to be Albanian. We just leave these kids alone. We don't help them if they have trouble with some of the other kids, and we don't respect them. They are not real Albanians.

The students' Albanian identity was also defined by their perceptions that teachers and non-Albanian students were discriminatory toward and ignorant of Albanians. Within Christopher Columbus High School, Albanian students are feared by students from other ethnic groups. They have developed a reputation among both students and teachers for being tough, violent, argumentative, dangerous, aggressive, and racist. Albanian students are fully aware of their reputation and complain that they are the victims of unfair stereotypes that result from a lack of understanding of their culture and their situation:

> FEYZI: People don't know anything about Albanians or Albania. We have a reputation for being tough and violent, and all the teachers assume that if you are Albanian then you are out to cause trouble. We stick together because we have a strong community and because we have to defend our people against other people who are prejudiced against Albanians.

> RAMAZAN: When Albanians first came to this neighborhood, people would make fun of us and disrespect us. Now people may not like us, but they respect us. Most people are scared of us.

These last two quotes are indicative of the ambivalent feelings that Albanian students have about being stereotyped as violent. On the one hand, they do not like being called "hoodlums," nor do they like negative things to be said about Albanians. On the other hand, they enjoy the sense of power they derive from their perception of themselves as the group that controls the high school and from the reaction people have based on their stereotypes. They also definitely feel a need to prove themselves within their own group. Being tough is highly valued both for the males and females, and it is important to demonstrate that one is willing and able to defend one's community, people, and blood.

> LEHMI: We have a sense of justice which tells us we cannot take any shit from anybody. We support each other which means if someone else has a problem, we all get together to take care of the problem.

> FEYZI: Look, there aren't that many of us in the school. So we have to watch each other's back. When you pick on one of us, you best be ready to take us all on.

> SABRI: We don't just defend our school or neighborhood. We defend our nationality, that's it.

The ALERT Youth at Christopher Columbus High School

The other group of students interviewed at Christopher Columbus High School are the picture of the "gorgeous mosaic" that New York City has been called. These students were all members of a student group called ALERT (American Leaders Easing Racial Tension). ALERT is a multiracial group of students who came together to make friends from different backgrounds, to try to improve the racial climate in their high school, and to learn more about people from other backgrounds.

ALERT youths ranged in age from fifteen to eighteen years old. Eight of the youths interviewed were black, four were white, seven were Latino, and one was Asian; there were eight males and twelve females. All came from working-class families, 75 percent of which were headed by single parents. Only 30 percent of them reported their father's occupation. Of those, three were professionals, one a skilled craftsman, one a transport operative, and one a service worker. Eighty-four percent reported their mothers' occupations: five professionals, two managers, one salesperson, four secretaries, and four private household workers.

The ALERT youths came from a number of different ethnic backgrounds; they included African Americans, Italians, Irish, Jamaicans, and Puerto Ricans. Most were good students who made passing grades, though a few were very good students. They all aspired to go to college. The group was an outgrowth of a leadership and cross-cultural awareness training workshop that some members of the group had participated in. At the end of the workshop, they decided to form a group that could address some of the interethnic and interracial conflict that occurred frequently at their high school.

They all had strong ethnic and racial identities, which they celebrated in the context of the group. The group encouraged cultural sharing and the exchange of information about different groups. Their ethnic and racial identities were not defined in opposition to or exclusive of another group. In fact, inclusiveness was one of the group's primary values and was one of the values of which they were most proud.

The Role of Peer Groups

Individually, all of the young people in this study—the Avenue T Boys, the students at Sheepshead Bay High School and John Dewey High School, the young people from Schomberg Plaza and the students at Central Park East Secondary School, the Albanian youths and the ALERT youths—were regular teenagers, not unlike other New York City teenagers, in their general interests, concerns, and preoccupations: relationships, their family situations, sex, music, TV, clothes, sports, jobs, violence.

Where they differ is in their life experiences as members of different ethnic or racial groups, their perceptions of the world around them, their sense of themselves and how they fit into that world, and their sense of the meaning of their ethnicity or race and of ethnic and racial difference. The differences among these groups of youths result from their varied experiences, from the different neighborhoods they live in, and most important, from the peer groups of which they are a part. It is in these peer groups that they form a sense of themselves as individuals and in relation to groups. Peer groups are among the primary institutions in which young people develop their individual identities and group affiliations. Most of the youths expressed a sense that their friends were the most important influence in their lives. This was particularly the case for those who had dropped out of school or who were doing poorly academically. Their participation in their peer group not only gave them a sense of belonging but was their main source of pride:

> RONNIE: I left school because I got tired of teachers who were always on my case. It didn't matter what I did, they thought I was causing

trouble. I didn't like school no way. It was boring, and you get sick of it after awhile. When I'm with my friends, there is none of that. They respect me. Not like with my mother. She's always on my case about something.

The development of a sense of racial and ethnic group identity and the development of a sense of the position of one's group in relation to other groups are critical processes for youth in multicultural, multiethnic, multiracial settings. Unlike youth in homogeneous environments, where ethnic and racial differentiation is a more abstract process that may not even occur consciously, youth in New York City are faced with issues of difference on a daily basis, and issues of race and ethnicity are central elements in peer group and individual identity formation.

The development of self-identity is an extremely important process during adolescence (Erikson, 1963, 1968; Vigil, 1988). The context in which this process takes place is critical to the development of attitudes toward self and toward others (Miller, 1969; Goffman, 1959; Edgerton, 1973; MacLeod, 1987; Vigil, 1988). For the young people at Sheepshead Bay High School, John Dewey High School, and Central Park East Secondary School, and for the members of ALERT, this development takes place within peer groups that are primarily school based.

In contrast, the Avenue T Boys, the Schomberg Plaza youths, and the Albanian youths are all members of peer groups that are based on ethnic or racial group membership and neighborhood residence. Each of these groups is integrally tied to its neighborhood. Members of these groups defined their identities in different ways. Their communities are organized and constructed around ethnic and cultural similarity. The neighborhood young people derive their sense of self from their attachment to the neighborhood. The process of the development of a racial or ethnic identity—of a sense of belonging to a group that has a particular position in relation to other groups—is readily evident with these young people.

The Avenue T Boys were all either high school dropouts, students in alternative high school programs, or marginal students. They are outcasts from the school system and within their community. For them, the street has replaced the home and the school as the context in which they develop their identities. The neighborhood peer groups supply the value models of what they should think and how they should act. The

Schomberg youths were also alienated from school. They spent most of their free time together, and their peers were the main source of information that they considered valid. The group was the arena in which they developed a sense of their racial identity and from which they internalized many of their values and ideas. The Albanian youths were an extension of their community. They functioned as an important support system in school, but they also acted as a mechanism of control against intergroup contact and socializing. Each of these peer groups served to reinforce the norms and values of the larger community. As we shall see, these peer groups functioned as important agents of the community for the reproduction of ethnic and racial attitudes and behavior.

three

Youth Attitudes

It's the end of the school day and students are streaming out of the build-
ing. Tensions run high as groups of students gather at different street
corners in front of the school. Black students assemble at the right of
the school and stare uneasily at a group of Albanian students across the
street. Down the street, at another corner, Puerto Rican students join the
afternoon ritual and a group of Italian students gather close by. An uneasy
calm is maintained by the presence of a couple of police patrol cars who
urge the students to move along.   —*Author's field notes from 3/7/90*

This is the scene on a normal day outside Christopher Columbus High
School. Most days the groups only engage in posturing. But sometimes
the scene is a prelude to intergroup confrontation and violence, which
can range from an exchange of racial epithets to individual and group
brawls. The confrontation may be sparked in response to an alterca-
tion between two students earlier in the day, or it may be a part of an
ongoing conflict between different ethnic and racial groups in the
school. Stories abound on both sides of one member of a group being
attacked by a group of youths from the other side. Sticks and clubs
have been found stashed in the bushes across from the school, a cache
of weapons for use in a gang brawl. Students have been knifed and
even shot in the ongoing conflict.[1]

This scene is all too common at many of the high schools in New
York City. Though only a small minority participate in these afternoon
rituals of posture and challenge, their actions have an effect on all students. Every student must negotiate the ethnic and racial politics of the
school and run the physical gauntlet of groups facing off against each
other each day outside the entrance to the school.

In this chapter I examine and compare the ethnic and racial attitudes of six groups of youth interviewed and surveyed in 1990 and 1991: the Avenue T Boys of Bensonhurst in southern Brooklyn; students at Sheepshead Bay High School in southern Brooklyn; youths from the Schomberg Plaza Youth Project in East Harlem; students at Central Park East Secondary School in East Harlem; Albanian youths attending Christopher Columbus High School in Pelham Parkway in the Bronx; and students who were members of ALERT, a student group at Christopher Columbus High School. I analyze the role of the structural economic conditions that these youths face, the ideological messages they receive about their situation, and their developing ethnic and racial identities.

Racial dynamics and race relations have a profound effect on young people in New York City. The "Study of High School Students and Educational Staff on Prejudice and Race Relations" conducted by the New York City Commission on Human Rights, the New York State Martin Luther King, Jr., Institute for Nonviolence, and the New York City Board of Education found that New York City high school students feel racially isolated, experience prejudice regularly, and have internalized prejudiced attitudes toward other ethnic and racial groups. According to the report:

> "You're on your own, and alone, in a prejudiced-filled and dangerous New York City": This is the report from city high school students. Prejudice is everywhere, in almost everyone, including those who say they are not prejudiced. Most say they believe in integration and have an integrationist attitude; but almost half are practicing a de facto segregation in the social setting of the school, and one in five believe in some segregationist ideas. . . . Prejudice has been internalized by these students. Some of them are aware of this; many are not. For these students prejudice is an inextricable part of their relationships with others. (New York State Martin Luther King, Jr., Institute for Nonviolence, 1990, p. 12)

Race affects these adolescents' lives in a number of ways. The racial composition of the New York City public schools brings young people from different backgrounds in contact with one another. Although there are some schools that are virtually all African American and Latino, many are racially and ethnically mixed. This is primarily true of schools located in white or mixed communities. These schools provide students with opportunities to experience cross-cultural interaction but also to encounter ethnic and racial conflict.

As young people travel around New York City, they have to negotiate a multicultural, multiracial landscape that presents a challenge to any young person who has little knowledge or awareness of different cultures. New York City youths must quickly figure out where they can go and where they cannot. There is an informal, unwritten map of the city that they learn as a matter of survival; Yusuf Hawkins never learned the map. Their perceptions about where in the city it is safe to go and where it is dangerous are based largely on racial dynamics:

> KEISHA (an African American student at Central Park East Secondary School): You learn where you can go and where it ain't so cool for you to be. Some of it's because of racial shit, and some neighborhoods are just dangerous for everybody. White people don't think they should go to Harlem, East New York, Bed-Stuy, Redhook, Brownsville, the South Bronx, places like that. I can't go to Bensonhurst or Howard Beach or Canarsie, and Williamsburg where those Jews (Satmar Hasidim) is probably the worst place.

> RONNIE (Avenue T Boys): You hear all this stuff in the papers about how bad Bensonhurst is for black people. What do you think would happen if I went up to Harlem? They would shoot me in a second.

> TERRELL (Schomberg Plaza): Lots of people think white people can't come to Harlem. White people live all up in Harlem. They're living further and further up, so there's no way you can say a white person is in danger in a black neighborhood, whereas, if I step into Bensonhurst I'm going to get shot by thirty white boys or get chased by twenty white boys.

Wherever I went during the two years I was conducting research for this book, I found that the young people were generally eager to discuss these and related racial issues. There are very few places where they are given opportunities to express their ethnic and racial attitudes and to dialogue about racial issues.[2] The young people I met were surprisingly open in describing their attitudes about racial tension in their schools, in their neighborhoods, and in the city overall. All had strong opinions about race relations, and almost all felt that race relations among young people in New York City were extremely poor. They perceived that race relations had worsened in the past decade and that presently racial tensions in the city were extremely high.

Youth in Southern Brooklyn
The Avenue T Boys

For the Avenue T Boys of Bensonhurst, race relations were clearly an important topic of discussion. Their neighborhood had been the focal point of media scrutiny and political action in the wake of the murder of Yusuf Hawkins. They felt a sense of outrage and anger at what they perceived as the "crucifixion" of their community and the unfair labeling of Bensonhurst youths as "racist." They all thought that race relations among young people in New York City were extremely poor. They listed five factors that they perceived to be the cause of heightened racial tensions in New York City: (1) the deteriorating economic situation, (2) blacks starting trouble, (3) a media that favors blacks, (4) racial prejudice, and (5) increasing black political and economic power in the city.

The Avenue T Boys consistently described economic constraints and economic problems as the primary reasons for racial problems in the city:

> SAL: The situation is more racial because the economy has changed. Some people are out of work and they don't like it.

> GINO: People in my neighborhood don't like how things are going. There aren't enough jobs. You got all these homeless people. When things get bad, it gets tense. Especially when the blacks get all of the attention. Except when some black guy gets beat up or somethin'. Then everybody's lookin' at us and callin' us racist.

These problems directly affected these young people's lives. With the exception of Sal, who worked with his father's construction firm, none of the young men I interviewed had secure employment; most were either unemployed or held short-term or part-time jobs. All of the Avenue T Boys complained that they were victims of favoritism toward blacks, of reverse discrimination, of double standards, and of increasing black power in New York City. Ronnie and Mario directly attributed problems getting a job to favoritism toward blacks:

> RONNIE: You know I been lookin' for work for awhile, but I can't get a job 'cause they're givin' them all to the black people.

> MARIO: Everybody is leaning over backwards to give the blacks everything. They get all the jobs. They get all the attention from the mayor. These days white people don't have a chance. Because blacks are controlling the city. You got your black mayor. The main police chief is black. They never do nothin' for us.

This sense of victimization was heightened by their fear that blacks are "taking over the city." Vinnie was particularly concerned about this because he planned to apply to the police academy:

VINNIE: You know, Italians used to run this city. We didn't have any problems 'cause we had political juice [power]. Now the blacks have taken over and we don't get nothin' from the politicians. Look what they're doing in the police department. They only want to hire blacks and Puerto Ricans.

The 1989 election of a black mayor, David Dinkins, was viewed as strengthening the political and economic power of blacks in New York City. The Avenue T Boys saw the mayor as working only to help black people; they perceived that city government was being run by black people for black people. The mayor's victory fueled preexisting prejudices and fears among whites that blacks were gaining control of New York City, which would make it more difficult for working-class whites like themselves to maintain the ethnic composition of their neighborhoods and, just as important, to achieve economic and job security:

ROCCO: My father told me that [as a result of the new black mayor] they are going to fire all the white construction workers in the city and hire all black guys.

GINO: Dinkins, he's all for the blacks, 100 percent. Not like Ed Koch who used to care about people in white neighborhoods.

SAL: Koch, he was for everybody. He went out into the neighborhoods and talked to people one on one.
ROCCO: When Dinkins was elected I wanted to move out of the city.
RONNIE: The black people will get more attention than they already receive—they get power.
VINNIE: That's right, the black people really think they got it now.

Although they lacked a developed analysis or ideology, these teens were convinced that they were in unfair competition with nonwhite groups, particularly blacks, whom they see as benefiting from "special" treatment. Their ideas and feelings and their resultant sense of victimization were based on their perceptions that blacks were taking jobs and housing away from whites. These themes came up over and over again in interviews with white youth from different neighborhoods in southern Brooklyn:

GINO: By sticking together they [blacks] get a job before a white person because they have to hire so many minorities. This frustrates white people. White people don't get together.

RONNIE: Blacks getting jobs when they are not as qualified makes more hostility.

The attitudes the young people have toward blacks are clearly linked to their sense of the position of whites vis-à-vis blacks in the city. Blumer states that "it is the sense of social position emerging from this collective process of characterization which provides the basis of racial prejudice" (Blumer, 1958, p. 4). This was clearly true for these white youth: Their attitudes toward blacks were significantly influenced by their perception that blacks were achieving success at the expense of whites:

MICHAEL: The situation is much worse for white people than it used to be. There is more competition. They are going to give blacks more jobs because people will be afraid of calling it racial.

MARIO: Companies have to give certain jobs to blacks even though they don't qualify as much as the whites, and I don't think that's fair.

FRANK: Why is it that black people think we owe them something?

They also felt that blacks were benefiting from preferential treatment in the media. They consistently described the media as distorting the image of white youth and white communities. They felt that the media unfairly portrayed young whites and failed to tell the truth about young black males. They perceived the media as only showing the bad things that happened in their neighborhoods and as reporting on events that these young people did not feel were racially motivated as if they were. They felt strongly that there should be "more equal and fair media coverage":

RONNIE: The media is more worried about what white people are doing to blacks than what black people are doing to whites.

SAL: If a white person attacks a black person, they throw the book at him. Meanwhile black kids are getting away with murder and nobody says anything about it, not the media, not the police, nobody.

GINO: There's a double standard in the media. If a black kid gets jumped by a bunch of white kids, they say it's racial. Friends of mine get jumped by black kids all the time and no one describes it as racial.

RONNIE: The media is pushing the black people's case and it's pissing off white people.

Many of the youths felt that the media contributed to racial tensions by sensationalizing racial incidents. They argued that by exaggerating reports of racial violence in the city, the media made young people feel like they had to defend themselves against other groups. Their perception of the media's treatment of them and their communities was reinforced by their perception of themselves as victims of a system that favors blacks:

> VINNIE: The media makes a little issue into a big racial shit. It's the media that does it all.
> GINO: Yea, it's the media that puts everything in our head that makes us want to be bad.
> VINNIE: That's right, they hype it all up.

> FRANK: When something happens to a black guy, it's like wham— everything's all hyped up. They don't put nothing about like when old white people get jumped in these neighborhoods.
> ROCCO: Or like in Central Park. If that was a black girl who got raped, forget it, they would have castrated those kids.

These youths saw blacks as causing trouble in two ways: Blacks commit crimes against whites, and black leaders "make everything racial." They felt strongly that blacks are responsible for crime in the city and that they are not being sufficiently punished for their criminal activity. Many of these young people focused on stories and accounts of crimes committed by blacks and saw these as a source of racial tension in the city.

There was widespread agreement among these youths that blacks are violent troublemakers who are especially dangerous and bold in large groups. Many told stories and anecdotes about blacks committing crimes that went unpunished by the police or school administrators.[3] They uniformly described blacks who ventured into their neighborhoods as "looking for trouble." According to them, everybody in their community believed that the only reason for blacks to come into their neighborhood was to make trouble:

> RONNIE: A group of black kids come into your neighborhood—they are looking for trouble. Why else are they there?

> SAL: The police know the blacks don't belong in our neighborhoods— everybody knows if they are here they must be looking for trouble. It's up to us to make sure they stay out of our neighborhood.

> MARIO (about Yusuf Hawkins): What is a sixteen-year-old kid without a driver's license doing walking into an all-white neighborhood at 9:30 at night looking for a used car? He was out looking for trouble and he found it. Those guys did what they had to do.

MICHAEL: If a white guy walks on my block, nobody will say any-thing to him. But if a black guy walks on my block everybody puts their heads out the window to make sure he leaves the block.
MARIA: Yea, if a black guy comes around, they are usually trying to rob or beat up on people. They would call the cops on a black guy if they see him. The black guy is probably better off if the cops show up than if the Avenue T Boys find him first.

GINO: Blacks just keep stealing everybody's sneakers. They will kill you for your sneakers. They start a lot of trouble. If they want trouble, they're going to get trouble.

The young people also pointed to the actions of black leaders as a factor in rising racial tensions. In particular, the Reverend Al Sharpton, an African American minister who led protests against the Hawkins murder, was perceived to be an instigator of racial tensions. The youths believed that Sharpton fueled racial hysteria about incidents that were not racially motivated. In every interview session with youths from southern Brooklyn, Sharpton was singled out as a troublemaker, and a number of youths stated that Sharpton needed to be killed.[4] They also felt that black people saw everything as racial. Blacks who marched through Bensonhurst to protest the murder of Yusuf Hawkins were criticized for disrupting the community:[5]

VINNIE: The problem in Bensonhurst is the blacks marching down 20th Avenue.

RONNIE: Sharpton is the problem. If he'd tell his people to forget about it, everything would be okay.
ROCCO: He's an instigator, he should be shot.

SAL: Sharpton started all the problems. You don't see him marching in Bensonhurst without a million police.
ROSE: I'd like to see him walk there by himself.
FRANK: I can't wait 'til watermelon season starts.

The data collected in this study reveal that the attitudes expressed by the Avenue T Boys are not restricted to Bensonhurst. Young people from other southern Brooklyn white communities hold similar atti-tudes, and these attitudes are shared by both the young men and young women in these communities. There was no substantive difference in the attitudes expressed by young women from southern Brooklyn in the interviews and on the surveys. Young people I interviewed in Canarsie and Gravesend expressed almost exactly the same sentiments about the economic advantages and power held by blacks, the problem of black crime, and the perception that blacks did not belong in their neighborhoods. It was clear that many white youths in southern Brooklyn have a strong desire to maintain the racial and ethnic composition of their neighborhoods and that they feel justified in fighting, if need be, to do so.[6]

These attitudes toward blacks reflect the neoconservative ideas and principles that have achieved national prominence in current debates over civil rights, affirmative action, and racial inequality.[7] While these teens were not well informed about the specificities of neoconservative analysis, they related to its images and symbols: a black person getting a job that a white person is more qualified for, blacks getting preferential treatment, young black males as criminals, black and Puerto Rican families as welfare-dependent, single-parent households with a violent culture and unclean habits. A couple of the youths referred to Professor Michael Levin of the City University of New York in their discussion of the violent, criminal danger that blacks posed to their neighborhoods.[8] These ideologies fueled their perception of blacks having power and justified their violent actions against blacks as "fighting back."

Blacks are not the only people that these youths view negatively. In fact, these at-risk white adolescents in southern Brooklyn expressed negative attitudes toward most Latino groups and most Asian groups; the only exceptions were other white ethnic groups, Puerto Ricans, Chinese, and Japanese.[9]

White In-School Youth in Southern Brooklyn

School-attending white young people interviewed at two separate high schools in southern Brooklyn displayed significantly more tolerant attitudes than did the at-risk teenagers who had dropped out of school. Though the in-school teenagers also felt that race relations among young people in New York City were not good, most of them said the main problems were ignorance, posturing, and fear of crime:

> LARRY: You're always faced with it. You have to deal with it as teenagers every day. Especially at school, where there are all these different kinds of groups and everybody is eyeing everybody else. Nobody wants to back down, so there's a lot of tension.

> GEORGE: Often times things that aren't racial at all turn racial because it involves a white and a black. Then everybody else gets involved.

TODD: Mainly it's ignorance. People don't know about each other so they feel scared but they can't show that they are scared so they put up a front.

In contrast to the at-risk youths who had dropped out, most of the in-school youths did not link racial problems to economic factors. Whereas the at-risk youths consistently brought up the subject of economic competition and conditions as a primary reason for racial conflict, the subject never came up among in-school youths. When asked directly about whether economic conditions and problems were contributing factors, the in-school youths dismissed it as an important factor:

GEORGE (a student at Sheepshead Bay High School): Things are bad in my neighborhood. There are a lot of people who don't have jobs, but it's even worse for the blacks. I don't think that has anything to do with the problems between young people. The problem is that a lot of kids believe the hype about racial problems. And they don't know anything about other groups except all this negative stuff.

Many pointed to fear of crime and violence as the major contributor to racial division. One of the few exchanges between black and white students developed when one white youth stated that the problem in his neighborhood was fear of black crime; the resulting discussion provides a glimpse into the gulf separating many black and white students:

WHITE STUDENT: People in my neighborhood are scared of blacks because of a fear of black crime. There have been a number of times when blacks from outside my neighborhood have come in and mugged and robbed people. People get tired of that.
BLACK STUDENT: See, that's the problem right there. You white people are always thinking that blacks are criminals. I can't walk anywhere in this city without people looking at me like I've done something or I'm going to do something. There are whites out there robbing and stealing, but you don't see people going out beating up just any white guy.

The survey and interview data clearly indicate that in-school white youths in southern Brooklyn held significantly more tolerant attitudes than at-risk youths.[10]

The Role of Peer Groups

The psychologist Erik Erikson analyzed the differences in ideological outlook among adolescents as the result of differences in school acheivement:

Adolescence, therefore, is least "stormy" in that segment of youth which is gifted and well trained in the pursuit of expanding technological trends, and thus with new roles of competency and invention and to accept a more implicit ideological outlook. Where this is not given, the adolescent mind becomes a more explicitly ideological one, by which we mean one searching for some inspiring unification of tradition or anticipated techniques, ideas, and ideals. And, indeed, it is the ideological potential of a society which speaks most clearly to the adolescent who is so eager to be affirmed by peers, to be confirmed by teachers, and to be confirmed as worthwhile. (Erikson, 1968, p. 129)

There are significant differences between these two groups of youths in southern Brooklyn that may account for the differences in their ethnic and racial attitudes. First, there is a difference in their attachment to school and their academic performance. Many of the youths who were still in school had not yet entered the job market and consequently had not experienced the same level of frustration and anxiety about their economic prospects and opportunities. It is also possible that the more integrated settings of the public high schools in New York City play a role in students' attitude formation. However, the integrated setting does not adequately explain differences in attitudes between the two groups. Most of the at-risk youths had attended integrated schools before they dropped out or enrolled in GED or alternative high school programs. Many of the at-risk youths whom I interviewed attended a special alternative high school or GED program with a dedicated, integrated staff and an excellent curriculum that included workshops on cross-cultural awareness and contemporary problems like sexism, AIDS, and homophobia.

Second, the neighborhoods that these youths come from is significant. Among the at-risk youths, those who lived in Sheepshead Bay exhibited more tolerant attitudes than did those from other southern Brooklyn neighborhoods (such as Bensonhurst, Canarsie, Kings Highway, Gravesend).[11] Of all the at-risk white youths interviewed in southern Brooklyn, Italian American and Jewish youths from Bensonhurst displayed the least-tolerant attitudes of any group. A third difference is the role that peer group dynamics play in shaping the attitudes of the two groups. The opinions of both the in-school and at-risk southern Brooklyn youths demonstrate that peer groups are an important factor in shaping their ethnic and racial attitudes. Both groups ranked peers and friends as the most powerful influence in shaping their ideas about other groups. However, although some of the in-school youths reported participating in neighborhood-based street peer groups, the majority did not appear to be relying primarily on street activities for the development of their identities, attitudes, and ideas. All were in school, all reported passing grades, and two-thirds maintained a C average or better. Most reported that their friends and peers were in school with them.

Attitudinal differences in the in-school and at-risk youths in southern Brooklyn appear to be related to three factors: (1) their ethnicity, (2) the neighborhood they live in, and (3) their attachment to school. Though a higher percentage of in-school white youths came from two-parent families and though they came from a slightly higher socioeconomic background than the youths in Bensonhurst and Gravesend, these factors do not appear to have a significant relationship to their ethnic and racial attitudes.

These three factors combine to produce negative attitudes toward other groups and provide a foundation for engaging in racial violence. Not all working-class white youth from Bensonhurst have negative attitudes toward blacks. Not all white youth who do poorly in school or who drop out have negative attitudes toward blacks. Only when ethnicity is combined with neighborhood support and participation in neighborhood-based peer groups that encourage and facilitate these attitudes is there the potential for ethnic and racial violence. So an Italian or Jewish youth who comes from a neighborhood with a history of conflict with blacks, who does poorly in school or has dropped out, who spends time on the street with a neighborhood-based peer group, and who has established a sense of his or her ethnic group position and sees his or her group as threatened by blacks is likely to have negative attitudes toward blacks and is more likely to engage in acts of racial violence.

Black and Latino Youth in East Harlem
At-Risk Black Youth in Schomberg Plaza

The attitudes of the Schomberg Plaza youths are almost a mirror image of the ideas expressed by the Avenue T Boys in Brooklyn. These young blacks have a deep distrust of white people,[12] and they described their distrust of whites as the result of three factors: (1) their personal experience with whites, (2) their careful examination of history, and (3) their observation of whites' behavior. They perceive whites to be responsible for the deteriorated social and economic conditions in which they live. They have a conception of white racism as responsible for an institutionalized system of oppression of blacks by whites. Fundamentally, they believe that white people cannot be trusted to treat blacks fairly:

TERRELL: African American people form their ideas about white people through history and from the things that they see and things that happened. Basically they just see that racism is being perpetuated. White people are suspect until they prove otherwise.

OSCAR: Black people base their ideas of white people on actual facts. When you read history, and you understand it, and you turn around and you see some white man, then you can see that that's the white man. All those things that he's done before, he's doing again. History has a tendency to repeat itself.

JEFFREY: My moms is race blind. You could be green with yellow polka dots, if you're nice she likes you. Me on the other hand. I mean, she's just more open-minded than I am. I just see the facts. I see how we are low on the totem pole. I think it's time for us to stop thinking of these people as being friendly. I'm saying collectively. White people, from reading history books, seeing what they have done, it's trickery to the utmost.

SHANEEQUA: You don't have to like white people. You don't have to dislike them. All I'm saying is be on your toes when you're around them. You cannot be slouching around them.

JEFFREY: I know the way a black mind thinks as opposed to a white mind. We know how black people scheme. White people scheme on a higher level. White people scheme for the long run. Chances are if it's a brother scheming on you he wants something, and he wants to get it quick. It's a chain or a watch or cash in your pocket. When a white person is scheming on you, they're trying to make you forget who you are. They're trying to take this [points to his skin] away from you, trying to make you forget all about this. They are out to get your head.

The Schomberg Plaza youths believe that white people are afraid of black people, an assertion that is confirmed by the attitudes of white youths in this study. One-third of the whites in the study stated that they felt they have something special to fear from blacks. The Schomberg Plaza youths believed that it is because of this fear and a desire for power that whites oppress blacks. They described a number of factors that they believed result in conditions being worse for blacks than for whites and that contribute to increased racial tensions between blacks and whites. They said that the projection of a negative image of young black males is an important factor contributing to the racial problems in New York City and in the nation. In their vision of U.S. society, young black males are the main target of white America's racism, and the destruction of young black males is a main objective of white racism:

> HABIB: White people are cowards. They will not fight you one-on-one. But they are afraid of you. White people are afraid of black people taking over. Even though they know that we are a distinct minority, they still got that fear of a black planet. And they are especially afraid of young black men like us. They will do anything they can to eliminate us.

> OSCAR: It is young black males like us that white people fear the most. Because of that fear, they try whatever they can to get rid of us. They bring drugs into our community, they miseducate us, they don't give us jobs, and then they put us in prison or kill us. This has gone on throughout history. The black man has always been the target of the white people. Even in slavery, they split up families and tried to break the black man.

> JEFFREY: Everybody is so scared of black youth wilding. If they provided a decent education and something for young people to do, then you wouldn't have all these kids on the street making trouble.
> TERRELL: Yea, well, I think that's just where they want African American youth. Out on the street making trouble so they can round them up and put us in prison. That's why they let the drugs come into our neighborhoods. They could stop it if they wanted, but they would rather we destroy ourselves on drugs and kill each other than compete with them for jobs.

Schomberg Plaza youths see the media much the way white youths in Bensonhurst do: as an institution that contributes to their victimization. They believe that the images of black males portrayed in the media contribute to white people's perception that black people, especially young males, are dangerous. They complained that the portrayal of young black males as violent criminals contributes to racial violence perpetrated against blacks by both the police and other people, providing an image of young black males that feeds the fear of whites:

> HABIB: It's [race relations] bad because of the media. Every time you see Afro-Americans on the TV, either we're a dope fiend or a pimp,

we're breakin' and entering, we're robbing cars, we're illiterate, we can't speak. And when other youth see that, it's like everybody else, they tend to look down on us. They start saying "well you niggers this and that" and there goes the friction right there.

TANIA: Also on the news, the media tends to put things in the spotlight which shows blacks doing something bad, regardless of whether they have any facts. They twist things. The media just tries its hardest to make African Americans look as bad as they can be.

TERRELL: You see how Bernard Goetz was portrayed as a hero after he, for no reason, shot four young African American males on the subway train because he figured that they were going to rob him, which is another stereotype in itself. And the way that Larry Davis was portrayed as a cop-shooting, wild maniac—when they came to get him, there were thirty cops to arrest one man which is really kind of extreme, they came to get him because he didn't want to do what they wanted him to do any more. He defended himself with guns that they had given him. Bernard Goetz has served hardly any time for his gun charge while Larry Davis has to serve ten years for his weapons charge.[13]

TERRELL: And what about that statement that white professor [Michael Levin] made about us not being intelligent?
HABIB: He said we didn't want to learn.
OSCAR: He said African Americans are inferior intellectually.
TERRELL: And that whites have reason to be afraid when they see a black person because chances are the black person is violent. And there are a lot of people that are going to think that he knows.

The ideas that Schomberg Plaza youths hold about the government are the flip side of the Avenue T Boys' view of black political power. Schomberg Plaza youths believe that the government serves white people but not blacks. They view government with suspicion, as one of the embodiments of white power and racism. They look at the lack of economic development in their neighborhoods, the poor level of city services, the actions of the police, the cutbacks in youth programs, and the flourishing drug trade as concrete examples of the interests that control government:

JEFFREY: The government of this country and this city caters to white people. It is white people that control it, and it is white people who benefit from it.
HABIB: That's right. That's why the police harass black youth only when some white person is the victim. Most of the money goes to white neighborhoods.

CARL: You could look at city government and point the finger at city government. Before there were so many empty lots in Harlem, it was a shame with buildings that were abandoned for years. And now the white folks are starting to move uptown, you see more rehabilitation and more renovation.

TANIA: Basically, the government and people with power are going to help white folks who move up here. As long as there's white people in the area and are using things, like they built a high-income co-op across the street and now they have all these stores right around it.

These attitudes persevered despite the election of an African American mayor. These youths stated that Mayor Dinkins had been forced by whites to pay attention to the white community at the expense of the interests of the black community:

JEFFREY: Dinkins is so busy trying to please the white people and show that he is not racist and does not favor black people, that he overlooks his own people who put him in office. It does not matter what he does, the white people are going to hate him and see him as a nigger anyway. They didn't vote for him in the election and they don't like him now—because he's black.

CARL: What happened to all those programs that were supposed to happen in the African American community? Dinkins is trying, but there is nothing he can do. Even with a African American mayor, all we see is our programs and our services being cut.

This contrasted sharply with their opinions about former Mayor Ed Koch, whom they viewed as a direct contributor to increased racial tensions and to the poor state of race relations. They felt that Koch clearly favored white communities and made statements that helped to increase whites' fears of blacks.

TERRELL: Koch was terrible. He was fanning the fire, throwing logs in the fire and making it hot. He never cared about black people in this city. He always was saying racist stuff about blacks. Like when he supported Goetz and said that young black kids on the subway were frightening and that he understood why Goetz would want to fight back against the terror that these young hoodlums were making on the subways.

KEITH: He was flimflammin'. He pretended that he cared about the problem but he never did anything about it. He made statements to the media about how black people were getting too powerful in the city; all the time while cutting funds to African American communities.

The Schomberg Plaza youths also blamed the school system for re-inforcing stereotypes of black people. They believed that schools con-tributed to both the negative attitudes that whites hold toward blacks and to a feeling of low self-esteem and a lack of self-respect among many young blacks:

> SHANEEQUA: All people hear about African Americans is negative. They never hear any of the positive contributions made by African Americans. That way, white people can keep thinking that they are superior.

> JEFFREY: We don't ever learn about ourselves. We never hear that we are the descendants of kings and queens, that Africa was the first and most-advanced civilization before it was destroyed by the Europeans. We don't hear about what we have given to this country. This coun-try is built on the back, on the sweat and blood of African people. All we hear is that we are violent, we are lazy, we are on welfare, we have a lot of babies, we are irresponsible. I am tired of hearing all that.

Distrust of whites runs deep for these youths. Many had developed a psychological barrier against all white people. This visceral reaction against white people was so strong that it created an ambivalence toward light-skinned African Americans of mixed parentage. An ex-change between one young man and the coordinator of the youth pro-gram, who is of mixed parentage, provides an example:

> COORDINATOR: What do you think about me?
> A.J.: Come on man, you ain't white.
> COORDINATOR: Let me hear what you think.
> A.J.: Truthfully? You're black and white, right?
> COORDINATOR: Yea.
> A.J.: The black side I can deal with but the white side I can't. That's how I feel. That other side I can't trust.

Yet despite feelings of distrust, the Schomberg Plaza youths do not think of whites as a homogeneous group. Though they distrust whites in general, they do make distinctions between white ethnic groups, and they rated particular white ethnic groups lower than others.[14] Many expressed feelings of resentment toward Jewish people in particular, whom they view as direct contributors to the problems of blacks:

> TERRELL: We always hear how much Jews have helped blacks, but they are often worse than everyone else. With Italians, at least if they don't like you, they say it to your face. But Jews claim they want to

help us but then when we try to help ourselves they try to stop us.
There's a lot of Jews who been robbing black people blind.

Structural conditions provide the context and shape the nature
(and function) of the interaction of different groups within the black
community. The attitudes that the Schomberg Plaza youths have about
Jews have been directly affected by structural arrangements and conditions. This is confirmed by the attitudes they now have about Koreans,
more recent migrants into their neighborhood. Jews, and more recently
Koreans, have had conspicuous roles in black communities throughout
New York City, including East Harlem, particularly as shop owners
and storekeepers. This role, labeled the "middleman" role by Edna
Bonacich (1973), has had an important impact on the attitudes that
these youths have developed toward these groups. For a number of historical reasons, when blacks migrated to northern cities, they settled in
neighborhoods that were predominantly Jewish. Though Jews moved
out of these neighborhoods, many retained their businesses and ownership of buildings in neighborhoods. The result was that many of the
shop owners and landlords in black communities were Jewish. Many
of these Jewish proprietors have been replaced by Korean and Arab
shop owners since the early 1970s. The position of tenant, customer,
or employee is often perceived as an exploited position. Many black
residents resent the lack of black-owned businesses and perceive that
their money is being taken out of their community. This resentment is
often directed at the groups who have been able to run successful businesses in the black community.

The youth voiced these sentiments and expressed their opinion that
Jews and Koreans are disrespectful of black customers and the black
community:

> CARL: I don't like Jews. They have contributed to making things bad
> for African Americans. They have tried to keep us from learning about
> ourselves. They used to own all the stores in my neighborhood. They
> never respected anybody in the community. Now it's the Koreans.

> JEFFREY: Anti-Asian sentiment does exist in the African American
> community because sometimes it's with good reason. A lot of these
> Koreans, they come here and they open these shops in our commu-
> nities, which is fine, except that some of them just don't like black
> people. Now, what are they doing in this community if they don't like
> us? They want to take our money and treat us bad at the same time?
> Uh-uh. You want my money, then treat me with respect.

Another structural factor has been the disproportionate number of Jewish teachers in the New York City public schools. There is a history of conflict around the issue of Jewish teachers in predominantly black schools dating back to the Ocean Hill–Brownsville controversy over community control of schools in 1968. Many of these youths hold their Jewish teachers responsible for their lack of education:

> OSCAR: Just about every teacher I have had in school has been Jewish. They don't want to teach us the truth about black people. Jewish teachers are the reason for many of the educational problems of black students.

All of the youths stated that personal experiences they had had with Jewish people were responsible for their negative attitudes toward Jews. But it is the structural relationship between the two groups, combined with stereotypical ideas about Jews that are prevalent in both the black community and in society generally, that influences and shapes these attitudes. Popular stereotypes about Jews, combined with broader social messages that portray Jews negatively, provide a context within which these East Harlem youths interpret their interactions and analyze their experiences with Jewish people. Many of the ideas they express have been put forth by a number of prominent black leaders. Most noteworthy among them are the Reverend Louis Farrakan, Professor Leonard Jeffries, and the rap group Public Enemy, all three of whom were cited as influences by the Schomberg Plaza youths. These leaders both help create and affirm these young people's perception that Jewish people are a powerful group. These youths strongly believe that Jewish people exert significant influence in New York City government. Though they recognized that Jewish people have a history of having been oppressed, and some expressed some respect for how Jewish people treat each other, they clearly felt that as a group Jewish people are racist:

> CARL: The Jews have been oppressed pretty bad. They are just trying to hide by blending in with everyone else and picking on us. You know it's going down the ladder.

> HABIB: The Jews are powerful. They control the media and they control the government. Dinkins is constantly trying to please the Jews. He won't criticize a Jewish leader when they are wrong. He won't criticize the Jewish community when they are wrong.

> JEFFREY: Jews never look down on each other. They stick with each other, they will not turn their backs on each other. That's one of the

best things that a people, race, or religion can do for themselves. But they don't like black folks. Some of them used to support the civil rights struggle but here in New York City, they're just as scared of us as the rest of the white people.

The process of attitude formation and expression takes place in a group context. For young people, attitudes toward other groups are discussed and figured out within the peer group. Though these black youth have interacted with Jews and are exposed to social messages about the position of Jewish people, it is in the peer group that personal experiences and messages are interpreted and channeled into a functional set of attitudes and beliefs about Jewish people. It is in the peer group that personal experiences with individual Jews are fused with stereotypical messages about Jews as a group and come to form the basis for attitudes about Jews as a group. At the time of this research, a similar process was producing and reinforcing negative attitudes among the Schomberg Plaza youths toward Asian groups in general and toward Koreans particularly:

TERRELL: There is a problem with Jews being a minority and progressing faster using things like nepotism like the Koreans are doing when they only hire their family or other Koreans.

The Schomberg Plaza youths were very aware of the controversy surrounding black–Asian relations, a controversy that has become particularly evident since the boycott of a Korean grocery store in a black community in Flatbush became front-page news in New York City.[15] There have been boycotts of Korean grocery stores in Harlem as well. Interestingly, the youths asserted that there is no anti-Asian sentiment in the black community. They believe that only particular stores are boycotted and that they are boycotted because the owners are insensitive or racist toward blacks who shop there, not because the owners are Asian. The youths believe that blacks should use their consumer power as an individual tool against a particular merchant who is racist toward blacks and as a collective strategy for social change:

TERRELL: It's [anti-Asian sentiment] no problem until they step over the line. The line is you do not disrespect me in my neighborhood when I am giving you money. When we are actually supporting you 'cause if we said we don't want you in this community and we are not going to buy from your store, then there is nothing you can do. When you disrespect us as a people, call us names like nigger, well, that's when the conflict comes.

JEFFREY: Our community is friendly, it comes from our heritage. That's how we got here, we were too friendly. Anybody can live in this community, no matter what your race. If you do not try to disrespect us in our community, then we will not have a problem with you.

HABIB: Anti-Asian sentiment does exist in the African American community because sometimes it's with good reason. For example, if you walk into a Korean fruit store and the guy is hawking you down. He's got his eyeballs on you, watching you, expecting you to steal something. That's when problems occur when people let the media shape their opinion.

TANIA: We only boycott the racist ones, the ones who disrespect us. There are plenty of Korean and Arab grocers all up through Harlem who do a great business because they treat us right.

However, the youths' assertions in the interviews that there is no anti-Asian or anti-Korean sentiment in their community are contradicted by the answers they give on the survey. Many of them distinguished between different Asian groups and ranked Chinese and Japanese higher than Koreans.[16]

The low ratings given to groups who have been present in East Harlem as merchants and residents (Jews, Italians, and Koreans) or as teachers in the schools (Jews) provide evidence of how the economic and social relationships of the black community have affected attitudes toward other ethnic and racial groups. The process of the development of a racial or ethnic identity—of a sense of belonging to a group that has a particular position in relation to other groups (Blumer, 1958)—is readily evident among the Schomberg Plaza youths. Their attitudes toward Jews and Koreans reflect attitudes that are prevalent throughout black communities. In sum, the images these youths have of Jews and Koreans are a direct result of three factors: (1) the historical and current structural relationship between black, Jewish, and Korean communities in northern cities, (2) personal experiences that are the result of the political economy of inner-city black communities and structural arrangements and inequalities at the local level, and (3) community-based ideological messages that are used to explain personal and group experiences and are supported by messages in the wider culture.

The importance of the structural economic relationships in shaping the racial attitudes of the Schomberg Plaza youths is also demonstrated by their attitudes toward Puerto Ricans, another ethnic group present in East Harlem. The youths said that the situation between themselves and the Puerto Ricans had improved with time. Many said they had close friends among Latinos of various ethnic groups, and Puerto Ricans received the second-highest rating from the Schomberg Plaza youths. Some maintained that there had been turf wars between blacks and Puerto Ricans, which had abated several years earlier, and that these struggles had been over control of territory among young people from different housing projects:

> JEFFREY: There's no friction between African Americans and Latinos. About six years ago, there were turf wars, but it was more like building against building or block against block. Black kids from Schomberg Plaza would fight Puerto Ricans from Tres Unidos and Metro Court. Like that. There are no turf wars, now.

Like the Avenue T Boys, the Schomberg Plaza youths live in a highly segregated world. This partly explains why there are similarities in the outlook and attitudes of the two groups. Both groups have a deep sense of having been victimized because of their ethnic and racial identity. Both distrust and dislike those groups whom they view as direct participants in the problems they face. Both have a sense that the media and government treat their communities unfairly. Both have a sense of individual and community powerlessness, which they connect to the power and actions of other groups.

Just as the Bensonhurst murder had an important impact on the youth of Gravesend and Bensonhurst, the Central Park jogger case was an important event for black youth at Schomberg Plaza. The Central Park jogger case supplied a concrete example and symbol of the power relations between whites and blacks and their position as blacks living in a white society.

Of all the young people interviewed in this study, those from Schomberg Plaza had the most developed analysis of race relations. There are several explanations for the high level of analysis and the relative complexity of their views. First, as black young people, their lives are defined by their racial experience. They live in a world controlled and dominated by the issue of race, and their ideas and attitudes reflect this reality.

Second, they have learned that white skin is a symbol of power and privilege. Almost all of them have grown up in poor families living in a poor community. Because of a weak public education system, their prospects for economic success are poor. They view their limited life chances as the result of white racism that has limited their opportunities and locked them in impoverished ghettoes. They view white economic power and privilege as the root of their community's problems and of their individual problems.

They live in a world where racial inequality is readily evident. They need only walk a few blocks south or venture into Central Park to see examples of white affluence. All of the Schomberg Plaza youths consistently pointed to the difficult economic conditions under which they live and the deteriorated conditions of their neighborhood as an important determinant of their attitudes toward whites.

Third, just as in Bensonhurst and Gravesend, peer groups play an important role for these black youths. They reported that they learn most of their ideas from each other. The process is similar to that observed among the white youths in this study. Issues of self-identity and racial identity are worked out in the context of the peer group. Attitudes toward others are internalized during the process of developing and integrating the collective ideology and belief system of the peer group. Young people develop a set of attitudes and beliefs that both conform to and support each other.

Fourth, these young people are maturing during a time of rising nationalism in a neighborhood that prides itself on being the lap of black culture. It is clear that they have been affected by ideas that have become prominent in the black community, particularly that black people are victimized by a lack of knowledge of their history. Their ideas indicate their exposure to a particular ideology that analyzes their situation in terms of power relations:

> TERRELL: The reason I don't speak about African Americans being racist is because racism to me is when you have the power to do something about your prejudice, against whoever you are prejudiced against. On the whole, white people have most of the power and they have done a good job of keeping us below them.

> JEFFREY: African American people cannot be racist because we don't have the power to act out on our prejudice.

The views and ideas expressed by Schomberg Plaza youths fit the analyses of internal colonial theorists.[17] Their perception of the political, economic, and social control of their community by white-dominated institutions and their portrayal of the effects of images of blacks on the minds of whites and blacks echo the theories of economic, political, and cultural exploitation described in internal colonialism theory. Though these youths are not familiar with internal colonialism theory, they respond to images, symbols, and analyses that have become prominent in their community.

Fifth, as with the at-risk youths in southern Brooklyn, there is strong community support for their attitudes. These youths live in a community with a long history and tradition of racial and cultural consciousness. Community leaders ranging from politicians to community organizers express ideas, attitudes, and ideologies that confirm and support the attitudes of these youths. Politicians, such as U.S. Representative Charles Rangel and Mayor David Dinkins, and community activists, such as the Reverend Herbert Daughtry and the Reverend Calvin Butts, present moderate analyses of the problems plaguing East Harlem and other black communities, analyses that depict historical racism in U.S. society and present-day neglect by the federal government as a primary cause of the depressed conditions of communities like East Harlem. Community activists, such as Elombe Brath, the Reverend Louis Farrakan, and the Reverend Al Sharpton, supply more radical visions of the role of white racism in the perpetuation of the problems in the black community. The youths easily relate to these messages and images, which provide an explanation of their sense of group position and an outlet and target for their frustrations, anxieties, and anger about that position. Just as neoconservative ideology, with its powerful symbols and imagery, supplies an explanation for their difficult situation to the white youths in Bensonhurst and Gravesend, Schomberg Plaza youths draw ideological support for their ideas from black nationalist ideology, which supplies an incisive analysis of the origin of their oppression.

Sixth, popular culture plays an important role in helping black youths interpret their situation and personal experiences. Whereas there was little reference to popular culture by young people in Bensonhurst and Gravesend, Schomberg Plaza youths often quoted rap artists to explain their own analyses. Cultural messages, which have become predominant in black communities in New York, are extremely important for these youths. Rap music has had a profound effect on the ideas and attitudes of many young blacks. Rap music is the most immediate source of black nationalist ideology for the Schomberg Plaza youths. Afrocentric and political rap music has contributed to a surge in racial consciousness and political awareness among young blacks in New York.[18]

Central Park East Secondary School

Central Park East Secondary School is an innovative high school with a diverse student population located in East Harlem. The young people interviewed at Central Park East Secondary School were from several different neighborhoods. The majority of the black youths lived in East Harlem, Harlem, and the Upper East Side—three adjacent neighborhoods. Those who did not lived in the South Bronx, Flatbush in Brooklyn, and Tremont and the Grand Concourse in the Bronx. They came from a number of different ethnic backgrounds: African American, Trinidadian, Jamaican, and mixed ethnicity. All of the black youths were doing well in school, with 92 percent maintaining a B average or better. These were young people who excelled academically, and almost all of them were college bound.

Like Schomberg Plaza youths, black youths at Central Park East Secondary School expressed distrust and distaste for the role they perceived politicians to be playing in the maintenance of racial inequality and racial tensions and for the role that some institutions play in creating and maintaining the problems of the black community. They analyzed this as a manifestation of racism. Yet their attitudes toward different racial and ethnic groups were different, and their sentiments about racism were directed toward government and other formal institutions. They did not translated these ideas into negative attitudes about whites as a group:

> CHERYL: Also, someone told me that they know someone in the sanitation department and they tell them to clean the streets good downtown but if they want to slack off, they can do that from 96th Street on because the black people live there and they will mess up anyway. Government works for white rich people and neglects all those neighborhoods with poor people of color.

> ANTHONY: Look at how this government has drugs in this community. You don't think the government could get these drugs out of here if they wanted to? There are different ways of oppressing people. Like bad Medicaid and increasing the infant mortality rate.

> TERRY: The system is racist. Government is supposed to be for all the people. But it serves the rich white community and neglects poor blacks and Hispanics.

Like the Schomberg Plaza youths, these young people believed that Mayor Koch did not care about their communities; that he both allowed government to neglect the needs of the black community and contributed to rising racial tensions in the city. And like the Schomberg Plaza youths, these young blacks believe that Mayor Dinkins was being unfairly attacked and criticized by whites in New York City:

ANTHONY: Koch hasn't done things in a positive way. He didn't do anything to make things better so that's negative.

LATASHA: Koch. He was terrible. He just added to the problems. Economically, he made it disgusting. And he allowed stuff like this to happen. He encouraged the racists.

LISA: Dinkins, he made a nice speech but he's not really doing anything. It's just to pacify the people.

LIONEL: I think it was a small step. At least he is aware of the problem and is giving it some attention. Koch never did anything but pretend that there wasn't a problem.

CHERYL: Everybody is picking on poor Mayor Dinkins. He's only been in office for a few months and already they want to blame him for all the problems. We had all these mayors who put us in this situation and finally we get one black guy and they want him to reverse the situation in one week. It took them decades to get us to this messed up situation.

But, in stark contrast to the Schomberg Plaza youths, black youths at Central Park East Secondary School did not express distrust and dislike of whites.[19] Their attitudes about Jews contrasted sharply with the attitudes of the young people at Schomberg Plaza. In fact, in their survey responses, Jews were one of the highest-rated groups. The majority perceived Jewish people to be different from other whites because of their history of persecution. They respected Jews for the role they have historically played in supporting the civil rights movement and for their history of enduring oppression:

LATASHA: I don't really see racial tensions with Jewish people because, like, on 125th and old Broadway, it's this Jewish synagogue, and then on 122nd there's this Jewish theological place. And people may laugh at them because of how they look but I don't think anybody bothers them.

TERRY: If anything, we should be closer to them 'cause they went through the Holocaust and all that, so they should have an understanding for what we're going through.

ANTHONY: Jewish people are friendlier to blacks than other groups. They have supported black struggles for equality more than anyone else.

The one exception was a student who stated that Jews have unjustly accused blacks of being anti-Semitic. When challenged by other students in the group, who asked whether blacks could also be accused of being too sensitive, this student maintained that Jews have little to complain about in comparison to blacks:

SAREETA (Central Park East Secondary School student from Harlem): Jewish people are so defensive. You can say any one little thing and it's like you are attacking them. Like they say Chuck D is anti-Semitic. Like Louis Farrakan. He is not anti-Semitic or antiwhite. He is pro-black. People don't understand this.

Black youths at Central Park East also expressed more tolerant attitudes toward Asians. Though young people from both Schomberg Plaza and Central Park East stated that anti-Asian sentiment was not widespread in East Harlem, the survey responses of the black youths at Central Park East Secondary School revealed less prejudice toward Asians than was expressed by Schomberg Plaza youths.[20] Nevertheless, black youths at Central Park East also recognized that blacks in their neighborhoods have problems with Asian merchants who were insensitive and racist toward blacks. For these students, the issue was a lack of respect, but they also thought that blacks felt angry and frustrated because of the dearth of black-owned businesses in the black community:

LATASHA: There has been a problem between African Americans and Asians in Harlem. It was not Asians themselves. It was a group of people who did something that they [blacks] did not appreciate and they did not think was appropriate. I feel that the media brought everyone's attention towards blacks against Asians just to try to say that it's not just white people who do it. It's not just a problem of white and black; they wanted to take the attention off of what white people are doing.

LIONEL: If they [Asians] are going to take all our money away from us, that's fine, but at least have respect.

SAREETA: Asians are opening more businesses and that's causing tension in the neighborhood. We look at it like, how can they come into our neighborhood and open a business and we can't? Then you add the insensitivity and racism of some of the Korean shop owners and it makes for more tensions. It spills over to other Asians.

TYRONE: The situation in the store that's being boycotted is out of control. The owners of that store were disrespectful of black people and they assaulted a black woman. Now everybody wants to say it's racial, but there are a whole bunch of Korean stores on the same street which black people shop in and nobody has any problem there. There wouldn't have been a problem if those Koreans in that store had not been racist and if they had been dealt with by the law. But now, it's been blown up in the press and people think blacks hate all Koreans. That just ain't the way it is.

In summary, though black youths at Schomberg Plaza and Central Park East Secondary School share the same racial background, there are marked differences between the two groups' racial attitudes and the levels of antagonism they feel toward other groups. Black youths at Central Park East had more tolerant attitudes toward other racial and ethnic groups than did youths at Schomberg Plaza.

Once again, neighborhood and peer group sentiments played an important role in the establishment of ethnic and racial attitudes. The sense of group position that young people develop is affected by the context and conditions within which the group is formed. Those young people who grew up in more integrated, affluent communities had a sense of racial identity and of the position of blacks in relation to other groups different from those of young people who grew up in communities that were predominantly black and poor. Where black youths at Central Park East did feel antagonisms toward other groups, they were related to the neighborhoods in which they lived, where they developed a sense of their group that was closer to that of the Schomberg Plaza youths. Just as neighborhood sentiment was an important factor as a source and a support of attitudes toward other groups for white youths in southern Brooklyn, so it was for the black youths in this study. Differences between black youths at Schomberg Plaza and Central Park East Secondary School stem not only from their structural socioeconomic status but also from their perceptions of the conditions of their group and how they analyzed the reasons for these conditions.

Interestingly, in a number of important ways, Schomberg Plaza youths were more similar to the Avenue T Boys than they were to black youths at Central Park East Secondary School. Black youths at Central Park East Secondary School were not faced with the high levels of economic and social uncertainty that the Schomberg Plaza youths and the Avenue T Boys were faced with. They felt more in control of their lives, and consequently, their individual identities were not as connected to their sense of their group's position in relation to other groups. Unlike the homogeneous racial environments that characterize the lives of the Schomberg Plaza youths and the Avenue T Boys, the multicultural environments of Central Park East Secondary School and Sheepshead Bay High School and of the neighborhoods in which their students lived facilitated both increased cross-cultural interaction and the development of an ideology that explains problems of societal racism and stresses the values of equality and tolerance of all groups. Most of the Central Park East Secondary School and many of the Sheepshead Bay High School black youths were members of heterogeneous peer groups that reinforced these ideas of integration and tolerance. Finally, students at Central Park East Secondary School did not derive their sense of self-worth and their identity primarily from activities on the street. Their sense of themselves was developing in contexts that stressed individual achievement and mobility and did not foster the development of an ethnic and racial identity based on differentiation from other groups. As a result, youths at Central Park East Secondary School have adopted racial tolerance and integration as values and displayed little antagonism toward other ethnic and racial groups. There are clear differences in the attitudes expressed by black youths surveyed at Schomberg Plaza and black youths at Central Park East Secondary School. The youths at Schomberg Plaza particularly, and those youths from East Harlem and Harlem generally, express a deep distrust of whites and showed negative attitudes toward Italians, Jews, and Koreans. These attitudes are linked to the structural economic and demographic conditions in the neighborhood, to neighborhood sentiment and collective community ideology, and to peer group interaction and dynamics that facilitated the development of particular attitudes and behaviors toward other groups.

Latino Youth in East Harlem

Latino youths at Central Park East Secondary School were from East Harlem, Washington Heights, and Williamsburg. The majority of the Latino youths interviewed were Puerto Rican, and the rest were Dominican. They all came from working-class and poor families. The Latino youths interviewed at Central Park East Secondary School were not as outspoken as the black youths. They all agreed that race relations among young people in New York City had deteriorated, but they maintained that they did not know about regular conflicts involving Latinos:

> ANNA: There used to be problems between blacks and Puerto Ricans but that has chilled out and now there's not really much happening around where I live. From time to time you hear about some whites or blacks, whites mostly, jumping Puerto Ricans—there were several problems up in the Bronx, but there is not that much going on.

Instead, the conflicts they spoke most about were interethnic conflicts between Puerto Ricans and Dominicans.[21] Puerto Rican youths at Central Park East Secondary School told many stories of tension and fights in their neighborhoods between Puerto Ricans and Dominicans. Most had no explanation for the animosity between the two communities.

> GLORIA: I don't think that there is that much racism. The media blows it out of proportion. Now we expect everything to be racial. Where I live there are Dominicans that work across the street, that sell drugs, and my neighborhood is mostly Puerto Ricans and they say those Dominicans come from the Dominican Republic or Santo Domingo just to sell drugs to the young people over here. It's just a stereotype that people have. I used to say that all Dominicans were nasty and stuff but now I know that that's not true. That's what I heard from people on the street. I changed my mind when I met Jackie [a classmate] and her family.

One young woman, however, offered the explanation that the tension between Puerto Ricans and Dominicans involved racism against darker-skinned Latinos:

> ROSA: The stereotype of Dominicans is that they wear those colorful shoes with no socks. They are always talking Spanish and yelling at their women out the window. Throwing rice out the window. It's true I guess, stereotypes are often based on reality, but I see the conflict as between the dark-skinned kinky-haired Hispanics and the light-skinned straight-haired ones.

Despite the evidence of negative attitudes on the part of some Puerto Rican youths toward Dominicans and of ethnic conflict between Puerto Ricans and Dominicans, Latino youths as a group, and Puerto Ricans in particular, exhibited more tolerant attitudes than did the white or black youths.[22]

As a group, the Puerto Rican youths had a range of different ethnic and racial identities—some self-identify as white, some self-identify as black, and most self-identify as "Latino."[23] Puerto Rican youths seemed to adopt the dominant attitudes of the peer group they hung out with. Those who lived in predominantly white ethnic communities appeared to self-identify as white and to be accepted by the youths in those communities—particularly Italian communities. Consequently, several of the most vociferous youths in southern Brooklyn were Puerto Ricans who hung out with Italian youths on the streets of Bensonhurst, Canarsie, and Kings Highway and strongly identified with their Italian American peers.

Those Puerto Ricans who lived among blacks likewise appeared to be accepted by blacks. Though there were stories of past conflict and violence between blacks and Puerto Ricans, most of the youths claimed that, currently, there were few problems between the groups.[24]

Pelham Parkway
White Albanian Youth in Pelham Parkway

Racially, the Albanian students at Christopher Columbus High School all identify as white. Their ethnic and racial attitudes reflect their community's experiences as a relatively new immigrant group. Like most of the other youths in the study, the Albanian youths felt that race relations among young people were very bad in New York City. Like the Avenue T Boys and the Schomberg Plaza youths, they expressed strong feelings of having been victimized, racially *and* ethnically. But in contrast to white youth in southern Brooklyn, Albanian young people expressed no anxieties about economic competition with other groups in the labor market. Though some of their sentiments echoed positions articulated by other white youth in New York City, Albanian youths did not see themselves as competing directly with blacks and Puerto Ricans for jobs:

> FEYZI: My future is certainly better than the life my parents have had. They came to the United States without much. My father and all my uncles had to work two and three jobs. They had it tough. I plan to go into real estate and own property.

> PHILLIP: Our parents had to work hard to establish themselves here. Now, I can go to college but they didn't have that possibility. I've got a lot more options than they did. I will probably become a lawyer, though my dad wants me to work in the family business.

Further, there was a noticeable difference between the two groups in terms of the relation between their ethnic and racial identity. Although Albanian young people in this study clearly felt victimized by other groups, they articulated their feelings of victimization differently than did the young whites in southern Brooklyn. In speaking about "being Albanian," they rarely linked it to race, to "being white."

Whereas the Avenue T Boys felt that they were victimized because they were white, the Albanian youths felt that they were victimized because they were Albanians and immigrants. Though both their racial and ethnic identities appeared well defined, the ethnic identity of the Albanian youths was not as integrally tied to their racial identity as was the case for the Italian American youths in southern Brooklyn. Whereas Italian youths in southern Brooklyn automatically linked being Italian with being white and spent most of the time talking about how *whites* were losing power in U.S. society and being unfairly treated in the city, the Albanian youths described problems that had to do with how other groups treated Albanians specifically. When they talked about why they thought race relations were so poor, the Albanian youths spoke mostly about the intolerance and prejudice they encountered as Albanians:

> LEHMI: Things are bad because people have a lot of prejudice against Albanians. They think we are stupid, that we are violent, when they don't know anything about us.

> PHILLIP: We have to deal with a lot of teachers and kids who don't like Albanians. They don't give us respect and they talk shit about us.

For the Albanian youths, their experiences as a newer immigrant group reflected a difference in the degree to which their ethnic identity was fused with ideas about race and attitudes toward other groups. As members of a new immigrant group, they had not assimilated to the degree that the Italian and Jewish youth in southern Brooklyn had. Part of the assimilation process is the incorporation of dominant societal values and norms into the ethnic culture of a group. Because race is so salient in U.S. society, white ethnic groups tend to adopt a racial identity as a part of their sense of ethnic identity. They are defined racially by others and compete for jobs, housing, and political power in a racialized context, all of which contributes to the development of a racialized ethnic identity.

Further, precisely because they are relatively new immigrants and have not assimilated as much as the Italian American and Jewish youths in southern Brooklyn, Albanian youths have a very clear and strong sense of their ethnic identity. This may account for differences in their attitudes toward different ethnic groups. With the exception of Italian Americans, to whom they relate closely, Albanian youths rated every single group lower than did other white youths.[25]

The separation of the ethnic and racial identities of the Albanian youths was evident in the course of the interviews. In response to general interview questions about the condition of race relations among young people, they spoke about being Albanian and the problems and prejudices they faced. There was no discussion of whites in relation to blacks. When they talked about conflicts with blacks, they did so in relation to power struggles over turf between blacks and Albanians rather than between blacks and whites:

> SABRI: The blacks don't respect our position at the school. They want to control the school, and so we have to fight them when they challenge us.

It was only after distinct shifts in the discussion that race as an issue was discussed. The tenor of the discussion changed when the youths were asked what they thought about Mayor David Dinkins. Immediately, the topic of discussion shifted from being Albanian to being white. At that point, these youths began to express racial resentment similar to the feelings expressed by the Avenue T Boys. It was only during the second part of the interview that Albanian youths discussed racial dynamics in New York City. Here, for the first time, they talked about blacks and Puerto Ricans in terms of race and racism, a connection that had been absent from their analysis of the conflicts they had with these two groups at their high school.

Here it was revealed that racial attitudes about blacks voiced by Albanian youths in the Bronx were similar to those expressed by the Avenue T Boys. Like the Avenue T Boys, Albanians at Christopher Columbus High School believed that blacks could not be trusted; they felt that blacks ruin neighborhoods and are out to cause trouble:

> FEYZI: You go to black neighborhoods, they're all bad.
> LEHMI: Yea, they don't care, they're like, fuck it, let's fuck up the place. There's a few of them that are working hard and going to college but most of them, they don't try to get out of the gutter. They blame their problems on racism.

RAMAZAN: We get along with all the white kids in the school. We get together with the Italians and the Irish—there ain't many of them, and the other white kids like Greeks and what not, and we take care of the blacks and spicks when they get really out of hand.

LEHMI: The blacks are ass kissers. Whoever is in power, they kiss their ass. So we don't get along with them because you can't trust them. First thing you know, when you turn around they stab you in the back.

The Albanian youths in Pelham Parkway sympathized with the Italians in Bensonhurst about the Bensonhurst murder case. Like their southern Brooklyn counterparts, they blamed the media and Al Sharpton for making the incident in Bensonhurst worse:

SABRI: They [the media] call fights racial that aren't racial.

PHILLIP: The publicity has made everything worse. If it wasn't for the publicity, Joey Fama wouldn't have gotten convicted [of murdering Yusuf Hawkins]. It's 'cause of Reverend Al Sharpton; that guy should be shot.

RAMAZAN: It's two ways, like, when a white kid hits a white kid, or say I was walking down the block and some black kids jump me, they'd just say that was a mugging. But say some black kid was jumped by white kids, then they say that's a bias racial attack. I don't get it.

Albanian youths also had similar assessments of the political situation as did the Avenue T Boys. They felt Mayor Dinkins was serving just the black community and preferred Mayor Koch, who they thought had been fairer to the white neighborhoods:

FEYZI: Koch was a good mayor. He didn't let the blacks push him around. He did a lot for the white neighborhoods. My dad said that when Koch lost to Dinkins that we lost a friend and gained an enemy.

LEHMI: Mayor Koch was much better than Dinkins. If Giuliani was mayor, he would have helped the people of Bensonhurst.

RAMAZAN: Dinkins is trying to be slick. He put all black people in his administration.

PHILLIP: That's right. Look at Mayor Dinkins' cabinet, now look, Mayor Koch had some blacks, some whites—it was mixed. Mayor Dinkins has all black people, there's no white guys in there. They let all the minorities have the jobs. And look at the cop test, a white guy has to score 700 and a black guy only 500."

SABRI: Yea, minorities get easier tests on college courses.

After the discussion shifted to white–black relations, the Albanian youths echoed many of the sentiments expressed by white at-risk youths in southern Brooklyn.[26] They too felt it was blacks who were racist, and they too complained of double standards on behalf of blacks and rising black power:

> DRITA: How come black people think we're so racist? Aren't they racist also? I think that they are more racist than us. They go make riots in the streets.

> RAMAZAN: They wear black power T-shirts but if we wear white power shirts they call us racist.
> SABRI: They wear Malcolm X shirts, why can't we wear Hitler shirts?

> FEYZI: Black people are coming on too strong, look what happened in Central Park. We didn't riot in the streets saying oh my God, racism. But as soon as something happens, like Yusuf Hawkins, they are out in the streets raising hell and disturbing the neighborhood.

> YASMINE: I think now that blacks are more racist than whites are now.
> LEHMI: They use racism as a tool now. For power.
> SABRI: They think they have the power now and they think, they want to . . . we're black, let's take them over.
> LEHMI: They're trying to pay us back.

Interestingly, the Albanian youths felt more animosity toward Puerto Ricans than did the white youths living in southern Brooklyn. Whereas in southern Brooklyn light-skinned Puerto Rican youths hung out with Italian youths and held similar attitudes toward blacks, Albanians in the Bronx viewed Puerto Ricans in their school and in their neighborhood as enemies.[27]

The attitudes of the Albanian youths clearly demonstrate the situational nature of ethnic and racial attitudes and relations. The context of community relations and conditions determines the nature of the relations. This context exists at the community level and is interpreted at the community level. Again, the roots of the youths' attitudes toward blacks and Puerto Ricans can be found in their local community.

One significant difference between the historical experiences of Albanians in the Bronx and ethnic whites from southern Brooklyn is that Albanian families moved into neighborhoods that were already inhabited by large numbers of black and Puerto Rican or other Latino residents as well as Italian residents. As relatively late settlers in the neighborhood, Albanians never experienced the "white flight" that characterized the experience of white residents in southern Brooklyn. On the contrary, Albanians gradually acquired real estate in the Pelham Parkway area, becoming the owners and landlords of many buildings where black and Puerto Rican families reside.

Many of the Albanian youths complained about the way blacks and Puerto Ricans affect their neighborhood and about the way they treat the apartments they rent from Albanian landlords. They also reported that although there are Albanian niches in the neighborhood, the area is ethnically and racially mixed. They reported occasional flare-ups of tension but few serious problems:

> FEYZI: There are sometimes problems along Allerton Avenue. There was a short period a few months back when it wasn't a good idea for black teenagers to go west of Williamsbridge Road on Allerton. That was because some blacks started some trouble on the avenue one night and the whole thing got racial and it took weeks to calm down. But normally, if they [blacks] are for the neighborhood, nobody bothers them.

Although Pelham Parkway is a culturally diverse neighborhood, almost all of the Albanian youths hang out exclusively with Albanians inside and outside of school. They all reported that they were discouraged by their parents and peers and by members of their community from having black or Latino friends. Although some socialize with blacks and Puerto Ricans at school, all reported that this kind of socializing was taboo in their neighborhood, where it could be observed by family, friends, and neighbors. Obviously, there are differences in the strictness with which individual families adhere to community values. For example, a few of the males claimed to have friends from different ethnic or racial backgrounds:[28]

> MEDIHA: Older people, like my father and mother, they only mix with Albanians.

> DRITA: There is a lot of pressure not to deal with, not to associate with, blacks and Puerto Ricans. If you are seen hanging out with them in the neighborhood, someone will take you to the side and say, "Look, you should be careful what kind of friends you keep."

> PHILLIP: If you [a black male] were to come to my house for dinner, well, my parents wouldn't like it but they would probably be polite. But my brother, he'd probably try to throw you out of the house. And everybody in the neighborhood would know in five minutes that there was a black guy at my house. It wouldn't be too big a deal if it happened once, but if I had a lot of blacks over, people would start to let me know that it wasn't cool and I should cut it out.

FEYZI: If you have a lot of non-Albanian friends, it will be hard to marry another Albanian, especially for the girls. It shows that you don't have respect for the values of the community. Later on in life, you might not get support for your business and you may be ostracized from the community.

RAMAZAN: The situation with the Puerto Ricans is the same as with the blacks.

LEHMI: That's right. You could never be close friends, because there's always going to be racial shit between you.

Another example of the importance of community sentiment in the production of ethnic and racial attitudes was evident in the attitudes the Albanian youths held toward Italians. It was clear from the survey and interviews that their attitudes toward other groups were not based solely on competition for resources or turf. Albanian youths have been in conflict with Italian youths for control of the high school for more than fifteen years. Yet this conflict did not produce negative attitudes toward Italians as a group nor toward individual Italians with whom they battle. In fact, it is clear that Albanians respect and feel an affinity toward Italians. Italians were rated extremely high by Albanian youths.[29]

Despite past and current conflicts with Italians over control of the school, Albanian students expressed respect and admiration of Italians as a group. Concretely, they respect and get along with Italian students who attend their school and live in their neighborhood. This affinity stems from the fact that many Albanian families spent time in southern Italy before immigrating to the United States. In addition, many Albanians feel that their immigrant experiences are similar to the experiences of Italians. The youths in this study especially admire Italian organized crime, which they perceived as able to support the Italian American community, enforcing its own cultural laws and norms, and wielding power as an ethnic group in U.S. society:

YASMINE: A lot of Albanians like Italians because their experience is close to ours. Many Albanian families stayed in southern Italy for awhile after leaving Albania before they came to the United States.

FEYZI: We really respect the Italians for the way they live here in the U.S. They have maintained their close communities and have developed a lot of power.

RAMAZAN: If you ask me what other group in this city do I look up to and admire, I'd have to say the Italians. And as for an individual, it would be John Gotti. Gotti takes care of his people and his community and he uses his power to help Italians.

Italians were the only group that the Albanian youth held in particularly high esteem:

> MEDIHA: We get along great with the Italians. They are a lot like us. Otherwise, there are no other groups which we really associate with. The Irish, the Greeks, the Polish—they are okay but we don't really have anything to do with them.

The Youth from ALERT

ALERT[30] is a multiracial group of students at Christopher Columbus High School. The lack of contact with other groups and the negative attitudes toward particular groups that characterized the Albanian youths at Christopher Columbus High School was the exact opposite of the behavior and attitudes exhibited by the members of ALERT. The ALERT youth demonstrate how important the peer group is in the development of positive attitudes toward other groups and as a mechanism for facilitating action based on those attitudes. These youths joined the group after witnessing the tension and conflict between different ethnic and racial groups at their school. They all credit the group with increasing their awareness and tolerance of other ethnic and racial groups:

> CHARMAIGNE: When I first came to Columbus, I was scared. There were all these different groups who seemed like they were ready to fight each other for nothing. I hung out with other black kids until I started feeling isolated. I was glad to find ALERT because I wanted to find some way to try to change this craziness.

> LUTHER: It's funny. I came from an all-black neighborhood, went to an intermediate school which was all black and Hispanic, and it wasn't 'til I got here to Columbus that I started to really be prejudiced. Here at Columbus, there are all these different groups and they all seem to be fighting each other. And while I know that not all the Albanians are violent or not all the Italians are racist, but those who are get you to thinking that a lot of them are like that.

> CARMEN: I just didn't like all the hate and hostility I saw in everybody. I found black people intimidating when I first came to Columbus. When I got my assignment, all my friends told me I was in trouble because blacks and whites don't get along here. But that's not true. It's only a minority of the students who get involved in these

racial situations. Most of the rest of the students just go about their business—though there isn't much mixing between groups. Now, with ALERT, I don't just have Puerto Rican friends, I know lots of different people.

As would be expected, the ALERT youths demonstrate more tolerant attitudes than other groups. They display tolerance toward most ethnic and racial groups different from their own. The exception was their attitudes toward Albanians, whom they gernerally looked upon negatively. Despite the group's goals and the best intentions of its members, their experiences with Albanians, combined with the stereotypes about Albanians that were prevalent at the school, produced less positive attitudes toward Albanians as a group:[31]

> ROBERTO: I had never even heard of Albanians before I came to Columbus. But you sure learn quick who they are. I got in a fight with a few of them my second week of school, because they saw me with some kid who they had a beef with. I guess they thought I was a new member of that group of black kids that hangs out across the street from the Albanians and gets in fights with them. But after that, well, I haven't met an Albanian yet who wants to know me for who I am. There is always the racial thing going.

> LUTHER: I'll tell you the truth, I don't trust Albanians in a group. One by himself can be okay, but get them in a group and it means trouble.

> CARMEN: There are a few Albanians who are okay. I'll bet deep down, they are all okay. It just so happens that they don't like Puerto Ricans, most of them, that is. There was this one girl in my class last year. She used to be nice to me when nobody was around, but when she was around some other Albanians, it was like she didn't know me at all.

Two other groups, Dominicans and Koreans, received ratings significantly lower than other groups by ALERT members from specific backgrounds. Both black and Puerto Rican youth in ALERT gave low ratings to Koreans. These youths were subject to the same factors that produced lower ratings of Koreans among black youths in East Harlem: They came from neighborhoods where Koreans were present as shop owners and storekeepers. Additionally, they were affected by the same ideological messages that provided a basis for the attitudes of the Schomberg Plaza youths.

Dominicans were rated lowest by Puerto Ricans. The attitudes of Puerto Rican youths toward Dominicans appear to be the result of three of the factors that help shape the attitudes of other youths in this study: (1) structural factors, which shape the type of interaction the two groups have; (2) neighborhood sentiment, which helps shape the attitudes toward other groups and the interpretation of interactions with members of other groups; and (3) peer group dynamics, which provide the mechanism for attitude development and expression.

Structural factors are particularly important in shaping interactions between Puerto Ricans and Dominicans. Puerto Ricans have lived in New York City for over a half century, with the largest influx coming to the city between 1940 and 1970. Dominicans, on the other hand, are relative newcomers to the city. Large numbers of Dominicans began to arrive in New York City after the U.S. invasion of the Dominican Republic in 1965. Many Dominicans settled in Puerto Rican neighborhoods and competed with Puerto Ricans for employment and housing. Dominicans who settled in formerly Puerto Rican neighborhoods were perceived as a competitive threat in the labor and housing market.

Neighborhood sentiments in the communities where these youths live are also important. The youths indicated that residents in their neighborhoods encouraged and supported negative attitudes against Dominicans and developed stereotypes about the group that had been internalized by Puerto Rican youths:

LUCIA: The Dominicans are strange. People call them Platanos because they dress funny and think they are still in the Dominican Republic. They wear these funny shoes, and pants that are too short. They're always making noise in the neighborhood and having fights and stuff.

CARMEN: There's problems between Puerto Ricans and Dominicans because they don't get along. Everybody says it's the Dominicans who are dealing the drugs in my neighborhood. I know it's not true, because I know some Puerto Ricans who are dealing drugs but the Dominicans do seem to be more violent.

ESPERANZA: My brother says that Dominicans are taking jobs from Puerto Ricans. They'll work for almost nothing and they don't take care of their homes, always throwing trash around.

ROBERTO: I used to hang out with a group of Puerto Rican kids who didn't like Dominicans. We used to yell at them and harass them and occasionally we would get into fights with them. I don't do it any more because I realized it was wrong.

Further, many Puerto Ricans perceived Dominicans as a threat to their employment and housing, contributing to negative attitudes toward Dominicans. In addition, there is an underlying racial issue alluded to by one student in Central Park East. Although Puerto Ricans are many different shades and colors, many identify as brown or white rather than black (Rodriguez, 1989). Dominicans, many of whom are predominantly darker-skinned, are looked down upon by some lighter-skinned Puerto Ricans, who hold stereotypes about Dominicans that are strikingly similar to those held by some whites about blacks: They deal drugs, they're violent, they throw trash all over, they are noisy, and so on.

Finally, the peer group functions as the mechanism through which these ideas are mediated to produce a particular result, in this case, negative attitudes toward Dominican youths, which can fuel intergroup conflict and violence:

> RICARDO: Normally, everybody stays with their own, but sometimes one of the Dominicans will try to talk to one of the Puerto Rican guys in my neighborhood. They don't like that. If the Dominicans don't back off, it can mean trouble.

> CARMEN: There are groups of Dominicans and Puerto Ricans in my neighborhood who just don't like each other. They fight each other all the time, so the Dominicans hang out down by the park and they look for young Puerto Ricans to jump and the Puerto Ricans hang out on the other side of Broadway and wait for some Dominicans.

Despite the apparently less tolerant attitudes of some of the ALERT youths toward Albanians, Koreans, and Dominicans, in general these young people exhibited more positive and tolerant attitudes than *any* other group in the sample. Not one of them was involved in activities directed against any of the groups. To the contrary, they embraced tolerance and ethnic and racial harmony as values toward which they should strive. This could be seen in the statements they made about groups they had problems with or whom they viewed negatively:

> LUTHER: I would like to get to know some Albanian kids. I don't think it's impossible for us to get along. We are more alike than we are different. We have the same problems as teenagers and I think eventually we could work together to make Columbus a better school instead of people fighting each other for no real reason.

> LUCIA: I feel bad about what I think about Dominicans. It's hard, because you know everybody is equal and the same, but at the same

time you have this experience of being attacked and beaten up by
them. I know that's just a few stupid punks and that all Dominicans
are not like that, but it's still hard to get rid of these prejudices.
ROBERTO: Yea, especially when all your friends in your neighborhood
think that Dominicans are bad, then, it's hard to go your own way.

Youth in the ALERT group provide an excellent example of the importance of peer group dynamics in the development and maintenance
of ethnic and racial attitudes and the facilitation of behavior based on
these attitudes. In this case, the actions being facilitated by the group
were not conflictual in nature; rather, they were designed to bring young
people of different ethnic and racial backgrounds together.

Once again, the peer group provided youths with a context in
which they developed their identity and felt they were taking control of
their ideas and actions. There was a certain sense of individual and
group power that they were able to feel as a result of their participation in the group. The group also fulfilled their need to belong; the
need to belong is a powerful motivation for adolescents to participate
in and identify with a group. In this instance, the peer group was organized with the specific intent of reducing ethnic and racial conflict and
increasing ethnic and racial awareness and tolerance.

Attitude change, like racial conflict, is a process. Puerto Rican
youths in ALERT were subject to contradictory messages from different
sources of ideas and values. Though they had joined a peer group at
school that encouraged ethnic and racial tolerance and cooperation,
they lived in neighborhoods where Dominicans were looked down
upon, and they had friends in those neighborhoods who were in conflict with Dominicans. Thus, the attitudes these Puerto Rican youths
held toward Dominicans were conflicted. They were in the process of
questioning their attitudes and ideas about Dominicans, much like the
Puerto Rican young woman at Central Park East Secondary School
who changed her attitudes toward Dominicans as a result of a change
in her peer group.

The fact that youths involved in the ALERT group had different attitudes toward different groups demonstrates that ethnic and racial conflict and ethnic and racial cooperation are processes on a continuum
affected by the factors examined thus far. When one or more of these
factors change, there is the potential for attitude change, and with attitude change comes the potential for long-term reduction in conflict
and violence. It is also possible in this context for attitudes to remain

the same and for conflict to decrease temporarily. In this case, structural conditions, such as job availability, can improve, potentially decreasing the level of competition between groups as well as lowering the level of anxiety and uncertainty among young people. If neighborhood sentiments and societal images and messages remain the same, and the youths maintain the same peer groups linked to those sentiments and ideas, it is doubtful that any reduction in conflict would be enduring. However, if enough young people change their peer groups—from a group that fosters a differentiative ethnic and racial identity based on a competitive and oppositional sense of the group's position, to a peer group that encourages ethnic and racial interaction and promotes an ethnic and racial identity based on an inclusive and cooperative sense of group position—then a long-term reduction in ethnic and racial conflict is possible.

Conclusion

The attitudes and behaviors of the young people described in this book provide insight into how structural factors, neighborhood sentiment and societal images and ideas, identity development, and peer group dynamics combine to produce racial conflict. The ALERT youths and the Albanian youths are particularly interesting because they exhibit two radically different kinds of behavior in the same institutional context. One group is insular and exclusive and participates in ethnic and racial violence that arises from and exacerbates divisions among different groups at the school. The other group is inclusive and open and promotes ethnic and racial cooperation and tolerance in their school.

These two groups represent the extremes of the youths examined in this book. While the ALERT youths exhibited the most tolerant attitudes of any in the study, the Albanians showed the least-tolerant attitudes.[32] The reasons for the difference in tolerance between the two groups can be found in the factors that are examined in this book.

Structural factors determine the type of interaction youths have with other groups and help shape the perceptions they have of their own group and of others. The changing demographics of Chistopher Columbus High School have had an effect on the perception of the Albanian youths, who perceive their group position as being threatened by blacks and Puerto Ricans.

Neighborhood sentiment is clearly important in the development of the attitudes and identity of the Albanian youths in this study. The

Albanians were the tightest, most insular group of youths in the entire study. They had the strongest ethnic identity, which is clearly linked to their sense of being victimized as an immigrant group. Their families, communities, and peer groups are selected on the basis of their Albanian (ethnic) identity. Ethnic identity also provides the foundation for their relationships with people outside their ethnic group. Fundamentally, these youths believe that only Albanians can be trusted. All other groups, with the exception of Italians, are seen as prejudiced against Albanians. Consequently, these young people have more negative attitudes toward all other groups than did any other ethnic or racial group in the sample. These attitudes often support acts of violence in struggles with blacks and Latinos over turf and control.

Neighborhood sentiment also plays an important role for ALERT youths in promoting particular attitudes and values. Those who come from neighborhoods and families whose sentiments and ideologies are consistent with those of the ALERT group have little trouble internalizing and expressing tolerant attitudes toward other groups and working for intergroup cooperation and awareness. Those who come from neighborhoods and families that are more intolerant and differentiative will eventually have to make a choice between new peer groups and old ones, new values and ideas and old ones. In this case, it is especially important that the youths differentiate between the ideas of the neighborhood, family, and old peer group and their own ethnic identity. The ALERT group facilitates this process by helping youths to understand that they can embrace their ethnic heritage and culture without developing a differentiative, oppositional sense of their group's position.

Fundamentally, conflicts at Chistopher Columbus High School are conflicts between ethnically and racially based peer groups who are all struggling to forge an ethnic and racial identity, to acheive a sense of group importance and power, to prove their racial and ethnic worthiness, and to establish a sense of power and control in their lives. The ALERT group was formed based on principles that allow youths to gain these same things in a positive context that allows for integration rather than separation of groups and fosters cooperation and tolerance rather than conflict and violence.

four

Racial Violence

It's 8 in the morning. A thirteen-year-old African American youth is wait-
ing for the bus to take him to school. A group of white youths who go
by the name of "the Albanian Boys" attack the youth and yell racial epithets. "Get out of this neighborhood, nigger." "This is a message from
the Albanian Boys. Albanians rule." "Fuck the niggers." After beating the
African American youth repeatedly, the white youths spray him with
white paint while shouting "white power" and "white is beautiful."
—*Author's description of an actual incident*

This incident was one of the more contemptible acts of racial violence
in New York City's recent past. A similar act occurred two days later
when a Latino youth was attacked on the way to school; after being
beaten, he too was sprayed with white paint. Both incidents occurred
in the winter of 1992. They renewed racial tensions in a city where
interethnic and interracial conflicts are periodically rekindled by high-
profile racial incidents such as these.

Racial conflict and violence are an unfortunate but constant reality for many New York City young people. The Study of High School
Students and Educational Staff on Prejudice and Race Relations found
that over one-third of the students in New York City have had a direct
experience in their immediate family with violence caused by prejudice
or racism (New York State Martin Luther King, Jr., Institute for Nonviolence, 1990). Seventy percent of the students reported that they had
"definitely" (46 percent) or "probably" (24 percent) witnessed violence that, in their judgment, was caused primarily by racism, bias, or
prejudice. Seventy-one percent of the students had at some time been
the object of prejudice based on race or ethnicity (New York State
Martin Luther King, Jr., Institute for Nonviolence, 1990, p. 46).

Most youths do not engage in racial violence and conflict, but they are directly affected by it. Some are the innocent victims of ongoing school-based conflicts between different racial or ethnic groups. Students at most New York City high schools must learn which groups are in conflict with one another, who controls which section of turf in the school, who they should be wary of, and what the implications are of their choice of friends:

> DAVID: When I first came to Sheepshead Bay High School, I had heard all kinds of stories about racial problems and fights, but I didn't know who was who. But you find out real quick what the deal is. My first month at the school, I was surrounded by a bunch of black kids who assumed I was with this group of white kids who they were fighting with because I had started to hang out with one of the kids in that group. They harassed me and threatened me, they didn't beat me up or anything but it was real scary. My friend Billy hears about it and is all set to get all his boys and go after these guys. I said forget it. I could see I was about to get into some long-term shit. I stopped hanging out with Billy and found some other friends at the school.

Some of the youths are involved in the conflicts and violence directly, participating in fights between different groups and often initiating the violence. These struggles take place both at school and on the streets in their neighborhoods. Though the venues are different, the fundamental causes of the violence are similar: a desire to control turf, a belief that the opposing group represents a threat, or a quest to exert power and achieve a sense of self-worth and importance within a peer group that embraces an oppositional sense of racial or ethnic group position.

The attitudes of the youth who engage in racial violence are linked to their sense of belonging to a particular ethnic or racial group and their conception of what it means to be a member of that group. There is little difference between the attitudes of young men and young women. The young Albanian women expressed the same attitudes as the young men in their group. Similarly, young out-of-school women in southern Brooklyn demonstrated similar attitudes as the young men in their neighborhoods. The difference between the young men and the young women was in the type of action they took based on their shared attitudes: what types of ethnic and racial conflict and violence they participated in. Action on the street is characterized by clearly defined gender roles. Neighborhood-based racial attacks were perpetrated almost exclusively by young men. Young women in these neighborhoods provided encouragement before and after the fact, but they rarely reported engaging in the attacks. The exception was a few of the young Italian American women in southern Brooklyn and young Albanian women in Pelham Parkway, who reported that they participated in racially motivated fights at school.

Racial Violence in Southern Brooklyn

For the Avenue T Boys, racial conflict and violence are a regular part of their lives. The conflict and violence are outgrowths of their negative attitudes toward blacks and other people of color. These attitudes help to promote social cohesion within their peer group since the expression of these attitudes provided positive proof that they were "down for the neighborhood" (that is, loyal to the neighborhood). Youths who express negative attitudes toward blacks and other people of color gain status and respect within the peer group.

The link between attitudes and the individual and group identity of these white youths was very strong. Many of them are viewed by adult members of their own community as "hoodlums" or "outcasts"; many were also alienated from their families:

> RONNIE: With my friends I get respect. I can't talk to my mother, that's why I moved out when I was sixteen. The rest of the people in my neighborhood think I'm crazy. They think we are bums who hang out on the street and cause trouble. In some ways they're right.

The place where they receive positive reinforcement is on the street, hanging out with other neighborhood teens in their peer group. As a result, they are constantly trying to prove themselves worthy to their peers. In the context of the street, that proof lies in their ability to express the collective ideology of their peer group and a willingness to back up these ideas with brute force, ranging from harassment to mayhem, sometimes tragically crossing the line to murder.

In the group interviews, several youths revealed that they were involved in an activity that they described as "going on missions." I first heard the term "mission" when one of the Avenue T Boys brought up the subject in response to a question about race relations in his neighborhood. When asked to explain what "missions" were, the young man described how the T Boys would get together at night to hang out. After several hours of drinking, and sometimes ingesting drugs, the group would look for people to harass and beat up:[1]

SAL: We'll just be hanging out, partying. And somebody will say "hey, let's go on a mission." That's when you go look for people who don't belong in the neighborhood and you beat 'em up. Sometimes, we go out lookin for blacks to jump. Sometimes we look for anybody who ain't supposed to be there.

The rest of the youths responded with noticeable enthusiasm to the discussion of "missions." They seemed to get excited by descriptions of these late-night searches for individuals who "did not belong in the neighborhood." They talked openly and excitedly about going on these "missions." The entire ambience of the interview changed when they began to describe these "missions" in detail.

When they first described these "missions," the youths steadfastly proclaimed that there was nothing "racial" about their actions. According to them, the media was responsible for making things "look racial." They claimed that they were simply "defending their neighborhood"; that they would attack whites as well as blacks, that their main objective was to "take care of outsiders." However, their perceptions that these "missions" were not racially motivated were contradicted by their own descriptions of their nightly group activities, during which they would go on regular searches for people of color, particularly blacks:

RONNIE: If we fight against Bay Parkway, that's because we don't like each other. When we fight the blacks, it's because we don't like their color. All of Bensonhurst unites against them.

SAL: You go out and you're lookin' for people. The best is if you catch a couple of black guys. Or if you can't find no blacks, maybe you find an Indian or an Arab or a Dominican.

The youths described a hierarchy of groups that were desirable targets for their assaults. Blacks were their primary targets. If they could not find a black person, then a Dominican, a Pakistani, or an Indian would do.[2] The youth said they would attack other whites as well, but only if they were from a rival neighborhood that had started trouble in their neighborhood:

ROCCO: Blacks, Pakistanis, everybody gets a little bit, racial slurs— like that. And if you're really hyped, you fuck them up good. Especially Dominicans.

VINNIE: We go after a lot of people. But, it's the blacks, mostly, who you want to take care of.

MARIO: The problem is mostly with blacks. There is not as much problem between whites and Asians or whites and Hispanics.
FRANK: We don't have no problem with Asians.

The language used by these youths reflects the centrality of race in their outlook toward other groups and provides an illustration of what Omi and Winant call "racialization." Omi and Winant define the term as "the extension of racial meaning to a previously unclassified relationship, social practice or group" (1986, p. 64). These youths describe their actions toward other groups as "getting racial"—an indication of the racially motivated character of these "missions" and of how they perceive the meaning of the racial differences between themselves and the people of color with whom they fight. Racial differences are the critical motivating factor in the choice of targets for these "missions."

These youths seem to get a sense of self-worth and individual power from going on "missions," a feeling that is otherwise lacking in their lives. When they beat somebody up, they feel powerful. Often, primed with alcohol or drugs, they seem to be itching to feel the elation of the sense of power, control, and status they know they would get from administering a beating to a neighborhood intruder. Their sense of group cohesion and group solidarity was heightened if the victim was from another racial or ethnic group high on their list of desirable targets. These young men consistently expressed feelings of economic powerlessness and of frustration that their community was politically powerless. These feelings of powerlessness, stemming directly from their economic position and prospects and from their social status within their own communities appear to contribute to the visceral nature of their attitudes toward people of other racial and ethnic groups.

What emerges from an analysis of the attitudes and behavior of white youths in southern Brooklyn is a picture of a relationship between (1) their negative attitudes and actions toward other groups, (2) their individual identity, (3) their developing ethnic identity, and (4) their perception of the role they play and their place in their community and in society more generally. For these youths, racial violence is essentially a group activity; it is rarely perpetrated by one individual alone. For these young people, establishing a strong, cohesive individual and group identity requires that they show the rest of the group that they are "down with the program." In this arena, the "program" includes concrete proof of being tough, hating the appropriate enemies, and a readiness to take those enemies on to defend one's principles and one's turf:

> VINNIE: You go on missions to impress your friends. You get a name as a tough guy who is down with the neighborhood and down with his people.
>
> RONNIE: You prove you're a real Bensonhurst Italian who don't take no shit, who don't let the wrong kind of people into the neighborhood.
>
> ROCCO: You do it to feel powerful, to feel like you're somebody. So people will respect you.
>
> FRANK: You do it 'cause you want to be cool.
> ROCCO: To get out their frustrations.
> MARIO: Because there is nothing else to do.

These young people claimed they were fighting to "protect the neighborhood" and for "unity in their community." They felt that they had the right and the obligation to defend their territory against blacks and others, that it was up to them to "stop the blacks," that if they attacked these outsiders, they would be sending a message to all blacks from outside the neighborhood to stay out of their communities. They had successfully translated the meaning of their delinquent behavior into acts of neighborhood defense. Their language reflected their feeling that they had a responsibility to protect their community, to defend their turf, and to keep undesirable outsiders (by which they meant people of color) out of their neighborhood. Numerous statements about doing "what they had to do" revealed this rationalization:

> RONNIE: I did what I had to do. I have a reputation as a tough guy who defends the neighborhood and I want to keep it. People know when you've taken care of people who don't belong in the neighborhood. You get respect. Especially if it is some of the blacks from Marlboro projects.
>
> MARIO: When you're hanging out with your partners and you see somebody who don't belong on your block, like a black guy or a Dominican, and you do him [beat him up], you feel real together. Everybody's together doing what we have to do.
>
> VINNIE: Everybody in the neighborhood knows what the deal is. The police don't care about it unless somebody gets killed. Everybody else figures we're just doing them a favor. As long as we don't bother neighborhood folks, it's no problem.

It is clear that these white youths see themselves as defending their community from individuals and groups who they believe do not belong in their neighborhoods. Consequently, they are able to explain and justify their actions as "helpful" to their community and in sync with community sentiments and values.

Like many teens, these youths engage in behaviors that are aimed at proving themselves worthy in the eyes of their peers. In this context, they demonstrate their toughness and their hatred of certain groups by beating them up.

By interpreting their racially motivated behavior as being beneficial to their community, they gain a sense of self-worth and raise their self-esteem. This is reinforced by the positive feedback they get about their actions from their peers and from some members of their community. I encountered evidence of community support in discussions with various community residents. One shop owner who was disgusted with the activities of the youth and complained that the problem was a neighborhood-wide problem:

> SHOP OWNER: The problem is that some of the people around here like what they are doing. People don't want blacks around here and these kids keep them out. These kids even get rewards from some of the shop owners for taking care of blacks who look suspicious. A fellah up the street gives away free pizza, if you can believe it.

The white youths from southern Brooklyn interviewed for this study provide important insights into the anatomy of a racially motivated attack and partly help to explain the increase in bias-related violence in New York City. There are four major factors contributing to these youths' involvement in racially motivated attacks: (1) structural economic conditions, (2) societal racial climate and national racial ideologies, (3) neighborhood history of race relations and the community racial ideology, and (4) participation in neighborhood-based peer groups that embrace negative attitudes toward other racial groups.

First, structural economic conditions frame these young people's lives. They face extremely uncertain futures. The prospects for employment for working-class youths, particularly males, have definitely constricted since the late 1960s as industrial jobs have been disappearing from the city's economy at an alarming rate. These conditions have laid the foundation for the rise in ethnic and racial violence by increasing anxiety and competition between racial and ethnic groups. Most of the youths in this study were doing poorly in school or had dropped out completely, placing them in a precarious economic situation in a labor market that places a high value on education. As a result of the changing structure of the labor market, the jobs that existed for their parents and older brothers or sisters were no longer available to them.

Second, these young white adolescents believe that jobs are scarce for them and other whites because of special treatment toward blacks. The overall context within which they view race relations is one in which affirmative action functions as reverse discrimination against whites and in which Third World immigrants are taking away additional jobs and invading their neighborhoods. Their perception is that it is *they* who are disadvantaged, while people of color are gaining political and economic power by getting special treatment.

It is in this context that they frame their violent attacks against nonwhites, interpreting their actions as "fighting back," though the tragic reality is that it is precisely because African Americans and other people of color lack the power to deter racially motivated attacks that they are vulnerable targets.

Third, they live in close-knit ethnic communities with a history of flight from neighborhoods where African Americans and other minorities have moved in. Though members of their community frown on their delinquent activities, there is evidence of tacit community support for the role these young people play in keeping unwanted minorities out of their neighborhoods, and there is no doubt that the youths definitely have the impression that neighborhood residents either look the other way or directly support their attacks on "unwanted" nonwhite outsiders.

For example, much of the Bensonhurst community rallied to the defense of the youths involved in the attack on Yusuf Hawkins, staunchly proclaiming that the incident was not racially motivated. A cloak of silence covered the events of 23 August 1989, resulting in an implicit understanding that the participants were not to be criticized openly.[3] In one focus group interview, a young woman inadvertently broke this code of silence and was immediately rebuked by angry stares and verbally reminded of the code:

> YOUNG WOMAN: Why do all the blacks want to put Keith [Mondello] in prison. He didn't pull the trigger, Joey did it.
> THE GROUP: Shhhhhhhh.
> YOUTH I: What are you talking about?

YOUTH 2: You know you shouldn't be saying that. We don't know who did it.

YOUNG WOMAN: At least that's what the police are saying but we don't even know if that's true.

Other evidence of tacit community support for the youths' activities can be drawn from an analysis of previous incidents that occurred in these neighborhoods. Bensonhurst, Gravesend, Sheepshead Bay, and Canarsie all have a history of racial tensions, and the 1970s and 1980s were marked by frequent racial violence at the high schools located in these neighborhoods, as the *Wall Street Journal* reported in a 22 July 1988 article. In 1982, an African American transit worker, Willie Turks, was attacked and killed by a mob of whites in Gravesend. In 1988, on three separate occasions, flyers asserting that "Orientals" were trying to take over the neighborhood were distributed throughout the Bensonhurst neighborhood; the flyers encouraged residents to boycott Asian businesses and to refuse to sell their homes to Asians (Mayor's Advisory Council on Community Relations, 1989). There was little coordinated neighborhood response to these incidents. In the absence of community control of racial violence, the youths of Bensonhurst and Gravesend feel as if they have encouragement and support for their racially motivated actions.

As in all communities, only a small minority of youths are involved in violent activity. However, in the case of white ethnic communities in southern Brooklyn, these youths often serve a function in their communities, and, as in the case of Bensonhurst and Howard Beach (where Michael Griffith was killed in 1985), they have a profound effect on the way their communities are viewed by outsiders. Their actions are well known in other parts of the city. As a result, these communities have a reputation throughout New York City for being inhospitable to African Americans. This reputation helps to deter African Americans and other minorities from viewing these communities as prospective neighborhoods in which to settle or even visit.

Fourth, the peer groups of which these white youths are members reinforce negative attitudes toward other ethnic and racial groups and facilitate the violence motivated by these attitudes. The youths gain a positive sense of themselves, a more cohesive group solidarity, and a heightened sense of identity from participation in group attacks against individuals or groups from different ethnic and racial backgrounds. It is through their membership and activity in the peer groups that they develop a racialized perspective on themselves and others, a perspective that is concretized through group action. The importance of having these attitudes is clearly linked to their developing self-identity and ethnic identity. As part of the identification process—the process of figuring out who they are and who they are not—these youths internalize and exhibit attitudes and actions that project the image of a tough, important, powerful member of the neighborhood who defends their community and receives tacit community support for doing so.

Processes of affiliation are often linked to processes of differentiation (C. Pinderhughes, 1982). In this case, the process of differentiation from African Americans and other groups by white youths is linked to the process of affiliation with the neighborhood and ethnic group. Thus, these young Italian American and Jewish working-class youth from Gravesend and Bensonhurst believe that disliking blacks is part of what it means to be a "good" Italian American or Jew within the context of their place and role in their communities. For many, the street has replaced the home and the school as the context in which they develop their individual and group identity, and neighborhood peers supply the value models of what these youths should think and how they should act. The behavior of these young people is a translation and extension to the street of neighborhood and societal attitudes and ideologies. The messages from their parents, other community residents, and political representatives at many different levels have been incorporated into a street ideology that provides justification for racial violence.

Restraint in East Harlem

Though there are similarities in the attitudes of the black youths at Schomberg Plaza and the white Avenue T Boys, there are radical differences in their behavior. Most of the youths at Schomberg Plaza expressed distrust and, in some cases, hatred of white people. With such strong negative attitudes, the potential for racial violence would seem to be high. Though the structural conditions of intense competition and economic hardship are present for both white youths in Bensonhurst and African American youths at Schomberg Plaza, there is a significant difference between the two groups in how they *acted* on their feelings. The white youth spoke freely and openly, without fear of punishment and at times with great pride, about going on "missions" and attacking different groups; they expressed feelings of justification, proclaiming that they had a right and an obligation to protect their turf. In stark contrast, though a number of African American youths professed to dislike or hate white people, there was not one black adolescent who knew about African American youths attacking whites because of skin color on a *regular* basis.[4]

Though there is a common perception among New Yorkers that Harlem and East Harlem are dangerous communities for whites to venture into, most of these youths disputed that notion, stating that whites are in no particular danger in their community. This view was discussed by members of the group as they spoke about whether African Americans in their community attacked whites in racially motivated attacks. Most of the youths maintained that whites who were attacked in their neighborhood were the victims of economic crimes rather than of racial violence.

> SHANEEQUA: It's not dangerous for white people to come up here.
> JEFFREY: That's not true. Black people tend to think about robbing white people, you can't deny it because like four years ago they used to rob every single white person that came by.
> SHANEEQUA: But that's different. It's about economics. If it was a black person who was up here with an expensive camera, flashing jewelry, they'd say yo, let's rob him, let's get him, he's a fix.
>
> OSCAR: I haven't heard of and I haven't seen on the news or read in the newspaper an incident where a white person got beat up just because they were a white person in a black neighborhood by a gang of black youths.
>
> JEFFREY: Most of the black youth on the street are not aware of the problem, they are out there, you know to rob somebody, to make this dollar. They're equal opportunity robbers. If you got a dollar in your pocket they are willing to take it.

In fact, these youths feel that their neighborhood is a dangerous place for everybody, most of all for community residents who must cope with the problem of crime and violence on a daily basis. The Schomberg Plaza youths said that the problem in their neighborhood was not racial violence between groups but black-on-black violence. They claimed that young African Americans were not attacking whites, Jews, or Asians. In stark contrast to the white youths in Bensonhurst, the African American youths at Schomberg Plaza said that most youths in their community found their enemies within the community. Most of the victims of crime in East Harlem are its African American and Latino residents. They stated that black-on-black violence is the norm in their community, and that whites have much less to fear than blacks. They attribute the high crime rate in their neighborhood to conditions of persistent poverty imposed on African Americans by whites:

> HABIB: Black kids don't go after white people, we go after each other. Black youth kill other black youth, and for what? For drugs and money. Sometimes it's over real bullshit like a coat or some sneakers or something. This is what the white man has done to us.

> JEFFREY: It's mostly black-on-black. It's a shame. It's a drug problem. You in my territory. You can't play me like that. Or you tried to scheme on my girl. I'm going to give you a quick beat down to let you know that's not happening.

> CARL: When you can't get no education. There ain't no jobs, except maybe flipping burgers downtown somewhere for a couple dollars an hour. They get rid of any opportunities and then they let the drugs into our community. What else are the young brothers going to do?

> TERRELL: For blacks, it's been mental genocide by making us forget who we are. By taking away our history. The majority of the problem for the young brothers is this drug thing that's been laid on us since we were dragged over here. They don't know who they are, don't know about our people, don't know the greatness of the African people.

Though the Schomberg Plaza youths asserted that they did not know anyone who engaged in racial attacks on a regular basis, they acknowledged that racial violence does occur in their neighborhoods after high-profile racial attacks in white neighborhoods, such as the murder of Yusuf Hawkins and the killing of Michael Griffith in Howard Beach. The youths maintained that periods of anger over the racial murders of African Americans in white neighborhoods were exceptions to the normal pattern of behavior for African Americans in East Harlem. In the weeks following these attacks, there were numerous reports of African Americans attacking whites while chanting "Howard Beach" or "Bensonhurst." Some of the youths admit to knowing people who claimed to have attacked whites in retaliation for the murders in Howard Beach and Bensonhurst:

> OSCAR: There were a few brothers who went off after Howard Beach and Bensonhurst. I believe there was tension between us. I would say they provoked it.

HABIB: Everything was fine and dandy until they went out and took the brother out in Howard Beach and Bensonhurst. I mean, they killed my man in cold blood. It was like, no thought about that. With things like that happening, you get pissed. There are other side factors such as low employment, bad housing. We're on the opposite side of the tracks, economically from those folks, they're on the good side, we're on the bad side. And for them to kill a brother made things just explode, from then on.

But overall, Schomberg Plaza youths maintained that racial attacks were uncommon in their neighborhood. There was a unanimous sentiment among them that African American youths understood that it was *extremely* dangerous to assault a white person in a racially motivated attack. The neighborhood that borders theirs is one of the most affluent white communities in the city, a distinct symbol for these youths of the powerful white world. Their community also borders Central Park, which they claimed is primarily for use by affluent whites. In the minds of these African American youths, to attack white people would arouse swift and severe punishment from the police and the criminal justice system. The events following the attack on the Central Park jogger confirmed their sentiments:

TERRELL: Most African Americans know if you attack a white person in a racial attack just because they are white, you see five-o [the police] real quick. The police protect white people from that kind of violence. If you racially attack a white person, then you are in for big trouble.

TANIA: Look what happened in the Central Park jogger case. That wasn't even a racial thing, but because it was a white woman supposedly attacked by a bunch of black male teenagers, the police have gone crazy.

In fact, the Central Park jogger case played an important role in confirming these sentiments. Each of the youths interviewed had been detained by the police and questioned about the incident. A number of them had been threatened and harassed by police in the wake of the Central Park jogger attack, and they all knew at least three of the defendants. The youths said that Schomberg Plaza had become infamous, much like Bensonhurst, as a result of the Central Park jogger case, which had served to further taint the image of young African American and Latino youths in East Harlem:

HABIB: White people have always been afraid of black teenagers, especially the guys. Now, since the jogger incident, everyone thinks that the youth around here are crazed hoodlums who get off on rape and wilding.

JEFFREY: There are some kids out there doing some crazy stuff, but most of us aren't into that thing. There are two things about this whole Central Park jogger thing that pisses me off. First, it feeds the perception that all young black males are animalistic criminals. The language they used about the kids involved, wolf pack and wild animals, you didn't hear them calling those white boys in Bensonhurst no wolf pack or animals. Second, now I'm sorry the lady got attacked and hurt, but they're only making a big deal about it because she's white and rich.

TERRELL: The police just went off after the rape happened in the park. It was open season on black male youth. Everybody got stopped, questioned, and some kids were taken for a ride by the cops. Black women get attacked in our community all the time, and you don't see the police out here rounding up every black male over the age of six. But when some white banker lady gets hit, they are all over us like bees on honey.

There are several important differences between the Avenue T Boys, who participated in racial violence against those groups they professed to dislike and by whom they felt victimized, and the Schomberg Plaza youths, who did not. First, there was clear consensus among the Schomberg Plaza youths that it was extremely dangerous to attack a white person in a racially motivated attack. Their perception that the criminal justice system severely punished young African Americans who engaged in racial attacks against whites serves as a powerful deterrent.

Second, there are important demographic differences between the two communities. Bensonhurst and Gravesend are part of a strip of working-class neighborhoods in southern Brooklyn that have poor and working-class black and Latino neighborhoods in close proximity as well as housing projects that house predominantly poor African Americans in the middle of their neighborhoods. East Harlem borders neighborhoods composed of more-affluent white residents and Central Park, which the youths claimed is primarily for use by affluent whites.[5] Thus, the potential for contact and conflict among white and black youths on the street is greater in Brooklyn than in East Harlem.

Third, whereas white youth in Gravesend and Bensonhurst receive support for actively defending their neighborhood, there is no evidence of community or neighborhood support for acts of racial violence in East Harlem. There is widespread condemnation of white racism and its effects on the East Harlem community, but I found little evidence of a perceived need to defend the neighborhood against encroachment. Though whites are gradually moving further north into Harlem from the Upper East Side, slowly changing the composition of the southern part of East Harlem, the nature of the interaction is different. The residents of Gravesend and Bensonhurst feel that blacks threaten crime, violence, lowering of property values, and deterioration of the quality of life in the neighborhood; African Americans and Puerto Ricans of East Harlem are facing gentrification by people perceived to have money and power. Thus, the power relations in the two situations are radically different and help to account for the differences in response.

In contrast to the Avenue T Boys, the Schomberg Plaza youths spoke at length about their vision of the future of race relations. This difference reflects the centrality and totality of race in the lives of black youths, which contrasts to its situational nature for white youths. The Schomberg Plaza youths were not optimistic about the future. Although they agreed on the need for education to foster cultural respect and understanding among ethnic and racial groups and saw the need for resources to be generated in order to improve conditions in the African American community, they saw no end to racial conflict. Rather, they anticipated an eventual race war between blacks and whites. Many felt that violence may be necessary to change the conditions under which African Americans live, and they had dire predictions about the future of race relations in New York City and throughout the country:

OSCAR: Things are going to get much worse before it gets better. Now everybody is sleepwalking. We're not attacking the problem. Laws have to work both ways. No more lopsided justice. There needs to be better education about cultural differences and the contributions of black and other people besides just white people.

TERRELL: Education is the key because ignorance is what causes most of these problems. We need to educate our own people. Like rapper KRS-One says, "When one doesn't know the other one's culture, ignorance swoops down like a vulture."

JEFFREY: Look at the history. They call us murderers and thieves, they got it backwards. They stole us from Africa, and killed millions of us. They stole our whole history. They almost killed every single Jew there was. They killed all the Indians. There are about three of them left. They destroyed everybody's culture. And they aren't about to stop now.

HABIB: I think we need reparations. Like my man Chuck D. [rapper and leader of the rap group Public Enemy] says, "That forty acres and a mule never came our way. It's due, with interest."

Though a certain amount of this may be bravado, these youths clearly felt that there was no interest on the part of white people to change the present arrangements, which they viewed as grossly unequal and unjust. There was a deep distrust of white society and white people. For these youths, white skin was a symbol of power and privilege. They expected whites to dislike African American youths and to fear African American males. They believed that white people do not care about African Americans:

OSCAR: We can't say that white people are going to give us anything. So we are going to have to fight for them. We have been trying this nonviolent thing within the system for a long time. It hasn't changed things. I think there will be more violence. But obviously we can't win a war which is black against white. We have less people and they have all the weapons. But there will be more violence.

JEFFREY: They're making us passive and peaceful. All this nonviolent trash. They never teach that stuff to white people. We may need to get rid of a few white people.

SHANEEQUA: There's going to be war. Blacks on one side and whites on the other.

CARL: If they want to avoid war, they have to give us what we earned. They have gotten rich off of our labor. We have to get what we deserve. They have to start catering to the African American community, not just in words but in actions. We need jobs, we need housing. See the white man, he doesn't have any limitations on him.

School-Based Racial Violence in Pelham Parkway

As it was for the Avenue T Boys, racial conflict was a regular occurrence for the Albanian youths in Pelham Parkway. It was apparent from interviews with the Albanian youths that there were major struggles over turf. Many of the students spoke about "owning" and "running" their school. Many had recurring conflicts with blacks, Puerto Ricans, Jamaicans, and Italian Americans in the school. In the past, many had fought with Italian American youth, who they claim used to "control the school." According to both Albanian students and the teachers at Christopher Columbus High School, before 1982, the school was "controlled" by the toughest Italian youth in the school. That year there was a fight between Italian American and Albanian students, which the Albanians won. After 1982, Albanian youth claimed that they "ran the school":[6]

> FEYZI: In 1982 we won the school from the Italians. We fought it out for three days, both in the school and on the streets. A lot of people got hurt, but we won.
> SABRI: Now we run the school, it's a sense of security, the ones who run the school, they don't have to worry about nothing.

Most of the conflicts the Albanian youths had at their school were with blacks and Puerto Ricans. One reason for these conflicts has to do with the demographics of Christopher Columbus High School. Since the early 1970s, the high school's student population had undergone a major demographic transformation from a predominantly white school—mostly Italian, Irish, Jewish, and Albanian—to one with a predominantly African American and Latino student population. Albanian youths see this demographic change as the source of racial tensions in the school. They charged black and Puerto Rican youths with destroying the school with drugs, crime, and vandalism:

> FEYZI: There are more and more blacks at this school and it is going downhill. It used to be well balanced, but now, you look around and there is graffiti on the walls and the place is falling apart; they need security guards because it's so dangerous. That's all because there are too many blacks in the school.

For these youths, the main source of conflict stems from their interactions with blacks and Latinos at school. Schools are the territory where issues of competition and conflict arose over "control of the school." Blacks and Puerto Ricans have been firmly established as the "enemy" as a result of their numbers and apparent lack of acknowledgment and respect for the Albanians' position (since 1982) as the "owners" of the school.

It is in this context that Albanian youths see themselves as "keepers of the peace." Their explanation of the conflict with blacks and Puerto Ricans is similar to that given by the Avenue T Boys: They defended their engagement in conflict and violence against blacks and

Puerto Ricans as a defense of the school. In so doing, they claim that they are trying to keep the school clean and the neighborhood peaceful. According to these Albanian students, "owning" or "running" the school means keeping the students in line and maintaining the peace in the school. They claim that their efforts help to keep drugs out of the school. They also claim that they have the most trouble with blacks and Puerto Ricans because they "bring drugs into the school," and because they "do not respect the leadership position of the Albanians," and because they "wanted to take over the school":

> LEHMI: We don't get along with the blacks. They always make us into the bad guys.
> SABRI: There would be less problems if they [the blacks] would just accept that we own the school.
>
> DRITA: There are more and more blacks in this school. And they don't respect us. They think they can come in here and take over the school. Are we going to let everyone walk all over us? We have to defend ourselves too.
>
> FEYZI: We keep the peace. If we weren't here, I tell you right now, you'd see the blacks and Puerto Ricans having it out.
> LEHMI: That's right. And the school would be filled with drugs. You look around, you don't see many drugs. That's because we don't allow it.

Like those of other youths in this study, the attitudes and actions of Albanian youths are the product of a confluence of factors. First, structural factors shape the type of interactions that they have with other groups. The locus of conflict occurs where Albanian youths come into contact and competition with black and Latino youths. It is only where competition is clearly present that the perception of a threat exists. For Albanian youths, this happens regularly at the school but not in their neighborhoods. Since the neighborhoods are mixed (and were mixed before the Albanians settled there), the issue of trying to keep blacks and Latinos out is moot. Though the groups don't live side by side on integrated blocks, the residential area, as a whole, is integrated. With the exception of a few occurrences, regular racial conflict on the streets does not occur. Though different groups don't mix, they are not attacking each other. There was little evidence that the "missions," which were a regular activity for the at-risk Italian and Jewish youths in southern Brooklyn, were a regular part of life for Albanian youths in the Bronx. When discussions of "missions" arose, the Albanian youths claimed that those few who did participate in "missions" were "hanging out with Italians and not with Albanians."[7]

The situation at the school, however, is very different. Blacks and Latinos form a majority of the school population, with fewer and fewer Albanians attending the school. Albanian youths see black and Latino youths as a threat to their position in the school—a position from which they derive a significant amount of their sense of power and self-worth as adolescents. Their "control" of the school is the source of much pride. It serves not only as personal validation for individuals but also as an important validation of the strength, power, and importance of their ethnic group. The most salient issues are power and control.

Once again, the conflict involves youths who are not doing well academically and who are members of a peer group that places a high value on toughness and combativeness. As in the case of the Bensonhurst and Gravesend youths on the street, the Albanians in this study achieve a sense of importance, power, and control, as well as validation from others that they are "good Albanians" who are defending their people, by participating in fights against blacks and Puerto Ricans. In the case of these Albanian youths, this perception is reinforced by cultural norms that validate the use of violence as a method of conflict resolution. The same could be said for the culture of the street that reinforces the use of violence against blacks and other minorities among at-risk white youths in Bensonhurst and Gravesend and reinforces the use of violence in black-on-black conflicts in East Harlem.

The role of neighborhood sentiment and support of societal ideologies is clearly also important. Albanian attitudes toward blacks and Puerto Ricans are, once again, the result of a combination of personal experiences filtered through ideologies and ideas that are accepted and reinforced at the community level and that provide explanations for individual and group experiences. In this case, the ideas that blacks and Puerto Ricans are lazy and dirty and that they are criminals who use and sell drugs is a result of stereotypes about these groups that confirm individual perceptions of blacks and Puerto Ricans in the neighborhood and in the school. The Albanian youths are exposed to the same messages, images, and symbols that youths in Bensonhurst and Gravesend are exposed to—the same images and symbols the African American youths complained about.

The key, once again, is the perception that these youths have of their group identity and group position. The Albanian youths' ethnic identity is reinforced in many different segments of their lives: their families, community, and peer group. Their perception of the position of their group is developed and maintained in the context of the peer group and the school environment, where they feel they are competing with other groups. In this context, Albanian youths view themselves as an oppressed and misunderstood group who must fight to maintain their position.

As with other groups of youths involved in ethnic and racial conflict, the most salient issues in these conflicts for Albanian youths were turf defense, personal power and self-worth, and a need to belong to a group. As part of the identification process, these youths internalize and exhibit attitudes that will project the image of the tough, important, powerful member of the neighborhood who defends the community.

The role of the peer group in the development of racial conflict at school is clear. Albanian youths stick together and relate to other groups as potential opposition. Of all the young people interviewed for this study, the Albanians were by far the most cohesive, close-knit group. The group interview proceeded like a discussion with a large extended family. The discussion would at times become quite raucous as everybody talked at each other at once; at other times, they deferred to one of the members of the group who functioned as a leader for the younger members. Their ethnicity was clearly the main factor in their group and individual identities, with friends being chosen according to membership in their ethnic group. Additionally, conflicts with blacks and Puerto Ricans in their school are seen as group conflicts, not conflicts between individuals. Racial conflict and racial violence, once again, take the form of a defense of group position, in this case in the hierarchy of groups attending a school.

Conclusion

Ethnic and racial conflict and violence among youth in New York City is a constant reality and major concern for most young people in the city. The causes of the ethnic and racial conflict and violence are rooted in their experiences in their respective communities, where they are exposed to community-based ideologies that supply racialized interpretations of their experiences and define other racial and ethnic groups in negative terms. These ideologies frame and provide meaning to their experiences with other groups and help to define their relations to other groups. Community-based peer groups are the arenas in which youth act out their aggressive attitudes toward other groups. It is the combination of these factors, when placed in historical, societal, and group context, that produces a given result: conflict or tolerance. Further, the confluence of these factors plays a role in determining how each young person feels about, and behaves, toward him- or herself and toward others.

Ethnicity also plays an important role in the development of conflict or tolerance. White youths who express the strongest ethnic and racial identification display the least tolerance toward other groups. These youths analyze their environment along ethnic and racial lines. Competition for turf, employment, housing, or control of the school is immediately placed in an ethnic or racial context, motivating ethnic and racial conflict.

The second part of the explanation for ethnic and racial conflict and violence is found in the psychosocial process of ethnic and racial identity formation and the development of a sense of the position of the group. If the sense of group position is based on an oppositional, competitive, differentiative perspective, then ethnic and racial identity can function to form the basis for fear, distrust, hatred, prejudice, discrimination, and violence.

It is tempting to conclude from the evidence produced by this research that ethnic and racial isolation or interaction is the most important factor in determining the ethnic and racial attitudes and behavior of young people. The least tolerant youths in the study were those who had the least contact with other groups.

However, it is not an interracial setting that produces tolerance but the way in which young people interpret that setting. All of the youths in this study have been in integrated settings at various points in their lives. Some have emerged from their experiences in these settings with attitudes of tolerance toward other groups. Others have developed intolerance, fear, and distrust. There are youths in southern Brooklyn who display tolerant attitudes toward blacks and other groups and who do not engage in or condone racial attacks. Though equal-status contact with other groups can be an important part of the process of the development of positive attitudes toward those groups, it does not inevitably lead to it. The messages that young people receive about how to interpret their reality is most important. These messages come from the social institutions with which they interact daily.

The most important social institutions affecting young people are their families, schools, churches, peer groups, neighborhoods, and the media (television, movies, and music). Black and Latino youths rated the family as the most powerful influence shaping prejudice; peers were rated second. White youth rated peer groups first and family second.

The peer group is most influential with youths who have left or are alienated from their families or other institutions. It is youths who spend most of their time on the street, who have left school and are ostracized by their own families and communities, who engage in racial attacks to achieve a sense of belonging to the group, a sense of importance, and a sense of power in their lives. Paradoxically, though these youths are outcasts in their community, they find sanction and support for their attitudes and actions from their parents, other community residents, and political representatives.

The power of the peer group was most vividly demonstrated by one Bensonhurst youth, who had vociferously engaged in the discussion of "missions," who pulled me aside after the group interview was over and said:

> I grew up in an all-black neighborhood and all my friends used to be black. Now I live in Bensonhurst and I can't tell my white friends what I used to think because I won't have any friends. The worst part is when I'm hanging out with my friends and a black person walks by and they want to do [attack] him, I have to do him too.

In summary, a number of key factors affect the racial attitudes and behavior of young people in New York City. Structural conditions increase anxiety, fear, and anger toward other groups. Peer groups play a critical role in the internalization of attitudes and in facilitating behaviors based on these attitudes. Familial socialization, neighborhood sentiment, and societal messages reinforce the attitudes and posture that young people develop and adopt toward other groups. Violence is an act of domination, the ultimate attempt to exert power over an individual or group. Ethnic and racial violence among the young are extensions of power struggles among groups in a racially stratified society.

Finally, the lack of a credible deterrent to violence—a lack of neighborhood opposition to racially motivated activities, ideological messages that supply encouragement, and ineffective police enforcement against racially motivated violence—allow some youths (particularly white youths) to consider acting on their attitudes without fear of punishment. Deterrence plays a critical role in the nature of conflict, circumscribing its form of expression. In the case of the African American youths, racial violence was not even a viable option because of the economic, political, and, most important, physical power held by the opposition groups. Consequently, the outlet for the expression of this conflict is through ideology and through cultural forms. One result is the occurrence of fantasies of violence and revenge in rap music.

However, the most important factor influencing how these youths view others is how they view themselves. Those who have a sense of purpose and power in their lives, separate and apart from their membership in a particular ethnic or racial group, are more tolerant than those who derive their identity, sense of self-worth, and sense of power primarily from membership in an ethnic or racial group.

Does this mean that strong ethnic and racial identities are inevitably oppositional and the source of intolerance and prejudice? The answer to this question lies in the context in which the meaning of identity and the sense of group position are formed. If a youth's ethnic and racial identity are based on an oppositional sense of group position that views other groups as a threat, then a strong ethnic and racial identity can reinforce intolerance and prejudice and provide a firm foundation for engaging in ethnic and racial conflict, as was the case for the Avenue T Boys and the Albanian and Schomberg Plaza youths. If a youth's ethnic and racial identity is based on an inclusive sense of group position that embraces other groups, then a strong ethnic and racial identity can be a source of both pride and self-esteem, as well as reinforcing tolerance and cooperation, as was the case for the ALERT youths and many of the young people at Central Park East Secondary School. Which type of identity young people develop depends upon the messages they receive from the individuals and social institutions that are influential in their lives: family, school, community residents and leaders, political leaders, and, most important for adolescents, friends and peers in their community.

The interplay of different forces and the importance of the peer group as a context for the development of ethnic identity and attitudes about other groups can be understood by reviewing two case histories of youths who were involved in racially motivated violence but who altered their behavior as a result of a change in peer groups. Both of these youths were students at John Dewey High School in Bensonhurst. The first was a young Italian American man who used to hang out with the Avenue T Boys:

> BOBBY: I couldn't stand black people. We used to fight with them all the time. I didn't know any better and that's what my friends were doing. We used to get together and look for some blacks to beat up. I spent most of my time on the street and had a pretty tough reputation. It all changed when I got involved with Bob DeSenna and the Council for Unity.[8] He really saved my life. I was involved in very self-destructive activities which hurt myself and other people. Luckily, nobody was ever killed. Things got real bad about eight years ago when we were headed for a race war of some kind and someone definitely would have been killed. That's when I met DeSenna who helped me to see that I was either going to kill somebody or be killed and that wasn't going to solve my problems. The Council for Unity was a place where I could do positive things and feel good about myself. I was never a good student so school was never a place that I felt comfortable. But the council showed me that you didn't have to hate and you didn't have to fight to be a good Italian. I had a black friend for the first time. It didn't happen overnight, but by the time I graduated, and I don't think I would have graduated if I had not joined the Council for Unity, I had a black friend whom I knew I could count on, who would watch my back, who would die for me.

Another member of the Council for Unity related a similar story:

> MARTIN: I'm half Puerto Rican and half Italian. I always hung out around my neighborhood with the Italian kids. There was one other kid that is Puerto Rican. You wanted to know why I changed? I don't know. I knew a kid who joined the Council for Unity. Before that I thought only kids who were soft joined the group. Then my friend joined and he got me to go to one of their events. They did this play about an incident that happened about eight years ago at the pizza parlor across from the school. There were racial fights between Italian kids and blacks which almost caused a race riot in the school. I saw myself in the play and where I was headed. I came to one of the meetings and that was it. The group gives you a sense of belonging, it's a family, really. And we support each other and grow as a family.

These descriptions, given by young men who had been involved in racial violence, demonstrate the importance of neighborhoods and peer groups in the formation, maintenance, and expression of attitudes toward other racial and ethnic groups. These youths were involved with neighborhood street groups made up of other teenagers like themselves who felt powerless in their lives, who were anxious about their situation, and who reinforced their sense of themselves and their ethnic identity from their participation in that group. These two youths were able to change their attitudes and behavior by finding a different group, one that supplied an alternative, positive context and a new set of peers with whom to bond.[9] The experiences of these two young men provide powerful evidence that ethnic and racial violence can be reduced by crafting strategies designed to address each of the factors that contribute to ethnic and racial conflict.

five

Conclusion

Contrary to the superficial evidence, there is nothing simple about the structure and dynamics of racism. . . . It is racism's very rigidity that is due to its complexity. Its capacity to punctuate the universe into two great opposites masks something else; it masks the complexes of feelings and attitudes, beliefs and conceptions, that are always refusing to be so neatly stabilized and fixed. . . . It is a way of masking how deeply our histories intertwine and interpenetrate; how necessary "the Other" is to our own sense of identity.   —*Stuart Hall, "Ethnicity: Identity and Difference"*

The problem of ethnic and racial conflict is both complex and enduring. Conflict is fueled by oppositional identities, kindled by structural circumstance, and fed by hostility and hatred. It is the confluence of these factors that makes ethnic and racial conflict so difficult to explain and to prevent. The objective of this book has been to examine these factors in the specific context of the increase in ethnic and racial conflict among young people in New York City and, more generally, to analyze how these factors *combine* to produce tension and conflict or tolerance and cooperation.

The factors that produce ethnic and racial conflict are found in what I have called "concentric spheres of reproduction": cultural, political, social, psychological, and economic spheres. Within these spheres, social and economic inequality, racialized ideologies, and oppositional ethnic and racial identities are produced and reproduced. These processes of reproduction take place within each sphere, which accounts for the continuity of ethnic and racial attitudes, relationships, and conflict. This process of production and reproduction of ethnic and racial attitudes, relationships, and conflict takes place at the societal, community, and individual levels.

The attitudes and actions of youths in southern Brooklyn, East Harlem, and Pelham Parkway demonstrate the importance of community-based ideas and attitudes in the construction of these young people's individual identities and of their perceptions of other groups. It is through community interaction that their ethnic and racial attitudes became associated with their ethnic and racial identities. The youth form and construct their attitudes toward other ethnic and racial groups as a result of their exposure to community-based social systems and ideologies.

For ethnic and racial conflict to occur, these ideological messages must be incorporated into a belief system that forms the basis of a group identity. Individual and group identities incorporate these ideological messages into structured belief systems that connect attitudes toward others with the individual's or the group's sense of self.

The attitudes of the Albanian youths, the Schomberg Plaza youths, and the Avenue T Boys demonstrate the importance of the relationship between attitudes toward others and individual and group identity. For the Albanian youths, membership in their community essentially precluded positive interracial interaction. Their ethnically exclusive peer group encouraged negative attitudes toward African Americans and Latinos, and engaging in conflict with these groups was seen as a measure of loyalty to the group. For the Avenue T Boys, the display of negative attitudes toward African Americans affirmed allegiance to the community and authenticated their ethnic identity. Their ethnic and racial identities were not based solely on which group they were born into, what ethnicity or race they were, but how they constructed and understood the meaning of their ethnicity or race.

The Italian American members of the Avenue T Boys and Bobby from the Council for Unity were all working-class Italian American youths from Bensonhurst. Yet they had different conceptions of what it meant to be an Italian American from Bensonhurst. The Avenue T Boys linked being Italian American with negative attitudes towards blacks. For these youths, attacking an African American was a form of cultural expression of their ethnic identity. Bobby shared this sense of identity until he encountered an alternative construction that allowed him to adopt a different conception of his Italian ethnicity in the context of a new peer group that could support his attitude and behavior change.

The attitudes of the ALERT youths demonstrate the central importance of peer groups and communities in the construction of ethnic and racial identity and the adoption of attitudes toward other ethnic and racial groups. Their attitudes also demonstrate the contextual and situational nature of ethnic and racial identities and attitudes. Many lived in communities whose members had ethnic and racial attitudes that contradicted the ideology of ALERT, their primary peer group. The attitudes of the Puerto Rican members of ALERT toward Dominicans and those of the African American members toward Koreans, for example, indicate that attitudes and identities are constructed from multiple, often conflicting sources of information and influence. The youth in ALERT who lived in communities where members held ethnic and racial attitudes that were in conflict with the group norms espoused by ALERT expressed confusion about their attitudes toward specific groups. These young people continued to hold some of the ideas that were prevalent within their residential communities and families even though they believed them to be "wrong," and they continually expressed a need to work on their prejudices to eliminate these ideas and to adopt attitudes more consistent with the ALERT ideology.

It is significant that none of the groups of youths examined in this book is denying differences that obviously exist among groups. Some groups reject and fear differences, basing their identities on the exclusion of and enmity toward groups who are different; others acknowledge differences and base their sense of selves on the inclusion and celebration of people from different backgrounds. Fundamental to each outlook is the meaning ascribed by different young people to ethnic and racial differences in a racialized society. These meanings are constructed through a process of definition and representation that happens at different levels in society. Young people are exposed to definitions and representations of the meaning of ethnic and racial difference through images in popular culture such as music, videos, television, and movies; through school curricula; and, most important, through community-based ideas and ideologies, which are communicated through everyday social interaction.

It is within one's chosen group that the basis and meaning of inclusion and exclusion, the definition of who is different, and the meaning of that difference gets defined. Individuals do not decide on their own who they are and who they are not. Young people do so through their interaction in a community of peers. The Avenue T Boys learned the importance and meaning of being Italian American through their interaction with their neighborhood peers. Similarly, the Albanian youths and the Schomberg Plaza youths learned the meaning of being Albanian and African American through their interactions with peers from their neighborhoods.

Ethnic and racial identity formation is a part of a process of understanding and making sense of one's situation and group position. For the Avenue T Boys, the Albanian youths, and the Schomberg Plaza youths, part of this process was making sense of their marginal economic and social position.

The actions of the ALERT youths, as well as of the Avenue T Boys and the Albanian youths, also demonstrate the importance of actions and behavior in the concretization of identity. The multicultural activities that the ALERT youth participated in and their organizing efforts within the school to promote ethnic and racial tolerance were an important part of the formation of their identities as members of a multicultural community. Similarly, the actions taken against African Americans and Latinos by the Avenue T Boys and Albanian youths were an important part of their process of identification of themselves as Italian American or Albanians.

The projection of attitudes, frustrations, and blame onto other groups obscures the very real pain and barriers that these young people face. The argument here is not that all young people face the same set of problems or that the identities and problems of white young people are the same as those that black young people face. Rather, the argument is that the factors that shape their identities and outlook toward others are similar. Their objective realities as white or African American youth in the United States influence their lives in different ways. The challenge is to address the problems that they and their communities face and to facilitate alternative ideas and understandings of the nature of those problems.

The factors and forces present in Bensonhurst, Gravesend, East Harlem, and Pelham Parkway exist in numerous other communities in New York City and throughout the country. The politics of ethnic and racial exclusion and reaction fueled a powerful community movement in the 1970s and 1980s in New York City and a powerful societal movement in the United States in the 1990s. The reduction and elimination of racial violence and conflict among young people in New York City and throughout U.S. society will require policies and approaches that address the various factors that have been discussed in this book.

Reducing Ethnic and Racial Conflict

Reducing ethnic and racial conflict and violence among young people in New York City requires that each of the concentric spheres of conflict and violence be addressed: economic anxieties and obstacles for youth employment must be reduced or removed, multicultural ideologies need to be promoted throughout the city and particularly at the community level, and peer groups and communities that embrace tolerant, inclusive ethnic and racial identities need to be promoted and encouraged.

For attitude or behavior change to occur, an individual must either change the group with which he or she affiliates and identifies, or there must be a fundamental change in the cultural and ideological perspectives in the community of which he or she is a member. This change could be brought about by the influence of an important member of the community who advances an alternative ideology, which would then be embraced as a cultural value by the rest of the community. It cannot happen without internal struggle within the community, and it cannot be the result solely of changes in economic structural factors; rather, it must entail a change in consciousness about the nature and reasons for their structural position and condition.

From a policy perspective, the results of this research provide the foundation for the construction of more comprehensive, holistic approaches to the problem of racial conflict and violence. The results point to three primary arenas for intervention: schools, employment, and the streets.

Theories about the role of representations and the importance of the definition of difference supply an important foundation for the link between theory and practice. Theories of cultural studies advanced by Giroux and McLaren (1994), among others, have emphasized the centrality of culturally based and generated beliefs in the maintenance of ethnic and racial inequality and conflict, as well as their importance for social change. These theories point to one of the primary areas of intervention to reduce ethnic and racial conflict and violence among young people.

In schools, education can provide an alternative interpretive frame to youths who are struggling to understand who they are and why they are in the situation they are in. Schools are among the only locations where young people come into contact with people from other ethnic and racial groups on a daily basis. Because of this fact, schools are uniquely situated to foster tolerant and open attitudes toward different groups among young people.

When young people from different racial and ethnic backgrounds are thrown together in a school setting, there are three possible outcomes: racial conflict, racial interaction and tolerance, or racial separation with little interaction. Schools have the potential to help shape how young people interpret the meaning of their experiences in such a multicultural setting.

Any efforts to address racial and ethnic conflict among young people need to focus on the factors that shape their attitudes and identity. Schools can play a crucial role in fostering more tolerant racial attitudes by actively and consistently encouraging cross-cultural interactions and supplying information to young people about cultural similarities and differences, which can help shape the way young people interpret their cross-cultural interactions. This is not merely an issue of acknowledging ethnic and racial difference; rather, we must analyze difference and interpret the various meanings ascribed to it, and we must analyze the social, economic, and political ramifications and results of various interpretations. Such an analysis would examine the role of competing and conflicting definitions and representations of the meaning of ethnic and racial difference in the reproduction and legitimation of relations of power, domination, and inequality. Schools and youth organizations need to commit themselves to dealing with the developing ethnic identities of school-age youths and the sentiments and ideologies in the communities that they serve. This would entail both the development of a multicultural curriculum that addresses the issues of ethnic and racial difference and racial oppression and a change in the traditional mission of educational institutions. This requires a pedagogical method that teaches critical approaches to the study of society, community, and self. The critical approach would incorporate an examination of the dimensions of power that affect relations, definitions, representations, and interactions (E. Pinderhughes, 1989).

Though normally the province of family and community, schools and youth organizations should pay particular attention to the construction of youths' ethnic and racial identities. Given the importance of the existence of an Other in the construction of ethnic and racial identity and the importance of issues of inclusion and exclusion for adolescents, the question of what type of identity to foster in young people is critical. Who will be the Other that helps to define an identity that seeks to include, tolerate, and accept all groups? In the context of multiculturalism, the Others are those who retain exclusive, opposi-tional, and antagonistic identities, attitudes, and relations. It would be important to foster not just a multicultural identity but an antiracist identity. The curriculum should locate, center, and anchor this identity in an alternative discourse and history, complete with a worldview, he-roes, and cultural expressions. This does not mean that individuals and groups need to give up their particular racial and ethnic identities as Italian Americans, African Americans, Albanians, and so on. Rather, it means that these ethnic and racial identities are constructed and de-fined as distinct parts of a larger pan-ethnic, multicultural identity and community.

Secondary strategies for reducing ethnic and racial conflict and vio-lence should be aimed at young people with limited economic oppor-tunities and futures who are most at-risk for engaging in racial vio-lence. This strategy targets youths who have dropped out or who are not doing well in school. Youth employment programs should func-tion as apprenticeship or bridge programs that focus on the transition from school to work for non–college bound youth by supplying job training for long-term employment in sectors of the economy where jobs are available and pay decent wages. These programs are most often neighborhood-based. They should be reconfigured as programs drawing youths from a wide range of neighborhoods. The programs would have multiracial or multicultural work teams, who would have gained their skills in a cooperative-learning environment. Essentially, these programs would be providing alternative peer groups at the same time they were providing job training.

Last, strategies must also be developed to deal with youths who are engaging in ethnic and racial violence. These strategies should in-clude both counseling and punishment. There is evidence that laws that designate bias crimes as specific crimes with a separate sentencing pattern work as a deterrent if aggressively enforced. Young people need to know that if they are convicted of serious violent bias crimes, they will do time. However, it is possible to get to many of these youths be-fore their crimes reach a lethal or even dangerous level. Youth workers need to be on the street where this activity happens. Diversion pro-grams for first- or second-time offenders should include counseling and mandatory racial and cross-cultural awareness workshops. Additionally, somehow, communities must be encouraged to participate in these programs and to find ways to disapprove of and clearly condemn racial violence.

The Council for Unity, which began in John Dewey High School in Bensonhurst, presents an important model of a more holistic program that deals with several of the concentric spheres of ethnic and racial conflict and violence among young people in New York City. The council provides a multicultural, multiethnic peer group for youths who attend the school. It promotes positive racial and ethnic identity and awareness through workshops and programs that the youths participate in. The program grew out of a mediation to defuse a racial conflict at the high school in 1979 between Italian youths and African American youths. As the conflict escalated through a series of racial attacks and fights, Robert DeSenna, a teacher at John Dewey, intervened with the leaders of each side in an effort to prevent further injury, a fatality, or a possible race riot. Having worked together to reduce tensions and promote better understanding among antagonistic ethnic and racial groups, DeSenna and the leaders of the conflicting groups formed the Council for Unity. The council is set up intentionally to function as a peer group that provides an alternative to street-based neighborhood peer groups. There are rites of passage, including an oath to the council, and induction ceremonies. The council has an established and articulated purpose and group identity that embraces multiculturalism, the understanding of difference, and the promotion of ethnic and racial tolerance. Members are expected to adopt and uphold that purpose and identity. An important part of the organization's goals is to promote multicultural awareness throughout the school and surrounding communities. For each youth that joins, the council provides the basis for a positive, inclusive sense of individual ethnic and racial identity; exposure to a multicultural ideology of tolerance, acceptance, and respect; and enhanced prospects for attending college through the improvement of skills or for finding a job through community networks it has established. Beyond the members of the group, the council promotes tolerance and acceptance in the communities surrounding the school through cultural programs and community service.

The Council for Unity is just one example of a program that is effective in developing tolerance and acceptance of difference and in reducing ethnic and racial conflict among young people. The ALERT group at Christopher Columbus High School is another excellent example.[1]

ALERT represents the crossing of borders within new spaces, spaces that have been deliberately created to address the isolation on each side of the racial lines.

The ideas expressed by the ALERT youths demonstrate the importance of the definition and politics of difference in shaping the attitudes and behavior of individuals and groups in a racialized society. In a very real sense, these youths' ideas and actions are an extension of political and cultural battles that are now being waged over the definition and meaning of difference. Differences in youths' attitudes reflect the different cultural milieus within which they come to understand the meaning of difference. For those who are developing their sense of self in peer groups that embrace the value of multiculturalism, there is a far less differentiative quality to their sense of self and their beliefs about others.

The ALERT youths are not only learning about different cultures, but they are doing so in the context of a group that does not ascribe differential values to the different cultural values and practices of different groups. The elements of power and privilege, and as important, of competition and threat are removed from the dynamics of the interaction, allowing for cross-cultural interactions on a more equal plane. This process includes the acknowledgment of different types of oppression and of differentials in power and position in the larger society that affect the material existence of their own and other groups and the interaction between different ethnic and racial groups.[2]

The strategies suggested here are based on an analysis of the combination of factors and forces that combine to produce ethnic and racial conflict. Complex problems require complex solutions. These strategies could be analyzed as utopian visions requiring large-scale societal change, or as practical, pragmatic programs that require a little creativity and a willingness to do things in a new way. The bottom line is that little change will be achieved unless we have the economic and social will to eliminate inequality and to provide authentic opportunities for the nation's non–college bound youth. Each of the programs in which I interviewed youths were run on minute budgets, continually competing for the same limited sources of funding. The idea of the adoption of multicultural curricula has itself become a racialized battleground. Funding for public education has been cut to levels where the learning of basic skills is impaired and social learning is a secondary consideration.

The concept of "social engineering" to decrease racial inequality and improve racial harmony has been undermined in recent years by the concretization of racial reaction in the form of a syndrome of white victimization and the resurgence of racial nationalism. It is unlikely that social, political, and economic conditions will change this reality in the near future. Economic competition and inequality have increased. Interest-group politics shows no evidence of abating. Ethnic and racial groups are becoming more entrenched in their oppositional postures.

What is crystal clear is that if the changes necessary to reduce ethnic and racial conflict are to occur, they must happen not just at a national level but also at the community level. Government attempts to reduce racial inequality and promote ethnic and racial harmony have encountered tremendous opposition. The failure of the social movements of the 1960s and 1970s to bring about a reduction in racial inequality and the recent resurgence in ethnic and racial conflict are partially the result of the reproduction and regeneration of racially oppositional ideologies and racialized identities at the community level:

> Ideology then governs people's activities within economic and political practices; so the idea of a social revolution that is not accompanied by a revolution in ideology is a recipe for disaster; a recipe for the return to the structures that have been overthrown, brought about by the way that people habitually and unconsciously act and relate. (Coward and Ellis, 1977, p. 72)

The battleground for racial change must be expanded to include communities across the nation. It is in their communities that young people learn about the importance and meaning of ethnic and racial difference. It is at the community level where are drawn the racial lines that provide the basis for intergroup conflict. For many youths in New York City, as well as for many youths and adults across the nation, the lines dividing different ethnic and racial groups appear more and more like borders to be defended rather than transcended.

Appendix A
Methodological Notes

I first decided to conduct this research after hearing a report in 1987 about the dramatic increase over the previous two years in reports of bias-motivated crimes in New York City. This study was originally designed to examine ethnic and racial attitudes among young people in New York City in order to explain the increase in racially motivated violence in the city. In approaching the research problem there were several methodological issues: first, how to verify the phenomenon of an increase in racially motivated violence; second, how to measure the ethnic and racial attitudes of young people; third, how to construct a sample that would allow for cross-racial, cross-ethnic, and cross-class comparisons; fourth, how to address the difficulty of establishing a link between attitudes and behavior. Specifically, I wanted to ask whether it was possible to demonstrate a link between the types of attitudes young people had and an increase in racially motivated violence, which was primarily the result of their actions.

Measuring the Ethnic and Racial Attitudes of Youth

The difficulties in measuring racial attitudes are well documented (Kinder and Sears, 1981; McConohay and Hough, 1976; Sears and Kinder, 1971; Schuman, Steeh, and Bobo, 1985).[1] Race is a highly charged issue in U.S. society. Social researchers have questioned whether racial attitudes can be reliably measured. The major problem in measuring racial attitudes is how to determine whether the subjects are telling the truth. How can the researcher distinguish between a genuine attitude and a response that is given because it is perceived by the subject to be socially acceptable? This dilemma has been most pronounced in political polls involving African American candidates. There is ample evidence that a small but significant percentage of white voters give answers on voter preference polls that do not reflect what they do in the privacy of the polling booth. Analyses of voting and of survey public opinion data suggest this was the case in Tom Bradley's loss to George Deukmejian in the 1982 and 1986 California gubernatorial elections (Pettigrew and Alston, 1988; Jaynes and Williams, 1989).

There is also evidence that the race of the interviewer can affect the responses of subjects (Hatchett and Schuman, 1975–1976; Schuman, Steeh, and Bobo, 1985). In this study, there was only one interviewer—myself, an African American male. However, in field testing the survey instrument, interviewers of different races were used, and I found no evidence of a reticence to speak about race on the part of the white youths. Additionally, the responses of subjects in this study were compared to the responses of subjects in "A Study of New York City High School Students and Educational Staff on Prejudice and Race Relations" (New York State Martin Luther King, Jr., Institute for Nonviolence, 1990).[2] That study used a team of white interviewers. A comparison of responses to the same and similar questions did not reveal the differences one would expect if the race of the interviewer were to have an effect: that is, responses indicating more tolerance toward blacks given by white respondents (Hatchett and Schuman, 1975–1976). This study yielded less tolerant responses on the part of white respondents, which can be explained by the difference in demographic background of the sample.

In fact, youths from many different ethnic and racial backgrounds responded more openly to me than to the other interviewers. Especially after they started sharing stories of racial attacks and criminal behavior, I began to continually ask myself the question, Why are they telling me this stuff? I addressed that question to several of the youths who had spoken at length about racial violence they had participated in. They gave three reasons for why they wanted to talk with me and why they were so open in sharing their ideas and experiences: (1) They said that "You seem pretty cool"—that I seemed to have some idea of what went down on the street. It was important to them that I had some basis from which to understand their opinions, actions, and experiences. (2) Very few people had asked them about their opinions of the racial situation in their neighborhoods and in New York City. It was an important issue for them, and I asked for their ideas and experiences without judgment and with full respect. (3) The white youths stated that I was different from the blacks whom they viewed as "the enemy." I was older and I dressed differently. This, however, did not deter a friend of one of my informants, who was the first to see me get out of my car on one of my first forays into Bensonhurst, from wanting to attack me until he was informed by Ronnie that I was okay. The youths also told me that if I showed up in their neighborhood with one or two more black people that I would immediately be "marked as a target."

Methods

The nature of the research problem required a creative combination of several methodologies. In an effort to deal with the dilemma of obtaining truthful answers to questions about ethnic and racial attitudes, two methods for gathering data on attitudes were used. Multiple methodological approaches were used to produce data that could formulate a complex explanation of the pattern of ethnic and racial attitudes among youths in New York City and enable an analysis of the linkages between the structural, cultural, and ideological factors that combine to produce the present climate of racial and ethnic conflict.

The two methods used for collecting data on the ethnic and racial attitudes of young people were (1) a survey questionnaire and (2) focus group interviews. These methods were combined to produce individual and group data from the 270 youths who participated in the study.

The survey questionnaire was administered first. Each youth filled out the questionnaire anonymously. After the entire group had completed the questionnaire and handed them to the interviewer, focus group interviews were conducted. These interviews lasted anywhere from fifty minutes to three hours. The interviews were taped and transcribed.

The survey questionnaire was developed to gather data about socioeconomic background, ethnic and racial identity, age, and attitudes toward other groups. The data produced by the survey revealed relationships between existing structural and cultural factors in the neighborhoods under examination and the attitudes of youths from those areas. The survey supplied a broad picture of the pattern and content of ethnic and racial attitudes among young people in New York City and produced data that allowed for comparative analysis of the content of the attitudes of the youths as well as of their demographic backgrounds.

Focus group interviews were conducted in groups, using open-ended questions designed to elicit information about the youths' views of race relations. Data from the focus group interviews supplied detailed information about the substance of ethnic and racial attitudes among young people in New York City. These data were used for the analysis of the role of ideological support for the youths' attitudes and the analysis of the process of attitude formation.

Using focus group interviews in conjunction with the survey revealed differences in public verbal responses and anonymous written responses, as well as the effects of responding within a group setting. The youths were surveyed and interviewed in preexisting groups: in classes and in peer groups. These settings more closely approximated the natural setting within which they consider these issues. In these settings, the effect of the peer group was observed to be the strongest factor in their responses. They were surprisingly candid in their responses to the focus group questions, exhibiting little desire to please the interviewer. The two primary methods are described in detail below.

The Survey

The survey instrument was constructed to collect both demographic and attitudinal data. Existing studies of racial attitudes were reviewed in an effort to locate existing survey questions that could be used for the study. Very few studies of ethnic and racial attitudes among young people have been conducted. The vast majority of attitudinal research has concentrated on adult attitudes (Kinder and Sears, 1981; McConohay and Hough, 1976; Sears and Kinder, 1971; Schuman, Steeh, and Bobo, 1985).[3] Most of the questions used in these studies were inappropriate for use with adolescents. The studies of adult attitudes asked questions about opinion on issues ranging from intermarriage to residential segregation. The questions were structured to relate to issues faced by adults rather than youths. In contrast, questions for this study needed to be structured in a manner that youths could relate to and in a language that they could understand.

Thus, the survey instrument uses a combination of questions from the questionnaire used in "A Study of New York City High School Students and Educational Staff on Prejudice and Race Relations" and questions developed specifically by the investigator for this study.[4] New questions for attitudinal variables were constructed after participatory observation in numerous discussions and workshops about race relations with youths. The questionnaire was field-tested and revised accordingly.[5]

The survey is divided into nine sections: (1) demography and background information; (2) personal expectations and aspirations; (3) contact and experience with other races/ethnicities; (4) comfort levels: dating; (5) attitudes toward ethnic and racial groups; (6) integration, segregation, and individual rights; (7) job competition; (8) prejudice and racism; and (9) bias violence.

The primary demographic background variables are age, sex, grade in school, race, ethnicity, religion, family structure, socioeconomic status (as measured by father's and mother's occupations), neighborhood, school, and grade average.

The attitudinal variables are constructed to gather data about the attitudes youths have toward other groups. These questions include issues relevant to young people, such as their attitudes toward dating individuals from different groups, the attitudes of their parents and friends toward their dating different groups, their attitudes toward segregated neighborhoods and job competition, their opinions of other groups, and their experiences with prejudice and racial violence.

Focus Group Interviews

Focus group interviews fall within the domain of qualitative research. The methodology differs from a traditional interview in that there is no strict adherence to an alternation of questions by the interviewer and answers by the subjects. Instead the interviewer plays a dual role of inquisitor and facilitator. The purpose of the structure is to allow the interaction within the group to develop based on topics and questions supplied by the interviewer. The utility of focus groups is the explicit use of group interaction to produce data and insights that would be less accessible without the interaction found in the group. Focus groups can be seen as a combination of interview technique and elements of participant observation (Morgan, 1988, 1996). The subjects respond to specific topics and questions, which yield standard interview data that optimally reveal what each individual participant thinks. Further, the subjects interact with one another as they react to statements made by other group participants. This allows additional issues to be raised if members of the group find them relevant and important. Additionally, the interaction itself provides data about how subjects deal with the topic of research in a group. The give-and-take of the interaction leads to relatively spontaneous responses from participants as well as to a fairly high level of participant involvement (Bellenger, Bernhardt, and Goldstucker, 1976; Morgan, 1988, 1996); it also provides insight into the natural language used by the participants (Levy, 1979).

The focus group interview is not a substitute for participant observation. Whereas participant observation allows the researcher to collect data about subjects in their natural environment, focus groups are conducted in unnatural social settings. Though they may take place in a setting in which the subjects would normally find themselves, such as a school classroom or pizza parlor, the structure of the interview itself produces an unnatural setting.

The optimum methodology would be to hold focus group interviews to gather data about attitudes and ideas combined with participant observation on the street of the behavior of the subjects. In this study, this was not possible because of access problems in white neighborhoods. Though the white youths interviewed were very open in their discussions about racial attitudes, I was informed that it would be impossible for me to hang out with them on the street, where my presence would be viewed with extreme suspicion by friends of the subjects.

One clear advantage of the focus group interview over the individual interview is the reduction in the focus on the interviewer. The interaction among participants can reduce the effect the interviewer has on the responses of the participants.

Therefore, the focus group interview was a particularly appropriate methodology for this study because it is possible that the young people would be intimidated by a one-on-one interview, increasing the bias effect of the interviewer. In the context of an individual interview, the pressure to answer questions to please the interviewer is greater.

This is a study of racial attitudes, which are developed and reinforced in a group context. Therefore, the best way to examine those attitudes is in the groups within which they exist. The most fruitful interviews took place when the groups were composed of youths who were friends with each other. In this context, the group took on a dynamic of its own. The young people made no attempts to please the interviewer with their answers. The groups functioned rather like a youth speak-out, with the young people in each group trying to be understood. It was clear that the subject is one that they are extremely concerned about, that is a part of their daily lives, and about which they have very strong opinions and attitudes. They are rarely asked their opinions on these matters and have virtually no chance to talk about racial and ethnic relations in the city. Consequently, they were extremely eager to discuss the issues in the focus group context.

The focus groups involved integrated, all-black, all-white, and all-Latino groups of youth. The most animated and engaging groups were those composed of one racial group. It was helpful if at least some of the subjects knew each other well, as this facilitated the group dynamic that they normally have in their peer groups on the street, in school, or in their neighborhood.

The focus group interview format allowed for a group dynamic to build within each group. The young people would respond to each other, and the process developed into part interview and part discussion. The group dynamic was critical because it revealed attitudes that might be hidden in an individual interview. As the youths respond to each other, the process of peer group reinforcement was observed within the context of the focus group interview. The format encouraged more truthful responses in a setting that more closely approximated the setting in which the ethnic and racial attitudes are developed, expressed, and acted upon.

The methodology made it possible for the researcher to learn about detailed behaviors that are illegal or considered taboo—such as "getting drunk and going on missions" in discussions with white youth. The discussion of "missions" arose out of a discussion of what groups are in conflict in these young people's neighborhoods. These behaviors were revealed because of the dynamics of the group discussion, and it is likely that they would not have emerged in an individual interview. Learning about "missions" was an important discovery, which revealed the role of the peer group in both the development and reinforcement of ethnic and racial attitudes and the resultant violent behavior. The dynamics of the groups changed when the subject of "missions" was brought up. Many of the youths would get visibly excited, and the discussion would turn from the ideas of the young people to the actions many of them had participated in. For these youths, "missions" were a medal of valor proving to themselves and others their importance, their loyalty to their neighborhood, their toughness, and their ethnic worthiness.

The Sample

The sample was composed of youths between the ages of fourteen and twenty-one who resided in New York City. It is a nonprobability sample that utilized a snowball technique. The original intent was to construct a random sample of New York City youths drawn from the citywide school and youth program populations. It was to be determined by plotting a geographic distribution of the bias incidents recorded by the New York City Human Rights Commission. The survey was to be administered to the neighborhoods with the highest and lowest frequency of ethnic and racial conflict among neighborhoods of similar socioeconomic background and ethnic and racial composition. This plan turned out to be flawed because it was based on the assumption that there was a significant difference among neighborhoods in the frequency of bias incidents. According to the New York City Police Department Bias Unit and the New York City Human Rights Commission, it is impossible to discern a pattern in the frequency of bias attacks. An additional faulty assumption was that a higher frequency of bias incidents would indicate a community whose residents had negative attitudes toward other racial or ethnic groups. In fact, there are a number of other factors that can affect the frequency of bias incidents. For example, contact between groups of different racial or ethnic backgrounds is necessary for conflict to occur. Highly segregated neighborhoods often have reputations for violence that are well known to outsiders, who avoid such areas, thereby decreasing the probability of the occurrence of bias incidents.

The revised plan was to draw a sample from as large a universe of New York City public high school students as could be generated. I compiled a list of high schools in all five boroughs, had the survey translated into Spanish, Korean, and Chinese, received approval from the Board of Education, mailed copies of the surveys to all of the schools, and followed up with phone calls to each school. For a variety of reasons, most of the principals in the New York City public schools did not want to deal with issues of racial and ethnic relations, as they were fearful it would stir up conflict.[6] As a result, I was able to gain access to only four schools and had to rely on contacts with youth workers in order to generate the sample.

A total of 270 youths were surveyed or interviewed. I conducted twenty group interviews at five different sites in the city; of these, 246 youths also responded to the survey. These numbers include fifty-eight youths at Sheepshead Bay High School in southern Brooklyn; eighty-eight youths at the Sixty-First Precinct Youth Dares program, an alternative high school program for at-risk youth and a GED program with students who live primarily in Bensonhurst, Gravesend, Canarsie, and Coney Island in southern Brooklyn; twenty youths at the Schomberg Plaza Youth Project in East Harlem; thirty-four youths at Central Park East Secondary School in East Harlem; forty-seven youths at Christopher Columbus High School in the Pelham Parkway section of the Bronx. The remaining twenty-four youths, interviewed at four additional sites, did not complete the survey questionnaire. These include six youths at the Council for Unity Youth Program at John Dewey High School in Bensonhurst; five youths in a park in Gravesend; five youths in a park in Bensonhurst, and six youths in a pizzeria in Bensonhurst.

The young people surveyed and interviewed came from thirty-seven different neighborhoods and twenty-five different ethnic backgrounds and included large numbers of Italian Americans, African Americans, Puerto Ricans, Jews, and Albanians.

One important aspect of the sample is that it included young people from areas that have figured prominently in the two most important court cases linked to the state of race relations in New York City: Bensonhurst (the home of all six defendants in the racial murder of Yusuf Hawkins) and Schomberg Plaza, a housing project in East Harlem (the home of three defendants in the Central Park jogger trial).

The limitations of the sample lie in its lack of generalizability beyond the groups represented. Although the sample does contain youths from a large number of neighborhoods, their demographic profile is not representative of the entire youth population of New York City. There are also racial and ethnic groups that are underrepresented. For example, there are very few Asians in the sample while Albanians are overrepresented.

The Link between Attitudes and Behavior

The problem of examining the connection between attitudes and behaviors is complex. There are few guidelines in the sociological literature, primarily because the link is a tenuous one. There are several substantive problems that make it difficult to link attitudes to behavior. It is extremely difficult to verify what type of behavior particular people have engaged in. This is especially a problem with criminal and violent activity, which may not be readily admitted by the perpetrators. This is an important problem for this study.

The study was designed to examine factors that contributed to the increase in racial and ethnic conflict and violence among young people in New York City. Originally, the research design did not seek to link the youths' attitudes with their behavior. Instead, I chose to avoid the issue altogether, as most sociologists have done. At this early stage, the intent was to garner data that would allow for an analysis of the general ethnic and racial attitudes of young people in New York City; any direct discussion of actions and activities would be left to the analysis and theory.

The causal link between attitudes and behavior has always been a difficult and tenuous relationship for social scientists to measure. Even if one can measure the attitudes of subjects and also observe their behavior, there is no proven method for establishing causation outside of a laboratory environment. Given these enormous problems, I originally decided that it would be best to avoid trying to establish a link between attitudes and behavior.

Having made this decision, I was surprised to discover that I obtained data that allowed for an examination of the relationship between attitudes and behavior as a result of using a number of varied methods. The focus group interviews generated data on behavior that made it possible to extend the analysis, in the case of some of the subjects, to the relationship between attitudes and behavior. The survey data allowed me to examine the attitudes young people had toward other groups as well as their predisposition toward ethnic or racial violence. The focus group interviews yielded surprisingly frank admissions of participation in racially motivated violence, especially on the part of young white males from southern Brooklyn communities. A comparison of responses to the survey by the individuals who participated in particular focus group interviews allowed for verification of attitudes and reported actions and facilitated the development of a picture of the composition of each group that could be analyzed according to discussions during the interview.

Structural Conditions

This study examines the role of structural conditions in three ways. First, structural conditions in New York City and in the neighborhoods under observation are examined to determine the relationship between key socioeconomic factors that have historically been viewed as the necessary conditions for ethnic and racial conflict in New York City.

Second, statistics about the structural conditions of different neighborhoods are used in the analysis of the survey and interview results. The structural conditions examined include employment rates, crime rates, dropout rates, average income, socioeconomic status, the settlement patterns of ethnic and racial groups in the areas of study, and demographic changes since the mid-1970s in the racial and ethnic content of the residents.

Third, historical research about the development of the ethnic and racial make-up of the neighborhoods studied was used to supply contextual data. Additionally, a short history of the relations between different ethnic and racial groups in New York City was generated in order to provide a context for an analysis of the present situation.

From a personal standpoint, conducting this research evoked a number of emotions in me as the researcher. I was continually struck by the paradox and contradiction of the white youths in southern Brooklyn who "liked" me enough to tell me about how they searched for and attacked people who looked just like me. I always returned, however, to the fact that when I got them alone, these young people seemed to be regular, average youths who mainly wanted to improve their lives.

One interview affected me more than the rest, and it stays with me even now, five years later. I did not include any portions of this part of the interview because the focus of this book is ethnic and racial attitudes and violence. Though there are some similarities between racial violence and antigay violence, there are also many differences. However, the accounts of antigay violence by five youths in a group interview was deeply disturbing. Here is what was said:

> YOUTH 1: We can't talk about this stuff [racial conflict] without talking about gays.
> INTERVIEWER: What about gays?
> YOUTH 1: We don't like them, we hate them.
> INTERVIEWER: Why?
> YOUTH 1: Because they have AIDS and they can give it to you, like if they are a waiter in a restaurant and they bleed on your food and you get AIDS.

INTERVIEWER: So what do you do about it?
YOUTH 1: Me and my friends we go to Manhattan and we beat them up.
INTERVIEWER: Let me get this straight. You live in Brooklyn. You leave Brooklyn and go to Manhattan to beat up gays so they might bleed on you because you're afraid of AIDS.
YOUTH 1: Oh no, we do it safely.
YOUTH 2: Yeah, we use baseball bats and we hit 'em in the knees so they fall on the ground so when we hit 'em in the head they bleed on the ground and not on us.
YOUTH 3: What we do is we chase them into the street and then my friend hits them with his car when they run into the street.

Hearing such testimonies of hatred and violence not only stir difficult emotions but also present serious ethical dilemmas. What should I do about young people who confess to regularly attempting to seriously injure other people? My response was to engage the youths in critical dialogues about attitudes they expressed and actions they described in the interviews. When possible, I would return and conduct workshops on cross-cultural awareness and issues of difference. I also strongly encouraged the schools or youth programs to address issues that emerged in the interviews, such as racial and antigay violence, with youth trainings and workshops designed to confront their ideas and encourage them to think more critically.

I always meticulously separated the process of data gathering from the process of teaching, learning, and consciousness raising. However, I could not leave these youths after the interviews with the idea that I agreed with, condoned, or did not care about their attitudes about other groups and their physical attacks on other people. Having gained their trust and respect, it was a unique opportunity for me to engage them in a dialogue about their attitudes and actions. I believe that, when structured well, the research process itself can be an agent of social change. That was my intention in conducting workshops after the interviews were completed.

One final methodological note: There has been far too little research done on attitudes among young people. Adolescence is a critical period in the formation of individual identity and the development of attitudes. Many social scientists shy away from attitudinal research with the young because they question the validity of their responses. Young people are seen as highly impressionable and more likely to be influenced by the researcher. My observations and experiences revealed that they tend to be more candid and truthful about their racial attitudes than adults when interviewed in groups. The influence of the peer group is far stronger than that of the researcher. In my experience, running workshops on racial awareness and conducting interviews on racial attitudes since the mid-1980s, young people have consistently been more animated, spontaneous, and forthright in their presentation of their ideas about race and racial conflict in U.S. society.

More important, if social science is truly interested in understanding ethnic and racial attitudes and ethnic and racial violence, it is critical to move beyond questions of validity and to take more seriously the ideas and behaviors of the young people in the United States.

Appendix B

New York Community Districts: The Bronx, Brooklyn, Manhattan

The Bronx Community Districts

1   Melrose, Mott Haven, Port Morris

2   Hunts Point, Longwood

3   Morrisania, Crotona Park East

4   Highbridge, Concourse Village

5   University Hts., Fordham, Mt. Hope

6   East Tremont, Belmont

7   Bedford Park, Norwood, Fordham

8   Riverdale, Kingsbridge, Marble Hill

9   Soundview, Parkchester

10   Throgs Nk., Co-op City, Pelham Bay

11   Pelham Pkwy, Morris Pk, Laconia

12   Wakefield, Williamsbridge

Brooklyn Community Districts

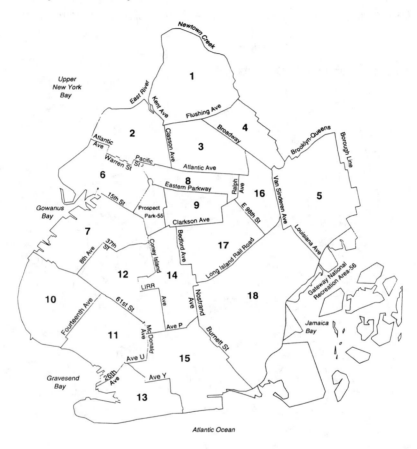

1   Williamsburg, Greenpoint
2   Brooklyn Heights, Fort Greene
3   Bedford-Stuyvesant
4   Bushwick
5   East New York, Starrett City
6   Park Slope, Carroll Gardens
7   Sunset Park, Windsor Terrace
8   Crown Heights North
9   Crown Heights South, Wingate

10   Bay Ridge, Dyker Heights
11   Bensonhurst, Bath Beach
12   Borough Park, Ocean Parkway
13   Coney Island, Brighton Beach
14   Flatbrush, Midwood
15   Sheepshead Bay, Gerritsen Beach
16   Brownsville, Ocean Hill
17   East Flatbush, Rugby, Farragut
18   Canarsie, Flatlands

Manhattan Community Districts

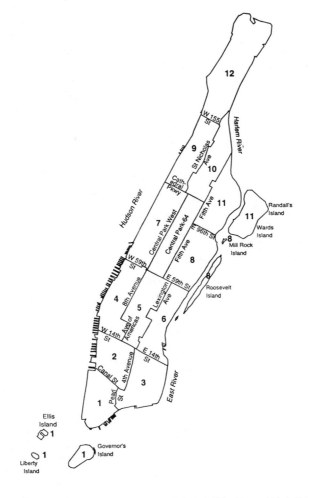

1 Battery Park City, Tribeca
2 Greenwich Village, SoHo
3 Lower East Side, Chinatown
4 Chelsea, Clinton
5 Midtown Business District
6 Stuyvesant Town, Turtle Bay

7 West Side, Upper West Side
8 Upper East Side
9 Manhattanville, Hamilton Hts.
10 Central Harlem
11 East Harlem
12 Washington Heights, Inwood

Notes

Introduction

1. This study uses statistics collected by the New York City Police Department Bias Unit and the New York City Human Rights Commission; these data establish that there has been a dramatic increase in the number of verified bias incidents. It is virtually impossible to verify unconditionally that the increase in the number of verified cases of bias incidents recorded by the Bias Unit and the Human Rights Commission was the result of an actual increase in the number of bias crimes being perpetrated. The increase in the numbers of verified incidents could be the result of an increase in reporting rather than an increase in the number of incidents. There are a number of factors that could affect reporting. Although there is no definitive way to address the "verification" of increased ethnic and racial violence, the evidence strongly suggests that an increase in racially motivated violence has occurred. Interviews with representatives of the police department, the Human Rights Commission, youth program coordinators, schoolteachers, and administrators yielded different interpretations of the meaning of the increase in reported cases of ethnic and racially motivated violence. Although the official opinion of the Bias Unit was that it is impossible to determine whether the increase in bias cases is due to an increase in reporting or an actual increase in the number of attacks, this view was not supported by officials at the Human Rights Commission, who view the data as evidence of increased bias-crime activity. Furthermore, virtually all of the individuals interviewed who worked with youth agreed that there had been an increase in racial tension, conflict, and violence among the youth they worked with. And finally, the study revealed that youth in New York City clearly share their perception.

2. The role of neighborhoods in the genesis and maintenance of negative racial attitudes among individuals can be seen in the organizational pattern and strategy of neighborhoods and political groups that organize around racial issues. The antibusing movement in Boston was ostensibly a movement to stop integration. It was also one of the first grassroots movements outside of white supremacist organizations to trumpet the rights of whites as victims. This was a radical departure from the notion of white privilege and superiority that was the cornerstone of the segregationist movement in the South. The organizational name is instructive: Restore Our Alienated Rights (ROAR). The significance of the antibusing movement in Boston is that it was largely a neighborhood-based movement whose purpose was to prevent the forced integration of Boston's public schools (Formisano, 1991). The language of the movement embraced the most sacrosanct values in U.S. society: individual freedom and individual rights. This linkage of in-

dividual rights to policies opposing government actions to achieve racial equality was a precursor to the development of the neoconservative ideology that gained prominence in academic and policy circles in the 1980s. J. Anthony Lukas's (1985) description of the strategy and ideology of Charlestown residents against busing provides a vivid example of the fusion of racial ideology into a group's identity. Lukas describes how antibusing activists challenged other residents to support a school boycott by invoking neighborhood and ethnic loyalty.

3. Intergroup interaction can be based on a recognition or denial of difference. The differences in these two perspectives can be traced to the values embodied in multiculturalism and assimilationism. Assimilationism is based on the adoption of a dominant culture that negates or denies cultural differences. Multiculturalism is based on an acknowledgment that cultural differences exist and are to be accepted and understood.

4. Each of these neighborhoods has been the site of high-profile incidents that have had an important impact on the racial climate in these communities particularly and in New York City generally.

1. The Neighborhoods

1. Proponents of the theory of invasion and succession describe a "tip point" that surfaces when the percentage of newcomers in the neighborhood surpasses the level of tolerance of the neighborhood's original residents. When this tip point has been reached, the neighborhood is quickly transformed by the rapid movement of old residents out of the neighborhood and their replacement by new residents who are members of a new group (Duncan and Duncan, 1957; Grodzins, 1958).

2. An article in the *Wall Street Journal* "Turf Defenders: The Mood Gets Nasty in City Neighborhood as Racial Tension Rises—Working-Class Bensonhurst, Next to New York Ghetto, Fears Drugs and Crime," 25 July 1988, painted a similar portrait of Bensonhurst.

3. The formation of ethnic and racial identities occurs when groups are confronted with their "difference" and when there is meaning ascribed to that difference. It is only when the racial issue becomes a community concern that racial identity becomes important for whites. According to Gerald Suttles, it is in their "foreign relations" that communities have to settle on an identity and a set of boundaries that oversimplify their reality (Suttles, 1974). The white neighborhoods of southern Brooklyn described in this book are classic examples of what Suttles labeled "defended neighborhoods." Defended neighborhoods are racially and ethnically homogeneous communities in which neighborhood residents organize to prevent the settlement of people from different ethnic and racial backgrounds. Rieder's description of Canarsie in southern Brooklyn provides a picture of a typical defended neighborhood (Rieder, 1985).

4. The term "whites" is used to refer to non-Latino whites.

5. Koch directly benefited from racial tensions in the city and was accused by some African American leaders of polarizing race relations in New York City with, for example, his criticisms of African Americans as "poverty pimps" (Mollenkopf, 1991).

6. I describe Dinkins's election as a deviation rather than a shift in political power and control because of the precarious state of the coalition that brought him into office. Dinkins lost a close election for mayor to Republican Rudolph Giuliani in 1993. Racial tensions and divisions among New York City residents, high rates of crime and violence, and an economic crisis prompted defections among traditionally Democratic white ethnic voters.

7. Bailey and Waldinger (1991) describe a polarization in the labor market for native-born African Americans. African Americans were underrepresented in the manu-

facturing sector and consequently were not as affected by its decline. The period since 1970 has been one of improvement in the labor market position of employed African Americans. Yet those African Americans who are not in the labor force have experienced a sharp decline in the structure of employment opportunity. This trend has had serious consequences for neighborhoods, like East Harlem, that have disproportionately high levels of poverty and unemployment. The public sector has been the most important arena of employment opportunity for African Americans in New York City, accounting for over one-third of the jobs held by African Americans in 1980. Government deficits and budget cuts have worsened the prospects for African American employment.

2. The Youth

1. More than any time before, inner-city children must deal with a myriad of barriers and hurdles. In New York City, they face an urban area in the process of severe decay. Though drugs have always been a temptation, they are now more prevalent, stronger, and more addictive than ever before. The violence that inner-city children face has increased since the early 1980s as violent crimes and especially homicide have increased. Inner-city violence has increased in urban areas across the nation. Among young people between fifteen and twenty-four years of age, homicide is the second leading cause of death, surpassed only by unintentional injuries (CDC, 1991). Homicide has increased 100 percent overall since 1960 and 300 percent for young black men. In a national survey in 1987, one of every thirty-six tenth-grade boys said they had carried a handgun to school in the past year, one in every hundred said they brought that gun to school every day, and in one U.S. city, one out of every fifteen eleventh-grade boys has carried a handgun to school at some point (Callahan and Rivara, 1992). In 1990, 2,861 children aged nineteen and under were murdered with guns, an increase of 114 percent since 1985 (Fingerhut, 1993). Another national survey reported that 15 percent of inner-city high school students said they were scared at school almost all of the time (Sheley, McGee, and Wright, 1992). From 1986 to 1990, 10,052 children between the ages of five and nineteen were murdered with guns in the United States. Issues of sex and sexuality have always been difficult ones for adolescents, but they have now become more intimidating and potentially more dangerous with the onset of the AIDS epidemic.

2. "Avenue T Boys" is a pseudonym, as are all of the names of the young people in this book.

3. Central Park East is an innovative secondary school with a diverse student population.

4. The Schomberg Plaza Youth Program is a project staffed and operated by the Manhattan Valley Youth Program, which provides youth services to young people from Harlem and East Harlem. The services offered by the center include educational and vocational counseling and referral, tutoring, crisis intervention, youth leadership sessions, cultural and recreational activities, and workshops on topics relevant to the community. The Manhattan Valley Youth Program has received recognition as one of New York City's most effective and innovative youth programs. The Schomberg Plaza Youth Program was one of very few youth programs that were available in East Harlem. A police officer in the Third Precinct had tried to put together a recreational program for the young people at each of the housing projects in lower East Harlem. His efforts were extraordinary, but he received little support from the city or the police department and was eventually reassigned to a street beat, which prevented him from working with the youth of the community.

5. "Rushin'" was the term used by these young people for the sprees of random

violence that had come to be known as "wilding" in the press. The youths said they had never heard the term "wilding" until it appeared in the media.

6. The Albanians who did drop out hung out just outside the school on the corner across the street. Those who remained in school all knew the dropouts who came from their communities. With few exceptions, they did not hang out together. However, whenever there was a racial dispute at the school, both groups participated in the conflict.

7. This was not true of all the Albanian youth. A number of the Albanian young people who had dropped out of school and who hung out across the street from the school used drugs, and a few dealt drugs. These young people were the real outcasts in the Albanian community. Their situation and lifestyle were very similar to those of the Avenue T Boys.

8. There were differences from family to family in the application of this practice. Among the second-generation Albanian families, there was a moderation of the practice by some fathers. Some would consult the rest of the family, and some even the prospective bride about the marriage proposal. The young people speculated that over time this custom would gradually be relaxed as the community became more and more assimilated.

9. This Canon of Albanian Law was described in a 22 April 1990 article in the *New York Times* entitled "Blood Feuds Boil in Albania." The article examined feuds that continued in ethnic Albania as a result of the strictures of this canon of law.

3. Youth Attitudes

1. This scene is not unique to Christopher Columbus High School. Columbus is, however, one of the more diverse schools in New York City.

2. I contacted all fifty-four comprehensive high schools in New York City to request permission to survey and interview students at the school. I followed up with phone calls.

3. This view was reflected in the Avenue T Boys' responses to the survey question asking them to choose one word to describe blacks. Fifty-eight percent chose "violent" as their word to describe blacks, and another 32 percent chose "pushy."

4. An attempt was made on Sharpton's life on 12 January 1991 as he prepared to lead the forty-eighth march through Bensonhurst to protest the sentencing of two defendants in the Hawkins case to time served.

5. The marches through Bensonhurst led by Sharpton were confronted by jeering crowds of neighborhood residents, and a number of Bensonhurst young people held up watermelons to mock the predominantly black marchers.

6. Their statements in the interviews were corroborated by the survey data: Although the overwhelming majority (80 percent) thought that people have the right to live wherever they choose, 51 percent agreed with the statement "It is better to have people of the same race living in the same neighborhoods" and disagreed with the statement "It is better to have mixed neighborhoods with people of different racial and ethnic backgrounds." Thirty-eight percent agreed that whites, blacks, Asians, and Latinos should stay in their own neighborhoods. Fifteen percent agreed that people have a right to physically prevent those who are different from them from coming into their neighborhoods.

7. In the last twenty years, neoconservative ideology has emerged as a strong current in public policy, academia, and politics (Omi and Winant, 1986). Public positions taken by the Reagan and Bush administrations on these issues, the emergence of the theories of neoconservative scholars such as Thomas Sowell (1990), Charles Murray (1984), and Nathan Glazer (1975), the imagery and language of the 1988 Bush presidential campaign, and the positions of politicians such as Jesse Helms and David Duke all

lend credence to these white youths' sense of victimization and provide a target for their anger, frustration, and economic anxieties.

8. Michael Levin is a professor of philosophy at the City University of New York. In the spring of 1990, he became the center of controversy when he gave several lectures and interviews in which he stated that whites have a justifiable fear of young black males because they have a higher propensity to be violent. Among other measures, Levin advocated reserving specific subway cars for young black males—a position that resonated deeply with the youths involved in this study.

9. Surprisingly, in response to a survey question that asked them to rate their feelings about twenty-three different ethnic groups, blacks were not rated significantly lower than most of the groups on the survey and eleven out of the twenty-three groups listed were rated lower than blacks.

10. Their average rating of all ethnic groups was almost a point and a half higher than the ratings of at-risk youths. Blacks received a significantly higher rating by the in-school white youths. Only 20 percent of the in-school white youths chose the word "violent" to describe blacks, and 38 percent disagreed with the statement: "It is better to have mixed neighborhoods with people of different racial and ethnic backgrounds."

11. Sheepshead Bay youths rated blacks over two points higher than did youths from Bensonhurst or Canarsie. There is a significant relationship between neighborhood and attitudes toward blacks. This indicates that neighborhood residence is an important factor in the development of ethnic and racial attitudes.

12. With the exception of Koreans, various white ethnic groups were rated lowest by the Schomberg Plaza youths. Although their rating of Salvadorans and Vietnamese was also low, the number of youths who had no opinion of these groups is high in contrast to their low ratings of Jews, Italians, Irish, and Koreans. It is significant that their lowest ratings were given to groups with whom they have had contact in their community: Jews, Koreans, and Italians.

13. Bernard Goetz became an overnight hero when he shot four black youths who he claimed were trying to rob him in a subway car. Goetz initially received support from many people including Mayor Ed Koch and U.S. Senator Alphonse D'Amato. In a controversial verdict, Goetz was acquitted of all charges except possession of an unlicensed handgun. Larry Davis is an African American who was apprehended by the police after a shoot-out with the police. Davis claimed he had evidence of police collusion with drug dealers in the Forty-Fourth Precinct and that the police were trying to silence him.

14. Jews, Italians, and Koreans were rated the lowest of all ethnic groups by these East Harlem youths.

15. The boycott began in December 1989 when a Haitian woman charged that the owners of the store had beaten her and accused her of stealing. When the police did not arrest the accused store owner, the boycott was called by the December 12th coalition, a small, militant black community organization that is best known for organizing the Day of Rage demonstration that blocked the Brooklyn Bridge in the wake of the Bensonhurst murder. The boycott leaders charged that the store owners had a history of disrespect for black shoppers.

16. Of all Asians, Koreans were rated the lowest and received the second-lowest rating overall. Of the Asian groups listed, only the rating for the Vietnamese approached that of the Koreans, with a large number of youths reporting no opinion.

17. For a full explication of internal colonialism theory, see Carmichael and Hamilton, 1967 and Blauner, 1972.

18. Rap music has quickly developed into an influential medium of expression for inner-city blacks and a source of political education for masses of young blacks. The

music indicates a rising racial and political awareness among black youths and may well presage increased militancy and confrontation in the black community.

19. In addition, Central Park East youths rated different ethnic groups far more evenly than did the Schomberg Plaza youths. Jews, who were rated lowest by Schomberg Plaza youths, were the fourth-highest rated group, after blacks, Jamaicans, and Chinese.

20. Among Central Park East students, Koreans were not rated significantly lower than other ethnic groups; Chinese and Japanese were among those groups rated highest.

21. In spite of the conflicts in their neighborhoods, Dominicans were rated highly by Puerto Rican youths at Central Park East Secondary School, behind only Puerto Ricans, Italians, blacks, and Salvadorans.

22. The responses on the surveys supported these claims, with Puerto Ricans receiving the third-highest rating by black youths. As a group, Latinos gave the highest average ratings to all groups, followed by blacks, Asians (though the number of Asians in the sample was extremely low), and whites. At each site where Latinos were part of the sample, they exhibited the most tolerant attitudes.

23. For an extended discussion of ethnic and racial dynamics affecting Puerto Ricans in the United States, see Rodriguez, 1989.

24. The position of Puerto Ricans as a swing group was reflected in the attitudes they had toward other groups. Latino youths, as a group, gave their second-highest rating to Italians, after Puerto Ricans, with blacks receiving the third-highest rating.

25. The one conspicuous difference was in their rating of Jews, which was almost 3 points lower than the average rating of Jews by all white youth in the sample. Perhaps this can be accounted for by the fact that 70 percent of the Albanians were Muslim.

26. The survey responses of Albanians confirmed their negative attitudes toward blacks in a remarkably consistent fashion. Four of the five groups whom Albanian youths rated lowest on the survey were of African descent: blacks, Jamaicans, Dominicans, and Haitians.

27. On the survey, Puerto Ricans were rated low along with other Latino ethnic groups.

28. Eighteen percent of the Albanian youths reported that they had a close black or Latino friend, and one also had a close Asian friend.

29. The rating of 9.62 received by Italians was almost 4 points higher than that received by any other group except Albanians, who received a rating of 10.

30. The ALERT group was formed in 1989 when a number of students who had participated in youth leadership training workshops run by the Panel of Americans, Inc., decided to form an ongoing group organized to deal with issues of ethnic and racial differences and tensions within their school. The Panel of Americans, Inc., is a nonprofit organization that conducts seminars and workshops in human relations training. The panel specializes in cross-cultural awareness and leadership training of youth.

31. Albanians received a rating from the ALERT youths that was more than 1 point lower than the rating of the next lowest group and more than 2 points lower than the average rating for all groups.

32. The ALERT youths gave an average rating of 6. 695 to all ethnic groups. The Albanian youths gave an average rating of 4. 01.

4. Racial Violence

1. The Avenue T Boys were not the only youths who participated in the practice of "going on missions." The description of missions was repeated over and over by youths from other southern Brooklyn neighborhoods.

2. In the description of "missions" by other youths, the list of preferred victims

varied in its order, with the exception of blacks, who were always at the top of the list. This exchange between young men from Gravesend is an example:

BENNIE: Every weekend, me and him and a group of others would go out and get racial with—against Mexicans.

MARK: It wasn't really racial . . .

BENNIE: Oh, yea, we were racial. All right, would you call this racial? Every Mexican we see, no matter what they were doing, if they weren't doing nothing, we'd still beat 'em up.

3. During the trial, prosecutors lamented that "Bensonhurst amnesia" was a significant impediment to the state's attempts to convict the participants in the attack on Yusuf Hawkins.

4. On the survey, all of the African American youths agreed that people have a right to live wherever they choose and disagreed with the statement that "whites, blacks, Latinos and Asians should stay in their own neighborhoods." Eighty percent agreed that it is better to have mixed neighborhoods, and 10 percent of the Schomberg Plaza youths felt that people have a right to physically prevent people who are different from them from coming into their neighborhoods.

5. It is important to note the differences between Harlem and other highly isolated black communities such as parts of Bedford-Stuyvesant, East New York, Brownsville, and parts of the Bronx. Since East Harlem borders the Upper East Side of Manhattan and Central Park, there are large numbers of outsiders who come through the neighborhood. Also, there are no working-class white communities in close proximity to East Harlem such as those that are the source of tension and competition in Brooklyn. There are no bordering communities with working-class white youths who hang out on the street and defend their turf such as we have seen in southern Brooklyn. There are poor and working-class communities of Latinos and West Indian blacks, but the youths reported that these were not sources of significant tension within their neighborhood.

6. It must be pointed out that the Albanians represent a distinct minority at Christopher Columbus High School. Their claims of running the school are supported by the accounts of teachers and other students, but their influence is certainly on the wane.

7. I returned to the neighborhood after the 1992 attack on two African American youths. I found no evidence that these attacks were a part of any pattern of regular activity.

8. The Council for Unity is an organization at John Dewey High School that was developed by Robert DeSenna. The council provides a multicultural, multiethnic peer group for youths who attend the school. The council promotes positive racial and ethnic identity and awareness through workshops and programs that the youths participate in. There are types of rites of passage, including an oath to the council and induction ceremonies. The organization also tries to promote multicultural awareness throughout the school and surrounding communities.

9. It is important to note that programs and organizations do exist in these communities that are attempting to deal with the problems outlined here. The Sixty-First Precinct Youth Dares Program and the Council for Unity at John Dewey are two such organizations doing excellent work with these youths. Unfortunately, funds for youth programs and recreation centers that provide young people with alternatives to the street have been slashed since the late 1970s, and that trend continues. The cut in youth recreation centers and programs may well have contributed to the rise in bias violence in the late 1980s.

5. Conclusion

1. Both the Schomberg Plaza Youth Project and the Sixty-First Precinct Youth Program also worked with the youths in their programs to increase their economic opportunities and to increase their cross-cultural awareness. At each of the high schools where I observed and interviewed youths, Central Park East Secondary School, Christopher Columbus High School, and Sheepshead Bay High School, the principals were employing various strategies and methods to reduce ethnic and racial conflict and to encourage tolerance.

2. This is an example in practice of what Chandra Mohanty defines as difference: "Difference cannot be formulated as negotiation among culturally diverse groups against a backdrop of presumed cultural homogeneity. Difference is the recognition that knowledges are forged in histories that are riven with differentially constituted relations of power; that is, knowledges, subjectivities, and social practices are forged within asymmetrical and incommensurate cultural spheres" (Mohanty, 1989–1990, p. 181).

Appendix A: Methodological Notes

1. This study is using the definition of attitudes outlined by Schuman, Steeh, and Bobo in *Racial Attitudes in America*. Attitudes are defined as "positive or negative responses toward some object, whether that object be another individual, a group, a policy, or whatever" (1985, p. 43).

2. The study was conducted jointly by the New York State Martin Luther King, Jr., Institute for Nonviolence, the New York City Commission on Human Rights, the New York City Board of Education, and the research firm the Michael Rowan Group, Inc.

3. Most studies either use the data or the questions from instruments developed by the three major survey organizations: Gallup, the National Opinion Research Center (NORC), and the Institute for Social Research (ISR).

4. The entire original survey that was developed for this study was constructed independently of any other instrument. The "Study of New York City High School Students and Educational Staff on Prejudice and Race Relations" was developed and conducted in October 1989. Since it contained many similar variables, questions from that study's survey instrument were adopted for this study to allow for a comparison of the results of both studies at a later date.

5. The survey was translated into Korean, Chinese, and Spanish in case any of the participants in the study were not proficient in English. The translated versions were never used.

6. The "Study of New York City High School Students and Educational Staff on Prejudice and Race Relations" was not well received. There were complaints from students, teachers, and parents about the manner in which it had been conducted. Many principals were wary of allowing students to participate in another study of ethnic and racial attitudes.

Bibliography

Abrams, C. 1966. "The Housing Problem and the Negro." In T. Parsons and K. Clark, eds., *The Negro American*. Boston: Houghton Mifflin.

Adorno, T. W., E. Frenkel-Brunswik, D. J. Levinson, and R. N. Sanford. 1950. *The Authoritarian Personality*. New York: Harper and Row.

Ajzen, I., and M. Fishbein. 1980. *Understanding Attitudes and Predicting Social Behavior*. Englewood Cliffs, N. J.: Prentice-Hall.

Alba, R., and M. Chamlin. 1983. "A Preliminary Examination of Ethnic Identification among Whites." *Annual Sociological Review* 48: 240–47.

Allport, G. 1954. *The Nature of Prejudice*. Cambridge, Mass.: Addison-Wesley.

Althusser, L. 1971. *Lenin and Philosophy*. London: New Left Books.

———. 1977. *For Marx*. London: New Left Books.

Amir, Y. 1976. "The Role of Contact in Change of Prejudice and Ethnic Relations." In P. Katz, ed., *Towards the Elimination of Racism*. New York: Pergamon Press.

Apostle, R., C. Glock, T. Piaza, and M. Suelzle. 1983. *The Anatomy of Racial Attitudes*. Berkeley: University of California Press.

Ashmore, R. D., and F. K. De Baca. 1976. "Psychological Approaches to Understanding Group Conflicts." In P. Katz, ed., *Towards the Elimination of Racism*. New York: Pergamon Press.

Ashmore, R., and J. McConohay. 1975. *Psychology and America's Urban Dilemmas*. New York: McGraw Hill.

Bailey, T., and R. Waldinger. 1991. "The Changing Ethnic/Racial Division of Labor." In J. Mollenkopf and M. Castells, eds., *Dual City: Restructuring New York*. New York: Russell Sage Foundation.

Banton, M. 1983. *Racial and Ethnic Competition*. Cambridge, Eng.: Cambridge University Press.

———. 1987. *Racial Theories*. Cambridge, Eng.: Cambridge University Press.

Barth, F., ed. 1969. *Ethnic Group and Boundaries: The Social Organization of Cultural Difference*. Boston: Little, Brown.

Bayor, R. 1988. *Neighbors in Conflict: The Irish, Germans, and Italians of New York City, 1929–1941*. Urbana and Chicago: University of Illinois Press.

Bell, D. 1975. "Ethnicity and Social Change." In N. Glazer and D. Moynihan, eds., *Ethnicity: Theory and Experience*. Cambridge, Mass.: Harvard University Press.

Bellenger, D., K. Bernhardt, and J. Goldstucker. 1976. "Qualitative Research Techniques: Focus Group Interviews." In D. Bellenger, K. Bernhardt, and J. Goldstucker, eds., *Qualitative Research in Marketing*. Chicago: American Marketing Association.

Bethlehem, D. W. 1985. *A Social Psychology of Prejudice*. New York: St. Martin's.
Blalock, H., Jr. 1967. *Toward a Theory of Minority-Majority Relations*. New York: Capricorn Books.
Blauner, R. 1972. *Racial Oppression in America*. New York: Harper and Row.
Bloch, H. 1969. *Circle of Discrimination: An Economic and Social Study of the Black Man in New York*. New York: New York University Press.
Blumer, H. 1958. "Race Prejudice as a Sense of Group Position." *Pacific Sociological Review* 1: 3–7.
Bobo, L. 1983. "Whites' Opposition to Busing: Symbolic Racism or Realistic Group Conflict?" *Journal of Personality and Social Psychology* 45: 1196–1210.
Bonacich, E. 1972. "A Theory of Ethnic Antagonism: The Split Labor Market." *American Sociological Review* 37: 547–59.
———. 1973. "A Theory of Middleman Minorities." *American Sociological Review* 38: 583–94.
———. 1980. "Class Approaches to Ethnicity and Race." *Insurgent Sociologist* 10: 9–23.
Bonacich, E., and J. Modell. 1980. *The Economic Basis for Ethnic Solidarity: Small Business in the Japanese American Community*. Berkeley: University of California Press.
Burgess, E. 1928. "Residential Segregation in American Cities." *Annals of the American Academy of Political and Social Science*, publication no. 2180: 1–11.
Callahan, C., and F. Rivara. 1992. "Urban High School Youth and Handguns." *Journal of the American Medical Association* 267: 3038–41.
Carmichael, S., and C. Hamilton. 1967. *Black Power: The Politics of Liberation in America*. New York: Vintage Books.
Centers for Disease Control (CDC). 1991. *Homicide Surveillance: High Risk Racial and Ethnic Groups. Blacks and Hispanics, 1973–1983*. Atlanta, Ga.: Centers for Disease Control.
Clark, K. 1965. *Dark Ghetto: Dilemmas of Social Power*. New York: Harper and Row.
Coward, R., and J. Elllis. 1977. *Language and Materialism*. London:Routledge.
Cox, O. 1948. *Caste, Class, and Race: A Study in Social Dynamics*. New York: Modern Reader Paperbacks.
Drennan, M. 1991. "The Decline and Rise of the New York Economy." In J. Mollenkopf and M. Castells, eds., *Dual City: Restructuring New York*. New York: Russell Sage Foundation.
Duncan, O., and B. Duncan. 1957. *The Negro Population of Chicago: A Study of Residential Succession*. Chicago: University of Chicago Press.
Edgerton, R. 1973. *Deviant Behavior and Cultural Theory*. Addison-Wesley Module in Anthropology, no. 37. Reading, Mass.: Addison-Wesley.
Erikson, E. 1963. *Childhood and Society*. New York: Norton.
———. 1968. *Identity, Youth, and Crisis*. New York: Norton.
Fanon, F. 1963. *The Wretched of the Earth*. New York: Grove Press.
Feagin, J. 1989. *Racial and Ethnic Relations*. Englewood Cliffs, N.J.: Prentice-Hall.
Ford, J. 1936. *Slums and Housing*. Cambridge, Mass.: Harvard University Press.
Formisano, R. 1991. *Boston against Busing: Race, Class, and Ethnicity in the 1960s and 1970s*. Chapel Hill: University of North Carolina Press.
Frazier, E. F. 1957. *Race and Culture Contacts in the Modern World*. New York: Knopf.
———. 1968. *On Race Relations*. Chicago: University of Chicago Press.
Fredrickson, G. 1988. *The Arrogance of Race*. Middletown, Conn.: Wesleyan University Press.

Gaertner, S. L., and J. Dovidio, eds. 1986. *Prejudice, Discrimination, and Racism: Theory and Research.* New York: Academic Press.

Giles, M., and A. Evans. 1984. "External Threat, Perceived Threat, and Group Identity." *Social Science Quarterly* 65: 50–66.

Giroux, H., and P. McLaren. 1994. *Between Borders: Pedagogy and the Politics of Cultural Studies.* New York: Routledge.

Giroux, H. 1994. Introduction to H. Giroux and P. McLaren, eds., *Between Borders: Pedagogy and the Politics of Cultural Studies.* New York: Routledge.

Glazer, N. 1975. *Affirmative Discrimination.* New York: Basic Books.

———. 1983. *Ethnic Dilemmas, 1964–1982.* Cambridge, Mass.: Harvard University Press.

———. 1988. *The New Immigration.* San Diego, Calif.: San Diego State University Press.

Glazer, N., and D. Moynihan. 1963. *Beyond the Melting Pot.* Cambridge, Mass.: MIT Press.

———. 1975. Introduction to N. Glazer and D. Moynihan, eds., *Ethnicity: Theory and Experience.* Cambridge, Mass.: Harvard University Press.

Goffman, I. 1959. *The Presentation of Self in Everyday Life.* New York: Doubleday.

Gordon, M. 1964. *Assimilation in American Life: The Role of Race, Religion, and National Origins.* New York: Oxford University Press.

———. 1975. "Toward a General Theory of Racial and Ethnic Group Relations." In N. Glazer and D. Moynihan, eds., *Ethnicity: Theory and Experience.* Cambridge, Mass.: Harvard University Press.

Grodzins, M. 1958. *The Metropolitan Area as a Racial Problem.* Pittsburgh, Pa.: University of Pittsburgh Press.

Hall, S. 1980. "Race, Articulation, and Societies Structured in Dominance." In UNESCO, *Sociological Theories: Race and Colonialism.* Paris: UNESCO.

———. 1991. "Ethnicity: Identity and Difference." *Radical America* 23(4): 9–20.

Handlin, O. 1959. *The Newcomers: Negroes and Puerto Ricans in a Changing Metropolis.* Cambridge, Mass.: Harvard University Press.

Harris, R. 1991. "The Geography of Employment and Residence in New York since 1950." In J. Mollenkopf and M. Castells, eds., *Dual City: Restructuring New York.* New York: Russell Sage Foundation.

Hatchett, S., and H. Schuman. 1975–1976. "White Respondents and Race-of-Interviewer Effects." *Public Opinion Quarterly* 39: 523–28.

Jaynes, G., and R. Williams, eds. 1989. *A Common Destiny: Blacks and American Society.* Washington, D.C.: National Academy Press.

Katz, P., ed. 1976. *Towards the Elimination of Racism.* New York: Pergamon Press.

Katznelson, I. 1981. *City Trenches: Urban Politics and the Patterning of Class in the United States.* Chicago: University of Chicago Press.

Kilson, M. 1975. "Blacks and Neo-Ethnicity in American Life. " In N. Glazer and D. Moynihan, eds., *Ethnicity: Theory and Experience.* Cambridge, Mass.: Harvard University Press.

Kim, I. 1981. *New Urban Immigrants: The Korean Community in New York.* Princeton, N.J.: Princeton University Press.

Kinder, D. 1986. "The Continuing American Dilemma: White Resistance to Racial Change Forty Years after Myrdal." *Journal of Social Issues* 42: 151–71.

Kinder, D., and D. Sears. 1981. "Prejudice and Politics: Symbolic Racism versus Racial Threats to the Good Life." *Journal of Personality and Social Psychology* 40: 414–31.

Kluegal, J., and E. R. Smith. 1983. "Affirmative Action Attitudes: Effects of Self-Interest, Racial Affect, and Stratification Beliefs on Whites' Views." *Social Forces* 61: 797–824.

———. 1986. *Beliefs about Inequality: Americans' Beliefs of What Is and What Ought to Be*. Chicago: Adeline Press.

Kovel, J. 1970. *White Racism: A Psychohistory*. New York: Pantheon Books.

Levy, S. 1979. "Focus Group Interviewing." In J. Higginbotham and K. Cox, eds., *Focus Group Interviews: A Reader*. Chicago: American Marketing Association.

Lauren, P. 1988. *Power and Prejudice*. Boulder, Colo.: Westview Press.

Levine, R. A., and D. T. Campbell. 1972. *Ethnocentrism: Theories of Conflict, Ethnic Attitudes, and Group Behavior*. New York: Wiley.

Lieberson, S. 1980. *A Piece of the Pie: Blacks and White Immigrants since 1880*. Berkeley: University of California Press.

———. 1988. *From Many Strands: Ethnic and Racial Groups in Contemporary America*. New York: Russell Sage Foundation.

Lincoln, C. 1984. *Race, Religion, and the Continuing American Dilemma*. New York: Hill and Wang.

Lukas, J. A. 1985. *Common Ground: A Turbulent Decade in the Lives of Three American Families*. New York: Knopf.

MacLeod, J. 1987. *Ain't No Making It*. Boulder, Colo.: Westview Press.

Mayor's Advisory Council on Community Relations. 1989. *Final Report*.

McConohay, J. 1982. "Self-Interest versus Racial Attitudes as Correlates of Anti-Busing Attitudes in Louisville: Is It the Buses or the Blacks?" *Journal of Politics* 44: 692–720.

———. 1986. "Modern Racism, Ambivalence, and the Modern Racism Scale. " In J. Dovidio and S. Gaertner, eds., *Prejudice, Discrimination, and Racism*. Orlando, Fla.: Academic Press.

McConohay, J., B. Hardee, and V. Batts. 1981. "Has Racism Declined in America?" *Journal of Conflict Resolution* 25: 563–79.

McConohay, J., and J. Hough. 1976. "Symbolic Racism." *Journal of Social Issues* 32: 23–45.

McLendon, M. J. 1985. "Racism, Rational Choice, and White Opposition to Racial Change: A Case Study of Busing." *Public Opinion Quarterly* 49: 214–33.

Miles, R. 1989. *Racism*. London: Routledge.

Miller, W. B. 1969. "Lower Class Culture as a Generating Milieu of Gang Delinquency." *Journal of Social Issues* 14: 5–19.

Mohanty, C. 1989–1990. "On Race and Voice: Challenges for Liberal Education in the 1990s." *Cultural Critique* 19: 179–208.

Mollenkopf, J. 1991. "Political Inequality. " In J. Mollenkopf and M. Castells, eds., *Dual City: Restructuring New York*. New York: Russell Sage Foundation.

Mollenkopf, J., and M. Castells. 1991. Introduction to J. Mollenkopf and M. Castells, eds., *Dual City: Restructuring New York*. New York: Russell Sage Foundation.

Montejano, D. 1987. *Anglos and Mexicans in the Making of Texas, 1836–1986*. Austin: University of Texas Press.

Morgan, D. 1988. *Focus Groups as Qualitative Research*. Beverly Hills, Calif.: Sage Publications.

———. 1996. "Focus Groups." *Annual Review of Sociology* 22: 129–52.

Murray, C. 1984. *Losing Ground: American Social Policy, 1950–1980*. New York: Basic Books.

Myrdal, G. 1944. *An American Dilemma*. New York: Harper and Row.

New York City Board of Education. 1984. Office of Student Information Services. *Annual Pupil Ethnic Census, 1960–1983*.

———. 1989. *Annual Report of the Office of Research, Evaluation, and Assessment*.

New York City Department of City Planning. 1985. Population Division and Office of Immigrant Affairs. Unpublished, untitled report.

———. 1993. *Socioeconomic Profiles: A Portrait of New York City's Community Districts from the 1980 and 1990 Censuses of Population and Housing*. New York: New York City Department of City Planning.

New York State Department of Commerce. 1985. *Business Trends in New York State*.

New York State Martin Luther King, Jr., Institute for Nonviolence. 1990. "A Study of New York City High School Students and Educational Staff on Prejudice and Race Relations." Unpublished document.

Olzak, S. 1986. "A Competition Model for Collective Action in American Cities." In S. Olzak and J. Nagel, eds., *Comparative Ethnic Relations*. Orlando, Fla.: Academic Press.

———. 1993. *The Dynamics of Ethnic Competition and Conflict*. Stanford, Calif.: Stanford University Press.

Olzak, S., and J. Nagel, eds., 1986. *Comparative Ethnic Relations*. Orlando, Fla.: Academic Press.

Omi, M., and H. Winant. 1986. *Racial Formation in the United States: From the 1960s to the 1980s*. New York: Routledge and Kegan Paul.

Park, R. 1950. *Race and Culture*. Glencoe, Ill.: Free Press.

Park, R., and E. Burgess. 1921. *Introduction to the Science of Sociology*. Chicago: University of Chicago Press.

Pettigrew, T. 1958. "Personality and Sociocultural Factors in Intergroup Attitudes: A Cross-National Comparison." *Journal of Conflict Resolution* 2: 29–42.

———. 1985. "New Black-White Patterns: How Best to Conceptualize Them?" *Annual Review of Sociology* 11: 329–46.

Pettigrew, T., and D. Alston. 1988. *Tom Bradley's Campaign for Governor: The Dilemmas of Race and Political Strategies*. Washington, D.C.: Joint Center for Political Studies.

Pinderhughes, C. 1982. "Paired Differential Bonding in Biological, Psychological, and Social Systems." *The American Journal of Social Psychiatry* 2 (3): 5–14.

Pinderhughes, E. 1989. *Understanding, Race, Ethnicity, and Power: The Key to Efficacy in Clinical Practices*. New York: Free Press.

Porter, J. 1971. *Black Child, White Child: The Development of Racial Attitudes*. Cambridge, Mass.: Harvard University Press.

Report of the National Advisory Commission on Civil Disorders. 1968. New York: Bantam Books.

Rex, J. 1970. *Race Relations in Sociological Theory*. New York: Schocken Books.

———. 1981. *Unemployment and Racial Conflict in the Inner City*. Birmingham, West Midlands, Eng.: S.S.R.C. Research Unit on Ethnic Relations, University of Aston in Birmingham.

———. 1986. *Theories of Race and Ethnic Relations*. Cambridge, Eng.: Cambridge University Press.

Rieder, J. 1985. *Canarsie: The Jews and Italians of Brooklyn against Liberalism*. Cambridge, Mass. : Harvard University Press.

Rodriguez, C. 1989. *Puerto Ricans: Born in the U.S.A.* Boston: Unwin Hyman.

Rosenwaike, I. 1972. *Population History of New York City*. Syracuse, N.Y.: Syracuse University Press.

Schuman, H., C. Steeh, and L. Bobo. 1985. *Racial Attitudes in America*. Cambridge, Mass.: Harvard University Press.

Scott, E. 1983. *Violence against Blacks in the United States, 1979–1981*. Washington, D.C.: Mental Health Research and Development Center, Institute for Urban Affairs and Research, Howard University.

Sears, D., C. Hensler, and L. Speer. 1979. "Whites' Opposition to Busing: Self Interest or Symbolic Politics?" *American Political Science Review* 73: 369–84.

Sears, D., and D. Kinder. 1971. "Racial Tensions and Voting in Los Angeles." In W. Hirsch, ed., *Viability and Prospects for Metropolitan Leadership*. New York: Praeger.

Sears, D., R. Lau, T. Tyler, and H. Allen. 1980. "Self-Interest or Symbolic Politics in Policy Attitudes and Presidential Voting." *American Political Science Review* 74: 670–84.

Sears, D., and J. McConohay. 1973. *The Politics of Violence: The New Urban Blacks and the Watts Riot*. Boston: Houghton Mifflin.

Sheatsley, P. 1966. "White Attitudes Toward the Negro." *Daedalus* 95: 217–38.

Sheley, J., Z. McGee, and J. Wright. 1992. "Gun-Related Violence in and around Inner City Schools." *American Journal of Diseases of Children* 146(6)(June): 677–82.

Silver, B. 1973. "Social Mobility and Intergroup Antagonism." *Journal of Conflict Resolution* 1: 607–14.

Simpson, G. 1972. *Racial and Cultural Minorities*. New York: Harper and Row.

Smith, A. W. 1981. "Racial Tolerance as a Function of Group Position." *American Sociological Review* 46: 558–73.

Smith, T. W., and P. Sheatsley. 1984. "American Attitudes Toward Race Relations." *Public Opinion* 7: 50–53.

Solomos, J. 1988. *Black Youth, Racism, and the State*. Cambridge, Eng.: Cambridge University Press.

Sowell, T. 1981. *Ethnic America*. New York: Basic Books.

———. 1990. *Preferential Policies*. New York: Morrow.

Spear, A. 1971. "The Origins of the Urban Ghetto, 1870–1915." In N. Huggins et al., eds., *Key Issues in the Afro-American Experience*. New York: Harcourt Brace Jovanovich.

Stegman, M. 1988. *Housing and Vacancy Report: New York City, 1987*. New York: Department of Housing Preservation and Development, City of New York.

Steinberg, S. 1981. *The Ethnic Myth*. New York: Atheneum.

Sullivan, M. 1989. *Getting Paid: Youth Crime and Work in the Inner City*. Ithaca, N.Y.: Cornell University Press.

———. 1991. "Crime and the Social Fabric." In J. Mollenkopf and M. Castells, eds., *Dual City: Restructuring New York*. New York: Russell Sage Foundation.

Suttles, G. 1974. *The Social Construction of Communities*. Chicago: University of Chicago Press.

Taylor, D., P. Sheatsley, and A. Greeley. 1978. "Attitudes Toward Racial Integration." *Scientific American* 238: 42–49.

Turner, J., and E. Bonacich. 1980. "Towards a Composite Theory of Middleman Minorities." *Ethnicity* 7, 144–58.

U.S. Commission on Civil Rights. 1983. *Intimidation and Violence*. Washington, D.C.: Commission on Civil Rights.

U.S. Department of Labor, Bureau of Labor Statistics. 1986. *Current Population Survey*. Washington, D.C.: Government Printing Office.

Van den Berghe, P. 1978. *Race and Racism*. New York: Wiley.

————. 1987. *The Ethnic Phenomenon.* New York: Praeger.

Vander Zanden, J. 1983. *American Minority Relations.* New York: Knopf.

Vigil, J. D. 1988. *Barrio Gangs: Street Life and Identity in Southern California.* Austin: University of Texas Press.

Waters, M. 1990. *Ethnic Options: Choosing Identities in America.* Berkeley and Los Angeles: University of California Press.

Weatherell, M., and J. Potter. 1992. *Mapping the Discourse of Racism: Discourse and the Legitimation of Exploitation.* New York: Columbia University Press.

Weiss, Lois. 1990. *Working Class without Work: High School Students in a De-Industrializing Economy.* New York: Routledge.

Wellman, D. 1977. *Portraits of White Racism.* Cambridge, Eng.: Cambridge University Press.

Wergel, R. H., and D. W. Howes. 1985. "Conceptions of Racial Prejudice: Symbolic Racism Reconsidered." *Journal of Social Issues* 41: 117–38.

Willis, P. 1977. *Learning to Labor: How Working Class Kids Get Working Class Jobs.* New York: Columbia University Press.

Wilson, W. J. 1973. *Power, Racism, and Privilege.* New York: Free Press.

————. 1978. *The Declining Significance of Race.* Chicago: University of Chicago Press.

Wirth, L. 1945. "The Problem of Minority Groups." In R. Linton, ed., *The Science of Man in the World.* New York: Columbia University Press.

Zenner, W. 1980. "Middleman Theories: A Critical Review." In R. S. Bryce-Laporte, ed., *Sourcebook on the New Immigration.* New Brunswick, N. J.: Transaction.

Index

Sullivan, M., 51
Suttles, Gerald, 178

theory: Blumer's theory of racism, 13–15;
  competition theory, 8–9, 11; concentric spheres of reproduction, 18–20,
  154, 158; cultural studies, 14–16, 158;
  internal colonial, 107–8; of invasion
  and succession, 178; power/conflict
  theory, 8, 10–11; psychosocial theory,
  8; racial formation theory, 10; structural theory, 10
threat, 147, 162; perceived, 19, 45, 125,
  130
tip point, 178
tolerance and intolerance, 16–18, 116,
  128, 151, 154. *See also* attitudes; ethnic and racial tolerance
Turks, Willie, murder of, 35, 137

uncertainty and anxiety in adolescence,
  50
unemployment, 45, 47

Upper East Side, 39, 41, 183; whites'
  movement from, to Harlem, 143

victimization, feelings of, 14, 116; Albanian, as immigrant group, 128; of
  Bensonhurst youth, 88
violence, 71. *See also* racial violence
voting, racially polarized, 48

Washington Heights, 31–32, 42
wealthier people, and housing, 48
Weatherell, M., 12, 18
Wellman, D., 7–8
West Indians: in Pelham Parkway, 42; settlement, 34
white flight, 47; and Albanians, 119
white racism, 98–99, 107; white supremacist organizations, 3
white victimization, 163
Williamsbridge, 71
Winant, Howard, 12–13, 133

xenophobia, 33

Howard Pinderhughes is assistant professor of social and behavioral sciences at the University of California, San Francisco. He is a William T. Grant Faculty Scholar and recipient of a Carnegie Corporation grant for the study of intergroup relations among adolescents. Pinderhughes is currently engaged in ongoing research on the meaning and construction of violence among inner-city youth. He is the author of numerous articles on race relations among youth.